Diaspora Online

Diaspora Online

Identity Politics and Romanian Migrants

Ruxandra Trandafoiu

berghahn
NEW YORK · OXFORD
www.berghahnbooks.com

First published in 2013 by
Berghahn Books
www.berghahnbooks.com

Library of Congress Cataloging-in-Publication Data
Trandafoiu, Ruxandra.
  Identity politics and Romanian migrants / Ruxandra Trandafoiu.
    pages cm
  Includes bibliographical references and index.
  ISBN 978-0-85745-943-5 (hardback : alk. paper) -- ISBN 978-0-85745-
944-2 (ebook)
  1. Romanians--Foreign countries. 2. Romanians--Migrations. 3.
Romanians--Ethnic identity. 4. Romanians--Cultural assimilation. 5.
Emigration and immigration--Technological innovations. 6. Romania--
Emigration and immigration. I. Title.
  DR214.2.T73 2013
  305.85'91--dc23

                          2013004346

British Library Cataloguing in Publication Data
A catalogue record for this book is available from the British Library
Printed in the United States on acid-free paper.

ISBN 978-0-85745-943-5 (hardback)
ISBN 978-0-85745-944-2 (institutional ebook)

Contents

Acknowledgements

I owe special gratitude to Rozalinda Borcilă, Gianfranco Germani, Marius Lehene, Ramona Mitrică, Iuliana Şchiopu, Maria Simona Toadere and Adriana Vidroiu-Stanca. This book would not exist without the numerous anonymous voices that have inspired and enriched it and therefore my thanks go to all Romanian diasporans encountered on- and offline. I would also like to thank the British Academy for a small research grant and Edge Hill University, especially Carol Poole and Nikki Craske, for a sabbatical that allowed me to complete this project. To my family, Ezra, Rodica and Steve, thank you for your love and support.

I dedicate this book to the memory of my father and Francesca.

Cover Image: Immigrant 1, by Marius Lehene (Romanian born artist and Associate Professor of drawing at Colorado State University). Reproduced with permission. 'The work Immigrant 1 was done during the time I was in the process of applying for my permanent residency in the US. The situation made me feel a weird species of anxiety. For some reason I thought of air layering – the plant propagation technique where roots are made to grow up the stem, away from the original roots. I dipped the t-shirt I was wearing in wet cement (the cement of the communist ghetto I grew up in and – up the stem - of American suburbia too) and laid it down with the envelope from the US Department of Homeland Security sealed on top; case closed.'

Introduction

This book chronicles the online cultural and political expressions of the Romanian diaspora, using websites based in Italy, Spain and the United Kingdom. The penultimate chapter reflects on the online Romanian presence in North America. A decade ago, the diasporic use of the then new communication technologies was still uncharted. However, I observed its first manifestation in 2000–2001, whilst working as a freelance interpreter for the Home Office, specifically the Immigration and Nationality Directorate (IND, which has now become the UK Border Agency) in Croydon.

The IND operated an 'Oakington List', an inventory of countries whose single, young, male asylum seekers would be eligible for detention in the immigration removal centre at Oakington, near Cambridge. A daily decision was made regarding the countries that would contribute inmates to Oakington on the day. Romania often featured on the list, but each time the first Romanian asylum applicant had been detained for transportation to Oakington, Romanian applications would dramatically drop and would not return to normal until some other country temporarily replaced Romania on the list. I then heard from solicitors that rumours successfully circulated via mobile phones; migrants chose carefully the day on which they applied for political asylum and preferred to wait for weeks rather than risk being sent to Oakington for 'fast processing'. A mobile phone was an immigrant's best friend even in 2001, when the cost of a handset was still high. Yet these recently arrived immigrants, who needed it for their successful survival, were happy to invest their life's savings into the new technology. Brinkerhoff's suggestion that diasporas are good at adopting cutting-edge technology (2009: 12) is very pertinent indeed.

In 2000, like many other Romanians in the UK, I used to check sporadically the old Romanian Yahoo Group (a cross between an electronic e-mail list and an online discussion board) where, via occasional online messages, news about Romanian cultural events was disseminated. By 2004, there was more than one diasporic website based in the UK and now (March 2012) *Români Online UK* has fifteen thousand members, up from ten thousand in July 2010, seven thousand in November 2008 and four thousand in October 2007, while the rival site *Români în UK* counts almost twenty thousand users. Out of an estimated one hundred thousand Romanians in the UK, the users of diasporic online discussion forums seem to make up a healthy percentage. The situation is similar in other countries – further proof that specialized websites have become a staple of diasporic life, in the same way the mobile phone was essential to recently arrived migrants a decade ago.

The Romanian Diaspora Online

Most Romanian diasporic websites started life as Yahoo Groups and by the year 2000 they had become a popular feature in the life of growing diasporic groups around Western Europe and North America. Websites and wikis with links, menus, forums and chat facilities, recognizable by the minimum standards that we expect today, became more prevalent by the middle of the decade. Diasporic websites not only multiplied, but also spread, mimicking the number and distribution of Romanians abroad. The size and concentration of the diaspora explains why in the UK both *Români în UK* and *Români Online UK* are based in London, since the diaspora is relatively small and concentrated in the capital, while in Italy, with its large Romanian community of over one million, web initiatives are spread between Rome, Turin and Milan.

From her research on Eritreans online, Bernal derives the conclusion that the Internet is the 'quintessential diasporic medium' (Bernal 2006: 168). Her statement is an attractive one. In comparison to other media, the Internet allows users to shape the medium in their image, so they stop being mere consumers and they start taking control of their social and cultural needs, in the same way they take control of their own destinies when they decide to embark on their journey of migration. Thus the features of the Internet fit and feed the immigrant imagination.

There are additional claims in the existing theory that are equally valid. The first claim refers to the relationship between migrants and host societies. According to Mitra, diasporic websites provide a space where marginalized voices speak for themselves (Mitra 2005: 378). This suggests that the Internet provides an important degree of freedom and accessibility, though obvious problems might derive from the fact that online diasporic spaces seem to exist outside and in parallel to the cultural and social spaces of the host society. A second popular claim arises from the link between the diaspora and its home. Cyberspace cannot be owned by the nation-state or national culture, and so online identity can be reimagined, different generations can meet and mingle, the community can be resocialized and mobilized (Graham and Khosravi 2002). On the one hand, citizenship and nationhood are reworked and reimagined (Bernal 2006) and a diasporic culture is free to emerge as a different entity. On the other hand, digital diasporic politics is increasingly shaping home politics through distance, reflection and criticism (Bernal 2006; Brinkerhoff 2009).

It is important to first understand the value migrants themselves place on diasporic websites and their accompanying discussion forums. One of the participants in a forum discussion on a UK-based diasporic website defined the forum as 'an outstretched arm, a place where you can share your view as Romanian immigrant . . .[;] a place where you can meet other Romanians like you, each with his/her own story in the UK' (Tudor, *Români Online UK*). Tudor's view of the forum is of a social space that fulfils the migrant's socializing needs. The theme of support and help provided by information and people online reappears in other accounts as well. One user thought that the website was 'a more reliable source than the Home Office or other institutions managed with the same incompetence. It's a refuge which makes me feel closer to home, a place where I am in contact with our language' (Silviu, *Români Online UK*). Migrants depict a cocoon or buffer zone, particularly essential for those newcomers who find the immersion into the host society difficult to cope with, which explains the frequent nostalgic references to a regained home and the symbolic rehoming strategies.

The administrator of *Români Online UK* claimed that the main aims of the site were to unite Romanians in the UK, offer them reliable information and represent Romania in an appropriate way. One of the participants in the forum agreed that it was

> born out of the acute necessity for information and 'networking'. The thing you need most when arriving in a foreign country is CORRECT information. Apart from that, you need a network of people, co-nationals with whom one can connect and create a familiar structure. It helps to surpass the initial huge shock. (Dante, *Români Online UK*, emphasis in the original)

Social structures and networking opportunities are important necessities to migrants, as Mihaela Nedelcu also found in her study of one diasporic website in Canada. *The Bans* website in Toronto became an important resource and a form of capital, made up of diasporic networks and the cumulative experiences of the online community (Nedelcu 2009: 198). The diasporic website, with its links, and the associated forum, with its discussions, become the repository of diasporic knowledge, which migrants can borrow from and add to.

In a thread initiated in October 2007 on *Români Online UK*, while users talked about the usefulness and necessity of a diasporic forum, it also became apparent that for both those preparing to emigrate and those recently arrived in the host country, the website acted as a vehicle of 'acclimatization' and helped readjust the representations one had about self and others (Nedelcu 2009: 226). Marieta thought that:

> The forum helped us prepare and we found the transition easier; the information on the forum helped us a lot. . . . I met wonderful people in the forum, I learnt from them, I had something to share. On the other hand, I also saw envy and hate, the misery we tried to escape when we left home; we had hoped that here we would be more civilized. . . . I propose that we meet at important occasions. . . . I hope that one day we will become friends, know each other and have the pleasure of meeting outside this virtual space. (Marieta, *Români Online UK*)

According to this contributor, the forum acted as an introduction to the diasporic group, before relationships were forged outside it as well. However, Marieta felt uneasy about the replication of certain Romanian traits and she inferred that there was a gap between the initial idealism and the subsequent realities of immigration. In a North American forum, another Romanian reflected in a similar vein:

> Well. . . this forum, among other qualities, also has the quality of filtering people a bit . . . [;] if you spend some time here . . . you start to understand who are the foes and who the good guys. It may be a forum and the discussions are online, but it can be a start for friendship outside it. (Aurelia, *RomPortal*)

One of the main traits displayed by diasporic online users is self-awareness and awareness of others, which are the result of migratory and diasporic experiences heightened by critical distance achieved online. This acuity often galvanizes the collective elaboration of solutions needed to solve specific problems (Nedelcu 2009: 169).

According to Anna Ferro's findings from her research with Romanian professionals in the diaspora, Romanians make constant use of the Internet. Almost everyone in her study was in online contact with other Romanians back home or in the diaspora, and the Internet provided the main source of information about the homeland. While relatively few Romanians were involved in diasporic groups and associations, most were active in online forums, exchanging information and experiences. These diasporans exhibited what Appadurai has called 'new patriotism', a combination of nationalism, politics and nostalgia (Ferro 2004: 388). My own research also reveals that diasporans continuously reflect on social and political realities in both home and adoptive countries, constantly locating their diasporic experience within a transnational space with fast-changing parameters.

Nonetheless, it often remains difficult to assess the true political value of some of these reflections. The Internet has a recognized organizational potential, but in the absence of clear political aims, such as forging a community of faith as a precursor to political affirmation, many groups are merely characterized by common, banal interests (King 2003: 180). I suspect this will remain a continuous problem when researching diasporic websites, which are not activist enterprises but social and cultural spaces lacking traditional structures and leaderships. During my research it became clear that the Internet encourages a different type of politics, as evidenced by numerous examples in the following chapters.

In an ideal world, the forum is the equivalent of the *agora*. As the Romanian philosopher Andrei Pleşu pointed out in a brief reflection, the online forum should fulfil an official public role, requiring responsibility from users who use convincing arguments rather than brutal fighting, and avoid private instincts and obsessions. The forum is not a 'virtual pub', but a social axial centre for the community (*Adevărul*, 16 March 2010). I believe that some of the following examples illustrate this aspiration. However, very rarely discussions remain at the level of rational argumentation. This speaks volumes about the openness of cyberspace, which welcomes a large variety of characters, with their unique experiences, purposes and foibles. Despite clashes of interests and personalities, as well as conflicts deriving somewhat from a traumatic baggage and a marginalized existence, online debates can, as Brinkerhoff observed in her analysis of the role of diasporic websites in conflict resolution, facilitate issue framing (Brinkerhoff 2009). The Internet may not provide an *agora* in the classic sense, but it offers a space of 'enunciation', which is a term that Bhabha appropriated from Bakhtin; a space where 'doubleness' can be negotiated and where hybridity can challenge inequity (Bhabha 1996: 58). These spaces become spaces of contestation (Mandaville 2003: 135–47) and affirmation of new cultural and political aspirations.

The Romanian Diaspora

Who or what is an immigrant remains open for debate, even more so in the case of Eastern Europeans. I never thought of myself as an immigrant. Like many Romanians of my generation, I considered myself to be a professional furthering her career in the West. Yet if we see identity as not only what we think about ourselves, but also what others think about us, I have to admit that on several occasions I have been prompted to revise that belief. Adrian Favell takes issue with labelling Easterners 'migrants' and prefers the term 'free movers'. His reasoning is that Eastern European migration is temporary and circular rather than permanent, stimulated by labour demands rather than asylum seeking (Favell 2008: 703). His views reflect those of Massey and colleagues, who suggest that the development of global cities requires the active recruitment of labour. The subsequent expansion of mobility routes and communication technologies not only contributes to the creation of migratory social capital but, in turn, according to the theory of cumulative causation, results in a self-perpetuating phenomenon (Massey et al. 1998: 279–80), which encourages circularity.

However, until less than a decade ago Romanians were still applying for asylum. In the first few years after 1989, Romanians were able to work temporarily in Turkey and Israel, after which working legally or illegally in Hungary, Germany and Italy became increasingly attractive. North America and Spain became favourites after 1996 (Sandu 2010: 86–7), but only the United States and Canada invited legal migration, with a well defined status immediately after arrival. Asylum seeking, on the other hand, was one of the few ways in which Romanians could regularize their presence in Europe. Until less than a decade ago Romanian emigration was largely a long-term project and Romanians could call themselves émigrés.

In January 2002 Romanians were finally allowed to travel without a visa in the Schengen area, which does not include the United Kingdom or Ireland. Even then, Romanians became 'noncitizens', to borrow a term from Rogers Brubaker, with privileged work opportunities in comparison to the less fortunate category of non-European work migrants (Brubaker 1999: 264). After 2002 Romanian migration tripled as a result of freedom of movement within Europe (Sandu 2010: 87), which also produced an increase in the number of those working illegally. Sandu puts the percentage of illegal workers after 2001 at 53 per cent of all Romanians working abroad (Sandu 2010: 105). However, it is important to note that among Romanians' preferred destinations, Italy and Spain have, in the last decade, made substantial efforts to regularize illegal migration and around one million Romanians have thus benefited from their policies (Anghel 2008; Culic 2008). In these countries, many Romanians are permanent residents, even citizens.

Although the opening of the Schengen area encouraged circularity, forming a well defined category of recurrent work-seeking migrants, illegality also fostered permanency. By prolonging their stay in Italy or Spain, many Romanians hoped to benefit from amnesties and regularize their status. For many, particularly those with children, migration became a lifelong project in countries where opportunities were more plentiful than in Romania. Temporary, work-seeking migration of the kind Favell contemplates became legally possible only after Romania's accession to the European Union in January 2007 and even then, work restrictions in several EU member states prolonged the uncertainty for, on average, a further five years. Unsure about their chances of emigrating again in the future, eager to obtain the coveted work permits here and now, Romanians tended to prolong their stay. Any plans to return have now been thwarted by Romania's descent into economic crisis. The anticipated mass return of diasporans has failed to materialize as a result, even from countries like Spain, where the construction industry has collapsed, causing the unemployment of thousands of Romanians. Recession is still more bearable in the West.

It is hard to put a reliable figure on the total number of Romanians now living and working abroad, comprising immigrants, residents, citizens, diasporans and circular migrants. As the then Romanian Minister for Foreign Affairs, Adrian Cioroianu, confessed during a round table in 2007, 10 per cent of Romania's population (more than two million people) could be somewhere in Europe at any one time (*22 Revista Grupului Pentru Dialog Social*, December 2007). Worldwide, taking into account older migration (between the two wars or during communism), the significant post-communist migration and the Romanian minorities who have been living just outside Romania's borders in neighbouring countries for generations, the Romanian diaspora amounts to ten million. A third of all Romanians now live outside their nation-state. Unverified data puts the numbers of Romanians in the countries this book focuses on at around eight hundred thousand in Spain, between one and two million in Italy and one hundred thousand or slightly more in the UK. What we know for sure is that by 2007 at least 15 per cent of Romania's population had worked abroad (Baldwin-Edwards 2007: 8) and that that figure has since increased. Data for 2008 put the number of remitting Romanian migrants in Europe at 2.8 million, in comparison to the 2.2 million who were sending remittances before Romania's EU accession (Sandu 2010: 37). One-third of Romanians now living in Romania have worked abroad at least once since the fall of communism and according to some polls, around 40 per cent of those with emigration experience intend to leave again (Sandu 2010: 96). As Sandu correctly observes, for Romanians emigration has become the preferred way to a quicker social transition (Sandu 2010: 35).

So are Romanians living abroad immigrants or free movers or something else? This question may not have a readily available answer yet. Until the EU accession, the Romanian press called them *căpșunari* (strawberry pickers), *macaronari* (macaroni eaters) or *stranieri* (foreigners, in Italian), although now the term 'diaspora' is more habitually used. For Romanians back home, these work-seeking migrants have now evolved to the status of diaspora. For the purpose of this research, they are all considered as diasporans, irrespective of how long or short their migration project is and irrespective of what prompted them to emigrate. It would be virtually impossible to carve reliable categories from among a large number of diasporans who may be born into the same social world, may carry similar states of mind and may construct communal identity strategies, but deploy individual strategies when deciding to emigrate and choosing their destination or emigration networks (Sandu 2010: 19). Nonetheless, they all feed into a diasporic project that is redefining Romanianness through migration. I agree with Rogers Brubaker that instead of a 'bounded' entity, we need to speak of claims, projects, expectations, loyalties and identities (Brubaker 2005: 12).

Massey, Goldring and Durand, who studied Mexican migration to the United States assiduously during the 1970s and 1980s, explain through the cumulative theory of migration that when migration grows in volume, it also becomes more diverse and finally causes permanent changes in social structures and individual motivations (1994: 1527). There are now too many migration waves, shifts in preferred destinations and strategies (see Sandu 2010) to construct classifications, but along with circular migration, we can deduce that permanent settlement has also become a favourite approach. However, it is important to remember that Romanians are all now European citizens and the term 'immigrant' will have to be revised sooner or later.

Some of the Romanians I interviewed offered a range of identity options, but their choices seemed to suggest a status that is still being reworked in the light of long-term arrangements. When I interviewed Camelia, she said:

> I define myself as Romanian. Even if tomorrow I get married, and I get a Spanish ID, or Spanish citizenship, if I have my children here and they become Spanish, I will still die a Romanian. You are born and die with an identity. I am Romanian from head to toe. I will never feel Spanish. I never felt I would become Spanish. I am not ashamed of who I am and where I come from. I think the Spanish see me as a Romanian girl who works hard and minds her own business. (Valencia, 28 August 2008)

Camelia avoided the term 'immigrant' and instead emphasized her Romanianness and personal value. Because she viewed national identity as a given, not a choice, she felt comfortable with preserving and enhancing it. Mia displayed similar feelings, but also elaborated on the various facets she portrayed to others:

> How do I define myself? I am Romanian. I am a tourist also. I also used to be a cleaner. Here it is just a job like any other. They really need cleaners.

My landlord would define me as a friend. Migrants have different values, they are distinct and maybe their children will not be Romanian anymore, but as for myself, I think that you stay Romanian, irrespective of what the passport says. (London, 27 September 2008)

Mia only alluded to her status as an immigrant, but did not define herself primarily as one. However, she implicitly accepted that this was how others might see her. Mugur and Adriana, on the other hand, who belong to a more mature generation and have been living in the West for longer, emphasized their migrant status. Mugur replied to the same question about self-definition with: 'I am a Romanian citizen, resident in Italy. Romanian blood flows through my veins; my country is Romania; my roots are in Romania. So here, I am an immigrant. I will never ask for Italian citizenship' (Rome, 2 July 2008). Mugur was the only person I interviewed who planned to return to Romania within a few years, if the economic climate was favourable. Adriana Vidroiu-Stanca, a poet and the founder of the *Nou Orizont* (New Horizon) association in Spain, talked about returning to one's roots as a way of surviving the immigrant condition:

Why do we always dream of going home on holiday? There is something that pulls you back. Unconsciously you recharge your batteries to last you another year and help you to survive your immigrant condition. Some may not want to acknowledge it, but being an immigrant is nothing to be proud about. (Valencia, 2 September 2008)

It is understandable why diasporans would choose to primarily define themselves as Romanians. It is one facet of their identities which is harder to challenge and is what sets them apart within their respective host societies. It becomes, through migration, their primary identity. The immigrant condition, on the other hand, is acknowledged as an important definer of status and experience, but is not the preferred self-depiction. This ambiguity reflects the difficult relationship Eastern Europeans might have with the assignation of 'immigrant'.

The European citizenship earned by many Easterners in the aftermath of two EU enlargement processes has not lifted the stigma. Symbolic political geography is still inescapable and one only has to turn to the tabloid press for confirmation. Popular opinion would have no difficulty in considering me an immigrant, but a friend who was born and grew up in East Germany will never be judged as one. As Balibar and Wallerstein remind us, in Europe an Arab is more of an immigrant than a Spaniard, a labourer more immigrant than a capitalist (Balibar and Wallerstein 1991: 221). In the introduction to their edited book, Triandafyllidou and Gropas (2007) arrive at the conclusion that what or who a migrant is, is very much dependent on national realities. In this context, it is clear that Romania's history keeps it and its citizens relegated to the realm of Orientalist fantasies.

On the other hand, Romanians cherish their cultural closeness to the West and aspire to be treated as equals. When in 2007 Romanians were finally given the right to travel and work freely in Europe as citizens, the future felt rosy; history was avenged. However, an incalculable disparity has now emerged between Westerners and Easterners in the expectations they have of each other. While the West was being made and remade in the Romanian imagination, a shift in migration patterns from the 'guest worker' model to more permanent settlement was producing a new 'self-awareness' in Western societies (Schierup et al. 2006: 23). Free movement of workers has been a key policy of Europe's common market, but in practice, sensitivities about immigration have resulted in restrictions imposed on Eastern Europeans after enlargement (Geddes 2007: 52).

The clash between idealized aspirations and rational protectionism is still making people like me wonder about their own identity and status in Europe today. Schierup et al. define 'differential exclusion' as the practice of accepting immigrants only for certain periods of time and only if they fulfil a purpose (Schierup et al. 2006: 41). However, if someone is not a full member of the polity and lacks citizenship, then their only function is to work (Sayad 2004: 204). This statement is incompatible with the idealized version of the world that, as a liberal and a democrat, I hold. This book results therefore from my wish to understand my own position within Western society and reveal the way other Romanians feel about their own diasporic experiences. I hope thus to contribute to a new diasporic theory, which accounts for the little explored area of post-communist East–West migration.

The Research Methodology

A specific research methodology for the study of diasporic websites was still undefined in 2006 when I took my first steps towards researching the diaspora, so the project had to find its own rhythm, mostly through direct experiences in the field. Originally, my inspiration was Terhi Rantanen's use of what she called 'mediagraphy' (2005): the analysis of personal global networks and media consumptions derived from a comparative multisited ethnographic research, examining how individuals, families and groups connect and disconnect via media technologies. Her mapping of individual life narratives (obtained via interviews and ethnographic observation) onto collective cultural, social and political phenomena put media and technology at the heart of globalizing experiences.

Participant observation online or a combination of interviews and online analysis were the methods that researchers were beginning to prefer. In his study of the Sierra Leone listserv *Leonenet*, Robert Tynes analysed a sample of over seven hundred e-mails over a period of two-and-a-half years (Tynes 2007). He derived some demographic data from the discussions, analysed the themes and inferred nation-building strategies from them. Androutsopoulos browsed several diasporic forums in Germany for several weeks, made a note of the popularity of certain topics, and identified key users and their language preferences (2006). Hiller and Franz studied internal migration in Canada by interviewing 350 migrants and monitoring sites suggested by respondents or found through keyword searches and links on other sites (Hiller and Franz 2004). Brenda Chan conducted several interviews (using snowballing) with users of two Chinese forums based in Singapore and conducted online participant observation for a period of eight months (2006). Emily Ignacio's study of the Filipino diaspora in the United States exemplified a similarly effective way of deconstructing identity discourses taking place online (Ignacio 2005). Ignacio monitored an online discussion group for a year. She informed participants of her presence, habitually reminded them of her research project and invited the participants to communicate with her. She regularly checked and saved discussion threads, kept a research journal and coded and analysed the conversations. Most of these studies utilize multisite ethnography, working across fieldsites, on- and offline, despite the dilemmas resulting from repeatedly crossing that boundary (see also Wakeford 2004: 46–7). In a another study, Oiarzabal has applied discursive and rhetorical analysis to an impressive ninety Basque diaspora sites based in sixteen countries, over two months. He focused in particular on textual, graphic and multimedia content (audio and visual), as well as the structure (Oiarzabal 2010: 338).

While Nedelcu's research with Romanian professionals in Canada (2009) was just being published as my project was coming to an end, I noted that she had used a comparable hybrid approach. Her multisite netnography included online observation of one website, e-mail exchanges, face-to-face interviews, an analysis of the relationship between the online and the offline and theoretical considerations on the emergence of transnational spaces, in relation to globalization and nationalism theory (Nedelcu 2009: 76–84). By 2009 the social analysis of virtual neighbourhoods or cyber-ethnography (Graham and Khosravi 2002) clustered around the now preferred term 'netnography' (Ignacio 2005; Nedelcu 2009; Kozinets 2009). Kozinets (2009) explains that netnography has its own distinctiveness since online experiences are significantly different from face-to-face experiences (Kozinets 2009: 5). However, he too observes that netnography can be contextualized with additional face-to-face interactions.

I had decided early in the project to follow up participant observation of several diasporic websites and discussion forums with more in-depth interviews, which would yield perhaps useful insights not only about people's migratory experiences, but also about their online participation and the meaning derived from such activities. Moving the research across various spaces of interaction also helped clarify some important ethical concerns, which I discuss further on. However, while Ignacio or Nedelcu concentrated on one website or discussion group, I chose a larger-scale, comparative approach. Jennifer Brinkerhoff's book *Digital Diasporas* was published while I was already writing my own, but she too chose to study nine digital diaspora organizations originating in five countries from Africa, the Middle East and Asia. She, too, chose interviews and discussion thread analysis as her methodology, with the aim of analysing the impact of digital diasporas in international affairs – their role in fostering democracy and security (Brinkerhoff 2009: 2).

Increasingly, widening the parameters to accommodate larger-scale research projects and capture macro phenomena seems a preferred option. My choice of Italy and Spain were default options, due to the scale of the Romanian diaspora in the two countries. The UK seemed an interesting addition for comparative purposes, due to the large number of professionals that until 2007 made up the majority of this diasporic group. I eventually decided to include a chapter on the Romanian diaspora in North America, due to the differences I observed in their online presence and the accompanying distinctive social and cultural contexts. Logistics and time constraints only made possible a few interviews. I recruited online, posting an open invitation to collaborate in my research project and whenever possible, I met those interested in expressing their views. I also conducted online interviews. On a few occasions I strategically chose or actively pursued people whom I considered to have specialist knowledge or a relevant position within the diaspora. They included representatives of churches and organizations, politicians and members of the intelligentsia. A total of ten interviews were conducted, as well as three site visits to Romanian organizations in Rome, Valencia and London, and they serve to inform, explain and contextualize phenomena observed online.

The initial stages of the project required a system of website selection. Previous diasporic research recommended a mix between user recommendations and search engine selections (Graham and Khosravi 2002; Hiller and Franz 2004; Siapera 2006). Using key word searches in Google, I compiled a short list of Romanian diasporic sites in the countries I intended to study. I confirmed the relevance of the websites by asking acquaintances and users about their preferences. In addition, I spent a couple of months browsing the selected websites to ascertain the amount of communication traffic and the spread and variety of discussion threads. I continued to browse new websites whenever I came across them and included them at a later stage in the research, if they proved relevant. This flexible approach came to be an advantage when websites (though not forums) stopped functioning while I was still conducting the project (*România Italia Net, Romanian Community of Ireland*), the forum depopulated to a degree (*Marea unire, Spania*) or the site became temporary suffocated by factional squabbles (*Identitatea românească* in Italy). By adopting a comparative approach, it became easier to understand the anchoring of most websites in the cultural and political specificity of the host country and the individuality of each diasporic group.

I chose two diasporic sites in the UK (*Români Online UK* and *Români în UK*), two in Spain (*Marea unire, Spania* and *Spania românească*) and three in Italy (*România Italia Net, Italia România* and *Realitatea din Italia*). In North America, I monitored a total of five sites in Canada and the United States (*BC Romanian Community Center, Québec Ro, Comunitatea română portalul diasporei române US, RomPortal* and *Romanian Portal US*). In addition, I occasionally browsed a Romanian diasporic site in Ireland (*Romanian Community of Ireland*) and one Moldovan site in the UK (*Acum*), because there had been instances of cross-referencing with the UK-based sites. In order to make my selection for North America, I browsed and analysed numerous other diasporic sites, but I do not quote from their forums in this book, although I do refer to their features. I also browsed the site and forums belonging to some cultural and political organizations. These offered an interesting case study, as they were placed midway between private initiative and official public image.

Netnography became insufficient when looking at the rich symbolism displayed by most diasporic websites. Online journalism research uses an approach that looks at various communication modalities (audio, video, text, graphics, animation), hypermedia (links, context), interactivity, dynamic content and customization (Pavlik 2001: 4–22). Web design psychology, on the other hand, puts emphasis on typography – typeface, layout, location on page, white space and colour (Smart et al. 2000: 602) – and proves how such elements not only have an impact on readability, but also can assign degrees of significance and meaning. Website structure can influence participatory functions (Wright and Street 2007), so the deconstruction of web design becomes part of web semiology and plays a part in understanding the interplay between content, structure and design. This approach is close to cultural decoding, which is accomplished through a 'hybrid' media analysis (Pauwels 2005: 609–10) comprising content and discourse analysis, semiotics and iconography (website design and navigational features, categories of topics, voices and their demography, hierarchies, links to other spaces, meaning). This methodology is used in the analysis of online visual symbolism in

Chapter Eight of this book, as well as thread discussions and user hierarchies throughout the book.

At the start of the project, the relevant research literature suggested that if the information was published online and thus already available in the public domain, then the researcher was perfectly entitled to use it (Mann and Stewart 2000; Hartman and Ackermann 2004). Some online forums exercised minimal vetting, with participants required to sign up in order to gain access. This practice is less of a security device and more the webmaster or administrator's attempt to keep track of the site's demographics. In most diasporic forums, one can still lurk at will, reading various discussion threads, since signing up is usually requested only for posting messages.

Since my initial steps in 2006, lurking has come to be viewed more critically (Gaiser and Schreiner 2009: 133–4) because of its voyeuristic and unethical quality. My initial approach was to sign up, take some time to read the posts and learn about each group and its main contributors. I knew that the time to contact the users and participate in the life of the forums would eventually come. After a few months, once I had selected the relevant and active forums, I contacted the webmasters or posted a note explaining my research and inviting participants to e-mail me privately for personal exchanges or interviews. I made sure I posted into relevant threads (Hewson et al. 2003: 116), usually the 'meet and greet' ones, which are frequented by newcomers but are also visited by seasoned users looking for fresh voices and ideas, usually at the beginning of each of their online sessions. I always promised anonymity and explained the published outcome of the research. The gathering of the main material took place in 2007 and 2008, although I have included some examples from 2009, when important events took place in Romanian politics.

Webmasters were always open-minded about the project. Although the issues of the confidentiality of data and trust in the researcher never came up, I always worried whether participants really understood or even cared about the possible outcomes. Writing up the research and publishing it in English, for example, would restrict access to this text for many. In only one case a forum member jokingly questioned the authenticity of my e-mail address, because I had made the mistake of using my private rather than university e-mail, but another user shortly dismissed his concerns. In turn, I posted a link to my university page to reassure him of my authentic intentions. Mistrust was clearly there initially, but my researcher badge was trusted.

Because all forums have archives and the information can be retrieved at any time, I kept logs as proof of monitoring (Hiller and Franz 2004), made a note of relevant threads and printed or saved electronically the posts I needed. I quickly accumulated hundreds of posts and when topics started to recur, I knew I had reached saturation point (Kozinets 2009: 116). Through routine comparative analysis, I identified gaps in my understanding of some of the issues. These were clarified either through personal posts, asking contributors directly for their views on the topic, or during face-to-face interviews. I do not have an exact number of the threads and posts I have read and analysed (I stopped counting when I reached three thousand posts), because I take Robert Kozinets' view that when studying social aspects, useful inroads can be made even with minimal material (Kozinets 2009: 116), which is not the case here, where the amount of data is now too large to quantify.

Current literature expresses great concerns about the distinction between what is public and what is private online (Mann and Stewart 2000; Hewson et al. 2003; Hartman and Ackermann 2004). The frankness of many unguarded posts made me realize that only too often participants were lulled into a false sense of privacy. They expected a familiar, semi-enclosed and secure space, which provided the illusion of privacy and lifted the burden of responsibility. Virtual communities have virtual boundaries. They bring together likeminded individuals, who share congruent purposes. The sense of security online may have to do with this sense of false intimacy and togetherness of purpose. Some sought the protection of pseudonyms/avatars; some posted information that would make them identifiable, but even then they showed little concern. Even during interviews, most participants remained ingenuous, although face-to-face racist remarks were drastically curtailed, and I kept wondering whether decades of communism made it impossible for Romanians to avoid expressing their convictions freely, no matter how outrageous.

The prevalence of flaming is an important argument for the preservation of anonymity (Hamelink 2006: 120) in this study and so is the prevalence of racism and intolerance which I found in many posts. I decided, early on, on the necessity to obscure the participants' real names and pseudonyms or avatars, despite a marked divide between my academic anxiety and users' *laissez-faire* attitude. My approach provides a 'minimum cloak' (Kozinets 2009: 154), where online pseudonyms are altered, but the name of the group or online community is mentioned and direct quotations are used. However, because all quotations have been translated from Romanian (by myself), it would be extremely difficult for anybody to be able to identify the online user, which I venture to say resembles more a 'medium cloaked' situation.

Members of associations or political parties feature under their own names and the appropriate permission was sought and obtained at the start of each interview. I never asked diasporans I met online for their real names and they all feature with pseudonyms. In one case I met online and then interviewed face-to-face a young Romanian who now lives in Valencia. We met in the city centre, from where she took me to her more familiar ground, a little café in an adjacent district. We talked for four hours. I met her cousin that night and they took me to an entertainment park outside Valencia, where we drank *orxata* and talked. We still e-mail from time to time, but I still do not know her real name. However, I made sure that everybody understood the outcome of the project and nobody ever objected to me using their thoughts and reflections in whatever way I saw fit, which I wholeheartedly appreciate.

My dual presence as participant-observer in the field and my double positioning, as Romanian and academic, brought home issues of Romanianness and foreignness, which normally I choose to ignore. My initial posturing somewhere between lurker and *flâneur* shifted to a more defined relationship between myself as researcher, webmasters and online participants in the forums, once I started to get involved in the project. However, I still felt uneasy about posturing as another Romanian migrant, because I had never thought of myself as one and because many participants have had a much tougher journey to the West than I did. It is also a cliché that most diasporic theorists seem to have 'foreign' names. In my defence, I have to say that being Romanian did allow me access to a community that would otherwise remain alien and being a researcher also became an advantage. Romanians wanted to tell their story and they trusted me to present it, because they trusted my professionalism. Slowly, I began to feel that being a Romanian researcher doing research about online Romanian communities was not an unrespectable endeavour. I hope this book proves it.

A New Diasporic Theory

From the perspective of post-communist Eastern European migration, diasporic theory is like a tree with two solid branches. On the one side, we have a phenomenal body of postcolonial theory produced by mainly British and French writers, with the contribution of US sociologists. On the other side sits the solid US theory based on the experience of primarily Mexican immigration. In an issue that the *Journal of Ethnic and Migration Studies* dedicated entirely to East–West migration, Adrian Favell (2008) suggested that the study of Mexican–US migration, especially Massey and Durand's classic Mexican Migration Project, was becoming increasingly relevant to theorists of Eastern European migration. He bases this assumption on a number of attractive propositions. Like Mexicans in the United States, he explains, Eastern Europeans increasingly fill low-end jobs in Western Europe. Due to cultural proximity, their presence tends to be more tolerated in comparison to non-European migrants. Migration policies also gradually aim to follow the North American model, where the selection process favours highly skilled migrants. Finally, like in the Mexican case, Eastern European migration has had certain economic benefits for the sending countries.

Favell's observations are correct, particularly if we look at economic disparities, migration patterns and cycles, remitting behaviour, immigration policy and macro-economic structures. Massey and colleagues (1998) are also very convincing when, in the conclusion to their vast analysis of migration theories, they highlight world systems theory, which attributes migration to local transformations under the impact of the penetration of capitalism into pre or developing capitalist markets, as the most likely explanation (Massey et al. 1998: 277) for emigration.

Attractive and likely as they are, these accounts fail nonetheless to explain specific qualities of Eastern European migration, and particularly of Romanian migration, such as: the emigration of a large number of skilled professionals, not just unskilled workers; the perpetuation of a Western mythology more complex than the simple 'American dream' and its role in encouraging a perpetual aspiration for migrating; the absence of coagulated settlement at destinations and hence the lack of neighbourhood ethnicization; the weak associative models but strong, albeit fragmented, online presences; or the ambiguity of national attachment and micropolitical activity based on conflict and ethnical fissures.

Postcolonial diasporic theory, on the other hand, may appear incongruous with the phenomenon of Eastern European migration, but many of its concepts could be usefully appropriated. Black cultures, Gilroy explains, are produced under conditions of oppression, racial exploitation and subordination (Gilroy 1987: 159). To a certain extent, the subordination thesis rings true for Eastern Europeans, who have always had a symbolic but unequal relationship with the West: this issue is explored further in Chapter One. European Union enlargement has also given rise to new forms of both racism and xenophobia (or xeno-racism) directed at Romany Gypsies and 'audible' Eastern European minorities – people whose physiognomies are undifferentiated from the general European type, but whose accents give them away as the 'other' (see, for example, Fekete 2009).

While exploring online diasporic phenomena, terms like 'Third Space', 'hybridity' and 'doubleness' from the arsenal of postcolonial theory help explain the visual, linguistic and textual anchoring of diasporic websites in dual or multiple realities. They are essential spatial representations of the way both locality and transnationalism are experienced symbolically, through shared meanings (Kennedy and Roudometof 2002: 24). They also depict inner diasporic ruptures and cultural duplicities on which migrants often reflect online. Postcolonial diasporic theory mapped the shift from premodern communities based on kinship, locality and state solidarity to modern delocalized communities, defined by voluntary participation and perpetual shifts and reinventions, according to economic and political interests (Kennedy and Roudometof 2002: 6–8, 13). Now, as contemporary diasporic groups continue to accumulate new experiences, current theory has to chart communities defined and brought together by movement, rupture and conflict. East–West migration needs a new theoretical corpus that would stand on the shoulder of previous giants, but would acquire its own language and momentum. What is now classic diasporic theory, focusing mainly on the African, Indian and Greek diasporas, may become insufficient for studying Eastern European migration. The following points summarize briefly common criticisms of existing diasporic theory and start to open up the discussion about possible new approaches:

- New research must dismantle what Sayad calls the 'moralization' of migration and migrants (Sayad 2004: 137) and discourage any attempt to ethicalize the act of migration;
- New research equally needs to abandon diasporic idealization; migration and foreignness lead to discrimination in both majorities and minorities; exclusively allocating racism to the camp of the majority obscures important diasporic formation mechanisms;
- New research has to abandon the myths: migration viewed in simplistic, cost–benefit terms or push–pull factors; the emphasis on Eastern European migration as purely 'labour' or 'work' migration; the belief that circular migration for work must end in return; ignoring the second generation for whom return is impossible; and the emphasis on the country of origin as the 'natural' home;
- New research needs to combine diasporic focus with understanding the renationalizing and institutionalizing attempts made by the homeland and study the formation of diasporic cultures outside national culture, whether diasporic culture emerges as an extension of national culture or as something completely different;
- New research should give a direct voice to migrants themselves: we should stop talking about migrants in their absence and in the abstract, and this needs a rethinking of our methodologies;
- New research should continue to develop an emphasis on the mental aspects of migration (lived experience, psychological phenomena) rather than exclusively focus on its physicality (numbers, jobs, remittances);
- New research needs a new language. It should talk more about emigration, not just immigration, as both Sayad and Bourdieu accentuate (in Sayad 2004); it should reconsider dubious terms like 'integration' or 'naturalization';
- New research should expand the meanings and facets of politics, starting with the fact that emigration/immigration is already a political act and generates a politics of its own (Sayad 2004: 97);

- Policy recommendations should call again for the global governance of migratory issues (see also Castles 2004);
- The role of the Internet as a predilect space for diasporic micropolitics merits further and detailed investigation, since social media are transnational, represent an opt-in technology and remain outside state control, though institutionalization attempts, both political and corporate, are on the increase.

This book starts to address some of these issues in the following chapters, building an understanding of the phenomena defining Eastern European migration from the perspective of the Romanian diaspora.

The Structure of the Book

This book talks about the anxieties, conflicts and realizations that have defined the post-communist Romanian diaspora in the process of foundation, partial maturation and incipient politicization. Emigration and immigration are about journeying, change and progression and therefore I have adopted a cyclical approach to the structure of this book.

Part One explores the historical and cultural context of post-1989 Romanian emigration. Chapter One explains the formation of a self-replenishing emigration ethos in response to the difficult post-communist transition, the interplay between Europeanism and nationalism and the rearticulation of Romanianness as a complex of both superiority and inferiority. Identity was thus reformatted to create an appearance of Westernization that could be performed successfully, while emigration became a political act of protest towards a bad mother country. Chapter Two explains the process of natural selection that the 'ideal' migrant undergoes. It continues to explore the issue of stigmatized citizenships by connecting migration to a discourse of illness and abnormality. A sick identity leads to the formation of a migratory pandemic. In its aftermath, a selective process takes place that allows only the fittest and those endowed with abnormal attributes to survive emigration/immigration. However, the Ulysses syndrome can also lead to the accumulation of transnational capital and to empowerment, transforming migrants into extraordinary subjects.

Part Two explores some of the features of the problematic adaptation to life as an immigrant. Chapter Three problematizes adaptation by highlighting the difficulty of talking about a complex phenomenon in the absence of an adequate language. The migrant body is found to be inadequate within a Western context and therefore a process of disjointing needs to be undertaken, through which those diseased limbs, which are unable to adapt, are racialized and expunged. The chapter addresses, therefore, difficult and rarely high-lighted issues in diasporic research: intradiasporic racism and diasporic can-nibalism. Chapter Four starts by discussing the liberal paradox that defines the relationship between Western economies and Eastern workers and influences the treatment of foreigners in modern democracies. It continues with a discus-sion of legal and policy arrangements affecting Romanians in Spain, Italy and the United Kingdom. The chapter ends with an analysis of the way diasporic associative models in these three countries have evolved in relation to the specific legal and social context.

Part Three explains the evolution from freshly arrived migrant to politi-cally reflexive immigrant subject. Chapter Five is dedicated to diasporic online activism and details the path chosen by each diasporic group in Spain, Italy and the United Kingdom on the way to becoming a diaspora. The numerous examples provided explain how online communities start per-forming as diasporas through political practices like contestation, negotia-tion, lobbying, decision-making and activism, self-publicity and public performance. Chapter Six discusses the politics of location and impossible return. It advances the idea that diasporans live an *atopos* existence in a self-generating purgatory defined by trauma and disillusionment, but also hope and anticipation. These feelings contribute to diasporic self-realization, which helps negotiate the relationship with the homeland and home politics. The role of the Romanian diaspora in the 2007 referendum and the 2008 and 2009 Romanian elections is described in the context of not only rena-tionalizing attempts by the homeland, but also the emergence of diasporic culture and the establishment of diasporic political representation. Chapter Seven focuses on a separate case study, looking at the Romanian diaspora in the United States and Canada. A migration of a different kind, shaped by historical, legal and social factors, has created different migratory and asso-ciative models. This difference is also observable online, where Romanians talk about similar things, but in different ways, and political activism is shaped less by events in the hostland and more by the relation with the homeland. The chapter finishes with a consideration of the way diasporic culture is represented in the North American context and resurrects briefly the themes of diasporic bodies, performance and representation.

Part Four concludes the book by exploring, in Chapter Eight, issues that have not been tackled elsewhere: the evolution of diasporic websites; common characteristics and unique selling points; ethnic representations in the visual language of websites; and the emergence of online hierarchies and rules, which enable political and identity expressions. The Conclusion further elaborates on the role of the Internet, offers two avenues for possible future research and provides a set of recommendations for various actors in the diasporic field.

PART I – DEPARTURES

The 'Great Escape':
Defining Emigration as Social
Transition and 'Natural Selection'

CHAPTER ONE

'Land without Horizon'

The Post-communist Transition and Emigration as Political Act

Pământ fără orizont (Land without Horizon) is the title of a poem written by Adriana Vidroiu-Stanca (2008), an immigrant and a writer who now resides in Valencia, Spain. The images and sentiments encapsulated in this phrase would have been familiar to Romanians during the communist period and for many it remains as evocative as ever. This chapter sketches the post-1989 social and political contexts that gave rise to emigration and argues that initially, emigration was the result of stalled social mobility and a slow post-communist transition, and then acquired a self-feeding character, mingled with new cultural and life aspirations. Migration became an act of protest, a no confidence vote in the new political system. However, it would be wrong to view emigration in simple functionalist terms, when emigration was also fed by the need to elaborate further an already problematic identity, split by historical ruptures and nationalistic exultations in tension with globalizing pressures. The resulting identity interrogations taking place within the cyber-diasporic space display a clear reflexivity, which tells the story of how online communities negotiate and organize their diasporic presence on- and offline. I define diasporic reflexivity as the ability to provide complex and continuous identity reflections as a result of the coexistence of the self within multiple spaces of interaction. The condition of marginality and assumed otherness, typical for the diasporic condition, create thus a perpetual diasporic consciousness and the ability to construct coherent political discourses.

Transitions

The euphoria experienced in December 1989, when Ceaușescu's unloved regime finally fell – those shared feelings of hope and opportunity – were rather short lived. Instead, the transition, like all transitions of this scale, came to be defined by uncertainty, instability and confusion. Romania turned into inhospitable social and political landscapes defined by contested political successions and a generalized crisis of authority, structural meltdown followed by decades of institutional rebuilding, widespread corruption, social upheavals and the public contestation of elites.

Romania was in a worse position than many of its neighbours, since its communist elite had not initiated the transition already underway in most other communist countries; there were no viable alternatives or prepared models; the civil society was almost non-existent (Tismăneanu 1992: 283–4). Living standards by the year 2000 were half of what they had been at the end of the communist period (Martin and Straubhaar 2002: 72). In 2001, more than a decade into the transition, half of the respondents in a national survey described themselves as disappointed with the regime change. This did not necessarily indicate communist nostalgia, but rather an expression of unmet expectations. The majority seemed to have been obnubilated by the belief that democracy must be the natural result of the revolution and had thus expected a magical transformation of society (Preda 1999). Romanians were left wanting when results were not delivered quickly. Almost 90 per cent blamed it on political failures (Ulram and Plasser 2003: 32, 34). The 'new' political class had emerged already corrupt, tinted by former communist associations, whilst many 'messianic' leaders had quickly crumbled under the weight of undeliverable promises (Tismăneanu 1992, 1997 and 1999). The strife to control the political transition led to a period of permanent electoral upheaval and prolonged social violence (Drăgan et al. 1998: 305). One migrant's online reflection summed it up thus: 'Romanians don't know how to live with one another anymore. . . . Communism and the transition have made them asocial, savage' (Severin, *Români Online UK*). However, it also made Romanians political.

Emigration is a political act (Sayad 2004: 88). Among all the possible political acts, emigration stands out as one of the most radical. Romanian emigrants cite the dishonesty of politicians, the widespread corruption and the lack of social protection in Romania among the main causes of emigration. 'They try to depersonalize, dehumanize us' (Gabi, *Italia România*), commented an online participant. 'They' seem to be the politicians, the elites, the intelligentsia – those undefined few who repeatedly fail the people. Such comments show that the economic and political collapse which started during communism and became evident during the transition also led to a social and moral disintegration that pitted elites against masses, majority against ethnic minorities, and those in authority against those feeling disenfranchised and powerless. It also pitted a rather passive majority, looking for some continuity and stability, against an active and vociferous minority, looking for radical change (Drăgan et al. 1998: 313–4).

For those feeling marginalized migration could bring an immediate change, a swift resolution for all their troubles. 'I know one could live there [in Romania]', said Mica, 'but why compromise? Why should I accept to taint myself . . . when I can live my life in dignity and have my contribution to society appreciated?' (*Realitatea din Italia*). 'We are "ill"', responded Lina within the same discussion thread, and 'as long as we continue to live without worth, without values . . . we will continue to "be ill"' (*Realitatea din Italia*). In another discussion forum Petrus mused: 'My great grandparents, grandparents and parents all had hoped for change. But some of us decided we could not wait for change anymore and we did what we thought best for our future' (*Români Online UK*).

Disillusionment and the lack of faith in politicians' ability to deliver compelled many Romanians to take things into their own hands and emigration became an act of protest. As one migrant explained: 'The biggest gain of emigrating was the feeling of national dignity – a live, powerful and clear feeling, that I could not have felt within the atmosphere of contemporary Romanian society' (Galina, *Realitatea din Italia*). One of the migrants I met online and then interviewed face-to-face suggested that Romanians needed to feel some self-worth; through migration they could learn how to feel national pride directly from other cultures:

I, too, had an idealised vision of the West, imagining things here to be perfect. But mistakes are being made here as well, people are not better or kinder, they just have more opportunities and means. They belong to a country that is important, means something on the world map. (Mia, London, 27 September 2008)

By comparison, Romania had become a land without horizon.

As the sociologist Dumitru Sandu observed, it is possible to achieve social transition through emigration (Sandu 2010: 35), so the initial vote of no confidence in the political class became a much more elaborate attempt to act in order to reverse the social stagnation and economic humiliations of the first decades after communism. Circumstances aided such strategic considerations. After years of isolation and banned foreign travel during communism, freedom of movement was taken advantage of whenever possible. Travelling abroad became a direct pursuit – for work, study and tourism – or indirect practice, through the shared experiences of friends and family (Brubaker et al.

2006). A mythology of destinations, opportunities and lifestyle narratives developed. Emigration may have had very specific causes, but its allure was also promoted through word of mouth and allusions to a 'promised land' of immediate social achievement. A higher social standing within their home community awaited those who left and the ability to grow in terms of personal learning, education and job opportunities opened up. As one migrant remarked, 'you cannot do things differently without changing something, changing yourself' (Lina, *Realitatea din Italia*).

Migrating abroad was the next natural step, after internal migration from rural to urban areas decreased due to lack of opportunities even in larger cities (Sandu 2010: 77). Ana-Maria's conclusion: 'in Romania you live from hand to mouth, month after month . . .[;] the salary is only enough to survive' (*Romanian Community of Ireland*), was shared by many diasporans. For certain categories, particularly rural youth with few qualifications and no opportunities for social and economic progress, migration became 'quasi-compulsory', very much 'a crucial and necessary act' (Horváth 2008: 774). Once migratory networks started to develop, it was easy to start taking advantage of them and migration became the preferred survival strategy (Sandu 2010: 80). The new economics of migration dictate that once the countries of destination become 'psychologically' attractive, entire communities start acting collectively to get involved in the phenomenon of migration (Massey et al. 1998: 21). In this sense, Eastern Europeans are no different from other migratory groups. As an online contributor explained, 'in 2000 it was fashionable to go abroad; everybody was leaving, so I left as well' (Gina, *Realitatea din Italia*).

Migration started to acquire a well known self-feeding character (Massey et al. 1994: 1493, 1496), aided also by individual characteristics, social conditions and technologies (Massey et al. 1998: 20). Romanians were 'ripe' for emigration both in terms of individual aspirations and social conditioning. 'There's just no way of making it here anymore', was an often heard leitmotif in the interviews conducted by Rogers Brubaker and his team in the Transylvanian town of Cluj, more than one decade into the transition (Brubaker et al. 2006: 316). As the research team noted, the theme of migration became part of everyday life, weaving narratives mostly of success, occasionally of hardship and humiliation. Whatever the story, the West came to Romania in the guise of remittances, consumer goods and particularly flash cars, often driven by diasporans coming home for a holiday after working in Germany, Italy or Spain. These became powerful symbols of prosperity and achievement through migration. Moreover, technology helped 'sustain' such collective illusions, helping to perpetuate migratory patterns (Sayad 2004: 73). Numerous premigrants joined diasporic websites to criticize Romanian realities, construct a network of information and support and prepare for the transit.

Technology enables 'mental emigration' (Sabry 2005). Satellite television since the late 1980s and, later, the Internet have translated Western experiences to Romanian audiences and the comparison has made Romanian realities unpalatable. In the first in-depth analysis of emigration causes and their resulting models, conducted through numerous interviews with Romanian emigrants and returnees, sociologists Zoltán Rostás and Sorin Stoica noted a keen aspiration for a better life, defined by not just economic but also social capital (2006: 8). Migration in search of social capital and mobility, economically motivated migration, the aspiration for feelings of national pride and a personal desire to grow, subsumed under the comment 'I wanted to change something in my life' (Gina, *Realitatea din Italia*), all share a yearning for 'the West'. Symbolic geography creates categories of rank. For many Romanian migrants, the West's cultural pedigree and evident material prosperity became the epitome of 'civilization'. An online participant clarified how he felt whenever he visited Romania and had the occasion to compare it to his life in the West: 'after a few days back home we couldn't wait to come back. We missed the CIVILIZATION' (Dan, *Români Online UK*, emphasis in the original). Another migrant explained: 'I didn't come for money only. . . . I also needed spiritual nourishment, otherwise I die little by little. . . . [T]he UK has remained my dream come true and with God's help I want to stay here' (Selina, *Români Online UK*).

The Europeanist Vocation

The West initially optimistically embraced Romania's return to democracy, partly mollified by the brutality of the 1989 revolution played on television screens worldwide. Nonetheless, it quickly became concerned by the economic collapse, ethnic conflicts, neo-communist sentiments and potential mass migration. Western media and politics displayed hints of Orientalism and Romania became associated with Balkanization – the return of tribalism and barbarity (Todorova 2000: 15). As Todorova explains, an earlier and inaccurate geographical knowledge and the First World War's negative political associations with the Balkans were thus stretched to include the period after 1989 (Todorova 2000: 21).

According to Larry Wolff, phantasmagoric constructions of the East have abounded in the publications and cartography of Western authors from Voltaire onwards, marrying the fantasizing of armchair travellers with the imaginative accounts of actual tourists (2000: 127). In Western travel accounts the East had a savage quality, with lovely but menacing landscapes, thus offering educated Westerners a comparison which helped reaffirm their own 'superior' identity. To this day, Dracula-type myths still survive. The colonial 'white man's burden' concept further contributed to the shaping of a supranational Western identity (Balibar and Wallerstein 1991: 43). The Balkan area emerged as a distinct entity, which also presupposed the homogeneity of the West (Todorova 2000: 221), as well as Western superiority.

The insidious myth of Eastern difference and Eastern inferiority was internalized in Romania both in elite discourse and in popular culture, provoking an underlying moral and psychological crisis in the Romanian collective consciousness. For a long time, Romanians had felt akin to Western culture, but the West's perceived rejection at a practical level, which Romanians experienced first and foremost when trying to travel and emigrate abroad, caused an incongruity often reflected upon by migrants and worth exploring further.

The West's Orientalist gaze occasioned the adoption and internalization of complexes of inferiority, without taking away the allure of the West. Historian Sorin Mitu exemplifies this self-flagellation through the writings of Transylvanian intellectuals since the nineteenth century, which reveal the existence of an established Romanian anxiety. *Suntem de batjocura lumii* (we are the butt of all jokes) is a self-stigmatization leitmotif based on the conviction that Romanians might be laughed at for their shortcomings (Mitu 1997: 59). Even today, in online diasporic forums, migrants use a similar mechanism. Mica, a Romanian migrant from Italy, quoted from a blog that displays a humorous take on Romanian identity:

> You are definitely Romanian if everything you eat tastes of onion and garlic . . . [;] in the airport you sit next to the two largest suitcases . . . [;] your house is full of doilies . . . [;] your mum tells you you're thin even if you weigh 110 kg . . . [;] you've seen the world from the toilet of a moving train. (Mica, *Realitatea din Italia*)

Another participant was similarly unforgiving:

> Many Romanians lack elementary civilization and minimum taste: you see how they dress in public (some look like they've just arrived from the miners' riots in the 90s), how they walk, talk in the street, gesticulate, the makeup they wear (the women), how they brag and laugh out loud and vulgarly, play it 'cool' (they think) etc. etc. Not to mention the thieves. . . (Mihu, *Realitatea din Italia*)

According to Mihu, this represents a *manelist* lifestyle. The juxtaposition between the word 'civilization' and the word *manelist* is very telling. *Manelist* (*manele* fan) comes from *manele*, a post-communist music genre, which combines Gypsy and Oriental rhythms with American hip-hop. Largely known as turbo-folk and popular in the whole Balkan area, the *manele* genre exhibits certain qualities that are taken to represent the Balkan spirit – a largely agri-cultural milieu, large, family-based communities, Mafia-style economy and corruption, rural passivity and traditionalism (Pecican 2003: 83).

The accompanying *manelist* lifestyle takes the Balkan symbolic geography further, to encompass references to: the post-communist transition defined by corruption and the collapse of moral values; a rural culture forced to modern-ize by globalization, dominated by kitsch and cheap cultural imports; the obsession with status symbols (largely financial); and the rise of a *nouveau riche* class that further confuses traditional social hierarchies. The fact that *manele* was first popularized by Gypsy musicians also adds an ethnic element, whereby Gypsy stereotypes are transferred onto those who love *manele* and 'bling'. By contrast, civilization alludes to a more restrained and sophisticated lifestyle. The implication is that you are civilized if your looks and behaviour do not single you out as a non-Westerner – if you blend in. This is echoed in the following online post as well:

> I was ashamed many times by the way Romanians behave and talk among themselves or with the Italians. But I was never ashamed that I am Romanian myself . . . [. W]hen people cross the border they forget the way they were brought up. (Silvana, *România Italia Net*)

The Romanian complex of inferiority shows through strongly. Migrants need to play up to the West's expectations of conformity, but this expectation does not come primarily and directly from Westerners; it comes instead from fellow migrants, fearful of being tainted by association. As a result, what can be described as a diseased and incongruous body, the migrant body, needs to be first healed and then remade in another's image.

Many nations share the dilemma of being both inside and outside the West, a doubleness that is almost impossible to 'synchronize' (Gilroy 1993: 30). Throughout much of the last two centuries, Romanians have strived to fit into and belong to what was their own imaging of the West. Even during the communist period, state propaganda emphasized Romania's contribution to European culture. As a result, both political discourse and popular media have attempted to find compelling justifications for belonging and recogni-tion. The myth of a Golden Age, an illustrious past heralding a better future, was the instrument that history handed Romanians in order to evade their inferiority complex (Boia 2002b: 68). Old topoi of Romanian popular culture, amplified by communist nationalism, were rescued in the post-communist period. According to them, Romanians are 'defenders of Christendom' and have played an almost messianic role as the 'bulwark' of Europe. Although the 'bulwark of Europe' motif is a commonly shared belief among all Balkan peoples (Tismăneanu 1999: 109), the wars fought against the Turks have remained imprinted on the national consciousness (Boia 2001: 65) and are used as a justification for outright European membership. Through 'historical amplification' Romanians are thus transformed from the West's apprentice into the West's defenders (Boia 1997: 37). Being a 'frontier' country, precariously perched between West and East, also speaks of extraordinary survival skills and a 'tenacity factor' (White 2000:153) that has come to define Romanianness.

As Adrian Marino sums up, between East and West, Romanian culture has been defined by two major complexes – Occidental and Oriental, both complexes of superiority but also inferiority (Marino 1995: 75). Internalized Orientalism may be a complex of inferiority towards the more 'civilized' and 'advanced' Western culture, but it can also become a complex of superiority (Marino 1995: 58), since Eastern culture has not only managed to maintain 'purer' traditions and a closer relationship with the environment, but also rescued the West from Islamization. Any current deficiency can be considered just a momentary shortcoming (Mitu 1997: 65). Enraged by the comments of an Italian Member of Parliament who suggested that Romanians should be excluded from the EU, an online migrant reacted with: 'Has this idiot forgotten that we were born in Europe?' (Adina, *Români în UK*).

Online, the European card is played forcefully and repeatedly in relation to perceived Romanian superiority and perceived inferiority. It is here that complexes resurface, probably spurred on by the participants' subaltern position in the host societies, but also as a recurring trauma. Despite making it to the West, despite a largely successful adaptation, online contributors continue to justify their presence in Europe, as is required of Romanians with a problematic national identity. One of the mechanisms of regaining symbolic European status is using racism to draw a demarcation between Eastern European and non-European migrants:

> Italians are right, Berlusconi especially . . . [:] migration only brings disaster, look at the English who brought over Africans, Asians etc. . . . [W]hat has become of them[?] . . . [N]ow they cry and vote for the BNP. TOO LATE, Babylon is here, hoards of barbarians are waiting at the gates of Europe . . . [. I]n about 100 years we will all be African and Asian . . . [,] converted to Islam. . . . I deviated from the subject. (Patriciu, *Români în UK*, emphasis in the original)

The post goes on to blame the Romany Gypsies for Romania's bad image abroad and displays throughout an appropriation of racist and anti-Islamic topoi. Paradoxical as it may be that this migrant faithfully reproduces the discourse of the right-wing press, it also conveys a strong Eurocentric superiority, which is typical of those Romanians who convert inferiority into superiority. I will return to migrant hierarchies and the appropriation of majority extremist discourses by migrants in Chapter Three.

The West has always been a point of reference in the Romanian imagination. In the nineteenth century, the Eastern elites' flirtations with the West prepared the bed for nationalizing and modernizing processes which continued until the period between the two world wars. In the first half of the nineteenth century, Romania could have easily been viewed as an 'extension' of Western Europe (Boia 2001: 12) due to the assiduous adoption of Western cultural models. During communism, nationalist exultations continued to place Romanian culture within the European pantheon of civilization, combined with socialist progress. In addition, many Romanians cultivated the myth of the Western 'duty' towards the East, accrued when the East was 'sold' to the Soviet Empire. As my mother often recounts, 'your grandfather always thought that the Americans would finally arrive and rescue us. He kept waiting for them. Only in the 1970s he finally gave up hope'. In 1989 it was time for the debt to be collected – the West 'owed it to us'. One migrant explained: 'Romania has been plagued by a restless history, otherwise we would be at a different stage' (Ionela, *Români Online UK*).

Romanians are not unique among Eastern Europeans to claim their outright membership of European culture. They have found, nonetheless, a unique entitlement. Being an 'island of Latinity in a Slavic sea' is seen to bestow imperial ancestry and the pedigree of belonging to a group of prestigious Latin cultures. It is through language that Romanians imagine their distinctiveness in Eastern Europe (White 2000: 119, 125). Language also gives Romania kinship with other neo-Latin peoples and the expected unconditional support of key European players like France and Italy. Through its neo-Latin family, Romania is a country ready to retake its place within the 'European family'. As diasporans often say: 'I don't feel inferior in comparison to the Italians, why should I????' (Mela, *România Italia Net*); 'I would also say that Romanians are comparable with the British' (Mia, London, 27 September 2008). Such views are imbued with the myth of Latinity cultivated by nationalist propaganda, but on the part of migrants, they are also a sign of a complex of inferiority turned on its head into superiority vis-à-vis other Eastern European nations and even the Spanish or the Italians who have the audacity to reject their own kin.

Europeanism was and still is articulated in two very different ways in Romania. On the one hand, Europeanism can be a genuine, elite project, which pushes for democratization at all levels and a realistic European integration. On the other hand, Europeanism is an appendix of the nationalist discourse, as expressed by the 'island of Latinity in a Slavic sea' metaphor, in which Romanianism (*Românismul*) is defined as superior through a process of exceptionalization. *Românismul*, the more nationalist view of Romania's relationship with the West, has in its turn two nuances. In its European-friendly form it is expressed through pride and appreciation for a people living on the edge of history, who are finally being vindicated and can expect better things in the future. It definitely has a dose of pathos and overindulgence, but it is also pro-European. In its ugly form, *Românismul* is a type of national discourse and a type of political culture based on feelings of inadequacy towards Europe. It has certain foundation myths, which give it an understanding of its enemies and the ways to treat them based on classification and stigmatization (Preda 1999). It is in its essence against the generous ideals that lay at the foundations of true Europeanist sentiments, sees Romania existing in a parallel history and constructs its uniqueness by claiming a mystical bond with a specific landscape and rural, ahistorical practices. Its narcissistic focus leads to a lack of understanding of outside contexts because 'any isolated culture' becomes 'a great mystery' (Mungiu-Pippidi 2002: 23).

Nationalist and exclusivist tendencies, which are shared, as we shall see, by many Romanian migrants, are a direct outcome of post-communist renationalizing processes (Brubaker 1996). With communism compromised, the only authoritarian ideology left was nationalism (Andreescu 1996: 91). As a result, Romania failed to move into a period of post-nationalism, defined by universalism and individualization, and remained prepost-nationalist: although the nation already exists, a renationalizing process is still taking place, as if the existence of the nation is still being threatened. Post-communist nationalism exploited 'a massified society, with atomized individuals, and a sense of universal helplessness' (Tismăneanu 1992: 302). The effects of communism, coupled with the nationalist rhetoric of the 1990s, can still be detected in the way some Romanians manifest their xenophobia, mistrust and inferiority complexes.

Reading online posts, I was often shocked by the way these complexes were being expressed by migrants online. However, they needed to be interpreted as part and parcel of the love–hate relationship that Romanians have had with the West. As Lucian Boia explains, three traumatic ruptures have affected Romania within the last 150 years. The first one is the split from the Orient due to an elite-led process of Westernization. The second is represented by the break with the West during communism and the third by the abrupt divorce from communism in December 1989. This triad has created a perpetual search for models (Boia 1997: 199) and a syncopated relationship with the West, which is commonly echoed in the online exchanges illustrated in Part Two of this book, which discusses the arrival and settlement of the Romanian diaspora in the West.

The idea of 'forms without substance' defines the first nineteenth-century rupture, in which two models were hotly debated. The polemic set in opposition the so-called 'traditionalists', who criticized imported European forms devoid of autochthonic substance, and the 'modernizers', who championed a synchronic approach, where modernization begins with the adoption of Western values and institutions, gradually filled with local content. The Romanian literary critic Titu Maiorescu wrote in 1868 against the fast but superficial appropriation of Western institutions and mannerisms, which he called 'forms without substance' (Boia 2001: 86; Lazăr 2002: 172). The literary critic Eugen Lovinescu responded with a 'synchronic' approach (Boia 1997: 17), which claimed that forms have a more profound impact on values than one might expect (Boia 2001: 83). Maiorescu's views were shaped by his ethnocentric illusions and the attempt to differentiate his views from a generation who industriously adopted many Western institutions, particularly in education (Lazăr 2002: 173). Ethnic exceptionalism based on the traditionalism and perpetuity of rural culture was thus exalted at the expense of the modernizing bourgeoisie's cosmopolitan claims. It is a classic example of a complex of inferiority converted into unwarranted (some may say) superiority and pride.

Maiorescu's traditionalist call returned in the work of twentieth-century Romanian philosophers. In a 1936 article, writer and philosopher Mircea Eliade maintained that Romanians needed to renounce their complex of inferiority vis-à-vis Europe and nourish Romanian creativity in order to establish Romanian culture as a major culture within Europe. Also in 1936, Transylvanian poet and philosopher Lucian Blaga wrote a panegyric of the Balkan *mioritic* landscape and the traditional rural life contained within (Blaga 1994 [1936]). *Miorița* (the name from which the attribute *mioritic* derives) is a magical sheep in popular mythology who warns the shepherd of a plan to kill him. The shepherd does nothing; he accepts the inevitable while contemplating the beauty of nature, thus passing on the message that the individual has little control over how power is exercised (Schöpflin 2000: 92–3). *Mioritic* is now a characteristic that sees Romanianness as being determined by the specificities of the landscape. In Blaga's view, the landscape and slow pace of life taught Romanians patience, resignation and fatalism in the face of external aggression. These traits ensured their survival as a nation.

Blaga's views are a eulogy of Romanian qualities, especially the defence of continuity in the face of adversity, yet they can also be interpreted as a boycott of history. Romanian life seems to run parallel to Europe's, outside normal time and space, bound to the cosmos and limitless. Blaga's philosophy is clearly centred on the notion of 'mystery' after finding inspiration in German philosophy (Hitchins 1997: 299). In relation to the way one might interpret Blaga's views, one Romanian migrant made the following astute comment:

I still think that the genealogical ingredients of the Romanian nation are those found in the *Miorița* pastoral ballad, as described by a (British) specialist who was referring to the traits of the Romanian people like so: envy, treachery, thievery and resignation. On the other hand, through extrapolation, as a Romanian you can consider yourself the 'centre of the universe', it doesn't cost you anything. (Dorin, *Români în UK*)

This contributor is obviously distancing himself ironically from well known stereotypes; however, in most online dialogues, a fault line appears between participants, mirroring the cultural controversy at the heart of Romanian identity.

Many other intellectuals in the twentieth century saw modernization as a type of 'rape' (Mungiu-Pippidi 2002: 154). This view was typical of Right-leaning intellectuals between the two great wars, who saw modernization as the annihilation of the Romanian essence or soul. Their exaltations about rural life were imbued with metaphysical considerations and paradoxically also became appealing to the communist Left, for whom references to an imaginary Romania were a way of distracting attention from the effects of social engineering (Mungiu-Pippidi 2002: 169).

The emphasis on traditional life remained therefore a permanent feature of the second major rupture in the Romanian consciousness, when the Romania of old was replaced with the 'new', communist Romania (Marino 1996a: 187–8). Some of the ideas about national specificities and the reconsideration of the Romanian village as the 'repository of the national soul' were recaptured in 1978 by philosopher Constantin Noica (1996), a sign of the lasting impact of the belief that Romanian identity is defined by land and folklore (Boia 2001: 220).

It is paradoxical that communism has destroyed the traditional Romanian village, first through collectivization and then through the attempt to 'resystematize' it and move the population to the factories and the urban high-rises. The village and its folklore remained nonetheless embedded within the rhetoric of communist nationalism, which needed to adopt unity and continuity as its defining elements (Boia 2001: 139). The downside was that the emphasis on uniqueness made Romanians distrustful of others (Boia 2001: 174). This phenomenon was accentuated by communist isolation and it developed into complexes both of superiority and of inferiority.

Rural symbolism also eschewed the importance of civic consciousness, the irrational attitudes of 'closed societies', the violence of the village and its treatment of women and children (Andreescu 1996: 114). The light fell instead on the landscape, which is of course suffused with nationalist metaphors (Outhwaite and Ray 2005). 'Environmental determinism' (White 2000: 138) or 'geographical determinism' (Boia 2002b: 43) included the Carpathians, the

Danube and the Black Sea, which featured prominently in communist iconography and rhetoric. The communist national anthem, for example, was all about the colour and shapes of the land determining the great features of a great people.

Many migrants have merged the deeply embedded rhetoric of environmental determinism with their nostalgia for their youth and childhood and the two together have become a strong protection or escape mechanism from the realities of migration. 'Some will remember what it was like for the sun to shine, to sit by the tent in the valley . . . [. E]veryone was gorgeous', reminisced one migrant (Tina, *Români în UK*). Online diasporic memory can also express multiple presences and parallel remembering (Outhwaite and Ray 2005: 179). One migrant illustrated this when he reflected comparatively, from the viewpoint of a double presence:

> Home for me means memories . . . [:] 20 years worth of memories. What does the UK mean? The place where I came to make money. . . . I do not want my children to be born here, in this country, I want my children to inhale the clean air of the Carpathians, to hear the same songs we used to sing in the mountains. (Călin, *Români Online UK*)

These instances of remembering but also forgetting, adopting and also rejecting, show the compound nature of migrant expressions of identity. Yet every nostalgic movement is counteracted by a realistic estimation: 'That Romania that some still dream of[,] . . . with good memories and wonderful landscapes, idyllic[,] . . . does not exist anymore' (Laur, *Români Online UK*). Zoe also rejected the received idea of geographical determinism: 'Unfortunately I like nothing there, not even the people, let alone the nature, not that out of the ordinary. To be honest I've seen more beautiful landscapes elsewhere' (Zoe, *Români Online UK*). Such contradictory views show the continuous interrogation of received beliefs that preoccupies migrant thinking and the constant parallels between here and there, East and West.

In the 1990s, the much mediatized polemic between nationalists and Europeanists was to return and polarize many Romanian intellectuals (Andreescu 1996). In view of the lack of viable alternatives, many expressed the belief that 'European and Occidental integration is the only acceptable solution' (Andreescu 1996: 26). However, among pro-Europeanists some expressed the fear that in the Romanian culture the overwhelming and most deeply rooted sentiment was the anti-European one (Marino 1995: 34). Romania was facing the enormous task of recapturing a lost identity, which included salvaging its own history, culture and religion, all perverted under communism (Andreescu 1996: 41). This recapturing, which included a generous dose of reinvention and reimagination, delved into an autochthonous past set apart by traditional folklore and the myth of its continuity through history (Boia 1997). This tendency has put Romanian culture at odds with more relevant cultural practices and has clearly fed nationalist feelings.

After 1989, the longstanding love–hate relationship with the West resurfaced in the collective consciousness as Western mimetism, but also as nationalism (Grancea and Ciobanu 2002: 364) and *ressentiment* (Greenfeld 1992). The response to the Orientalist gaze of the West was, as we have seen, anxiety about identity and belonging, the rolling out of nationalist topoi and the remaking of inferiority into a complex of superiority, by falling back onto claims of traditionalism and authenticity. As we shall see in the final part of this chapter, the search for identity is exacerbated by migration, which brings Romanians face-to-face with their own demons. Romanian migrants display very little healthy patriotism, which they envy in their Eastern European neighbours, such as the Hungarians, and instead feel resentment towards both the homeland and the hostland. In terms of identity they become moored in a no man's land brought about by their double alienation. Such feelings are freely expressed online, the virtual space without flags or borders, where the search for identity can continue unabated, as illustrated below.

Romanianism in Transition

Contemporary Romanianism is defined, as we have seen in intellectual debates and migrant reflections, by recurrent ruptures at the level of the collective consciousness, where feelings of both inferiority and superiority have defined the tensions between Europeanism and Romanianism. Online diasporic cultures reverberate most poignantly these identity dilemmas, which are articulated through the lenses of diasporic specificity from a double positioning by Eastern migrants living in the West. The Romanian case is not unique. Brinkerhoff mentions the same love–hate relationship with the homeland in the case of the online Somali community (Brinkerhoff 2009: 121). Migrants have, therefore, the capacity to interrogate received identities and propose what nationalist purists would probably consider identity aberrations, which nevertheless more accurately describe the dilemmas migrants face around nationhood and citizenship.

The following few excerpts exemplify a mutating Romanian identity. While we might expect migrants to express alienation vis-à-vis the contexts they encounter in the host society, some in fact choose to articulate their own Romanianness as burden, curse and alienation. The fixities of national identity start to appear incongruous with some of the new aspirations cultivated in time by mental emigration, transition fatigue and diasporic experiences. However, some migrants also reveal their realistic assessment of advantages or gains derived from citizenship and belonging. These migrants seem free to make choices based on what is best for them and their families. Undeniable nostalgia is thus neutralized by a sense of calculation and realism about the future.

In the first instance, migrants expressed their separation, presumably painful, as the result of a mismatch. 'I cannot find my place in Romania anymore' is a recurrent theme among this group of migrants: 'every time I go back home, I am happy not to live there anymore' (Grecu, *Italia România*). A premigrant who used one of the diasporic websites to prepare for emigration, reflected in a similar vein: 'I do not feel represented by anything here, in Romania. . . . Romania does not give me any chance to be happy. . . . I want to leave, so much. . . . I feel more and more alien, misunderstood by people around me' (Gabi, *Italia România*). Sometimes tasting life in the West is the precursor to realizing an inescapable destiny. Decea, a migrant who had spent one year in the UK doing voluntary work before deciding to live in Britain permanently, explained:

> At Băneasa Airport I felt as if I was burning my bridges and I had no way of returning, I had nothing to return to . . . only the MOUNTAINS and the NATURE. Unfortunately, in Romania I have met too many people who made me sorry I was Romanian . . . Why? Because I am different . . . [. M]aybe during the year spent here as a student my mental hard disk was formatted according to British principles. (Decea, *Români în UK*, emphasis in the original)

The formatting metaphor speaks of a transformative process, during which the old life is rejected in favour of a superior existence and a more relevant persona. Migration requires the shedding of the original national skin, although what it is in favour of is not always clear. The first identity aberration arises therefore in the form of extreme dislike for the country perceived as a bad mother. One migrant simply said, 'the mother country offered me nothing' (Dan, *Români Online UK*), while others, like Lucica, who was a premigrant, attempted some justification: 'I'm fed up with everything Romania stands for, the indifference of the authorities, lack of competence and so on' (Lucica, *Români Online UK*). Evdochia also explained: 'Romania is dominated by snobbishness, lack of culture and lack of care' (Evdochia, *Italia România*).

Other migrants raised the issue of belonging in relation to personal gain. Enache asked:

> Would you go back to a Third World country where the state steals even the air that you are trying to breathe? Does it really matter that you speak

your maternal language? Be serious, man, if you came here, stay and work for yourself and your family, not for a government and a piece of land called homeland, a homeland that never did and never will do anything for you. I decided to Live [capital in the original], not survive for others, for a state, an ideology, in fact for nothing. (Enache, *Marea unire, Spania*)

This post constructs another identity aberration. Love and allegiance for one's country is not a given or a must; it is a function of what the homeland can offer. It is not just the citizen who has to perform duties in exchange for rights, but the homeland, too, has a duty: to provide an appropriate context within which citizens are happy to perform their own duties, their nationhood.

The theme of fair exchange, giving only after receiving, echoes in many online posts. 'My country offered me nothing', commented one migrant (Dan, *Români Online UK*), while another elaborated: 'it's tough in a foreign country but I would not return to Romania . . . [. I]t's a beautiful country, but what can you do . . . when your parents offered you everything but the country nothing' (Tara, *Români Online UK*). Sever also assessed in a very practical way what he, as a citizen, could extract as profit from the unwritten contract he had entered. He thus compared the given homeland with the new country of his choice when he posted, 'once I will become a citizen of this country, this country will protect me. . . . I can't see Romania protecting me any time soon, not with the government it currently has' (Sever, *Români Online UK*).

Some migrants, like Mircea and Ceanu, made a sharp distinction between the country and the country's subjects: 'Romania as a country gave me very little[;] . . . its people . . . a lot!' (Mircea, *Italia România*); 'Romania is a beautiful country, even sublime, pity it's inhabited' (Ceanu, *Italia România*). Enache gave the impression that he shared a similar view, although he was unable to make up his mind about whom or what he hated most: 'You see the poverty, the crisis. . . . I'm sorry I went back and I am sorry I was born there. I am not against Romania as a country, maybe just against its people. . . . I would never give my life for that country' (Enache, *Marea unire, Spania*). Giving your life for your country, one of the central theses of nationalism, is discarded by Enache, together with the whole baggage it presupposes.

Migrant views, frankly and forcefully expressed online, show that outside the nationalizing space of the nation-state, identity becomes a matter of choice, not a given or a must; it moves away from 'an inescapable dependence' and becomes a 'selective association' (Georgiou 2006: 148). The online 'diasporic habitus' is detached from closed (state) definitions of identity and instead fosters 'reflexive racializations', which encourage the continuous revision of identity (Parker and Song 2006). Augustus echoed this freedom when he wrote: 'the fact that you are born in a certain country is an occurrence, not a choice' (Augustus, *Români Online UK*). Lori also said: 'Even if we need not forget where we started from, at the end of the day, your *patria* is where you feel best' (Lori *Marea unire, Spania*). 'I am not denying my origins', reflected a migrant from the UK, 'but as someone already mentioned, at the end of the day being born in Romania is an accident' (Miriana, *Români Online UK*).

One of the online participants raised another identity aberration, that of nationality as artificial performance, brought about by diasporic reflexivity and the ability to concomitantly reflect and interrogate the self and the collective:

> Being 'Romanian' differs from one person to another and may be anything: from cooking Romanian and attending the Romanian church, to watching Romanian TV and reading this forum. . . . This new year we did more than we did in the last five years: we watched a Romanian film (4-3-2) [4 Months, 3 Weeks and 2 Days, 2007], made *salade de boeuf* ['Russian' salad], *cozonac* [Romanian-style *panettone*] – it even turned out OK this time, and my wife made pigs' trotters in jelly, which she ate, because I don't like them. That's all. Do I feel more Romanian? No. Should I? (Ilie, *Români în UK*)

In this thread Ilie described identity as a performance with fixed, required attributes. However, the performance did not necessarily reflect his actual feelings brought about by diasporic experiences.

Enache dispelled, as well, the authenticity of performing your national allegiance: 'Patriotism is a mirage, entertained by those who do not want to change their lives, a motive to remain a slave and feed those who become rich by exploiting others' (Enache, *Marea unire, Spania*). Here the leitmotif of slavery is reversed. The slave is not the migrant, who works for the benefit of the West, sells his soul to the Devil and loses dignity – not an uncommon standpoint in many interviews with migrants (Rostás and Stoica 2006) – but the one who stays and endures, giving allegiance to an ungrateful mother country. Patriotism as burden is a theme, which is also evident in another post by a premigrant:

> It's true that once there, you become smaller and more insignificant than in your own country, but then even at home, we are small and taken advantage of. A friend who lives in the UK told me, 'rather than being a scorned citizen of my own country, I'd rather be belittled elsewhere[:] . . . at least I know what the motive is'. (Toma, *Spania românească*)

Other migrants displayed the aberration of a split personality, which is more akin to what we expect from the effects of diasporic experiences. 'Yes, I'm still Romanian and I also love the UK, God help us if we sin by wishing to stay here, rather than in Romania' (Ovidiu, *Români în UK*). Other migrants, like Rus, exhibited a somewhat expected confusion: 'I always speak nicely (but realistically)☺. . . . I try, but I do not insist, to teach my child Romanian' (Rus, *Români în UK*).

The intervention of premigrants also helped to diffuse some of the love–hate feelings displayed by diasporans. One participant who claimed that she had made a deliberate choice to stay in Romania said:

> News about illegalities and lack of professionalism will always pop up in Romania. Moreover, after you've known another culture it is more difficult to accept such realities. . . . Romania is still a country in which you can live. A dose of compromise goes without saying if you want to live here. (Lina, *Realitatea din Italia*)

Berciu, who was a premigrant, wrote just before arriving in the UK:

> I like what I read in this forum, happy to see that wherever we are, we don't forget we are Romanians. I can't stand those who, having left Romania, talk badly about it, or even worse, deny they are Romanian. If we have a precarious economy and an overindulging political class interested only in pilfering what they can, it doesn't mean that Romania is not a beautiful country worth living in. Maybe in a few years' time. . . (*Români în UK*)

From this post it is evident that migrants also look at their own and others' attitudes towards the mother country. A continuous reexamination of how their Romanianness is negotiated between outright rejection and nostalgic attachment is carried out by diasporans themselves. In a way, the last two examples match our expectations of what diasporic sentiment should be. However, they can also be interpreted as criticism of a country that falls short of expectations, a land with no horizon in view.

There are, of course, as many nostalgic voices as there are critical ones. Very touchingly, Lara declared: 'I miss Romania every second' (Lara, *Români Online UK*). Crossing into the territory of more serious identity debates, Babu reflected: 'We experience an illusory personal benefit, we contemplate calmly, self-sufficiently the phenomenon of uprooting' (Babu, *Români Online UK*). In a separate post he added: 'We have so many cultural, spiritual values. Here I am in danger of losing myself, caught in the routine of material gains'. These comments seem to be in direct contradiction to Enache's previously quoted calculations of the pitfalls of illusory collectiveness versus the advantages of personal benefits. Babu's view was echoed by Ionela, who posted: 'Although I've had various interesting experiences in other countries . . . in RO [Romania] I feel somewhat more "solid"' (Ionela, *Români Online UK*).

Once more, although these posts conform to the classic understanding which expects the diasporic condition to be defined by nostalgic attachments, in them we can also read an unforgiving assessment of available identity choices. Migrants and premigrants alike constantly justify their feelings and thinking behind their choice of citizenship, behaviour and homeland. These reflections are expressed in a number of identities, some anomalous with regard to our classic understanding of nationhood. However, their choices have also to be understood in the context of historical and cultural fractures, the polarization of East and West in symbolic geography and the mental emigration that precedes *de facto* migration. Migrants endeavour to find a better fit between dream and reality, between present difficulties and future hopes, in an attempt to escape the fatigue induced by a long transition to democracy.

Conclusion: Online Is the Predilect Space for Identity Interrogations

Emigration becomes an act of protest against the political elite and the economic and social realities still plaguing Romania, two decades after the anti-communist revolution. Migrants' perpetual interrogation, rejection and proposition of transformative identities are not just typical, but a necessary constituent of the diasporic condition and the virtual 'diasporic habitus' that invites reelaborations of static identities. 'Making it' and 'civilization' become key themes linking migrants' contradictory reflections. Both themes indicate that economic circumstances are not enough to explain Eastern European emigration; we also have to look deeper, into the social and cultural capital of migration.

As we have seen, migration is a function of stalled social mobility and denied cultural aspirations for personal growth and achievement in a country which has not yet found its feet among other European nations. As a result, migration can be described as a clear political act. However, it is online that we have to look for a display of all subtleties encompassed in the passing of identity from one state to another. Online reflections mediate the transition and adaptation to the hostland's realities. They also allow the freedom of reflexivity from a space with multiple anchors but ultimately free of identity fixities, defined by liquidity in the way the self and the collective are perpetually reconfigured. The online also interrogates the offline, providing the necessary critical discourse and a much needed gaze turned inwards.

From the views of premigrants who enter online diasporic spaces and engage in conversation with those who have already made the geographical and mental shift, it is also clear that online diasporic spaces allow premigrants to cultivate and deepen their feelings of isolation and inadequacy 'at home'. The premigrants then use these spaces to justify their choice and validate their emigration plan. Online diasporic reflexivity also allows for a 'critical counter-public' (Parker and Song 2006: 589) to emerge, thus adding a new dimension to the search of identity. From their diasporic positioning, migrants and premigrants alike reelaborate what it means to be Romanian in Europe today. The individual is thus in tension with the community, those inside with those outside, the perceived immutability of the nation with the flexibility of those in perpetual transit.

The online dialogue between various reflexive positions – here and there, then and now, at home and abroad, online and offline – tells us something about the way the Romanian diaspora shapes itself, how it interacts with others and how it constructs its future in the context of multiple cultural anchorings. It tells us that the idealism of the Europeanist vocation is in tension, but also in a dialogue, with the realism of social mobility, leading thus to identity aberrations, which find online the ideal place for further elaboration.

CHAPTER TWO

'Taking the Bull by the Horns'

Migrant Pathology and the Role of Diasporic Websites

Anton's Story

I go mad here. . . . It seems like I relive the same day over and over again. . . . England . . . [is] a country for making money[,] . . . nothing more. I never felt I was living here for one moment[;] . . . here I forgot what happiness is[;] . . . here I learnt how evil the whole world is. . . . I don't want to turn 30 here[,] . . . terrorized by the past[,] . . . stressed . . . [and] scared of people.

This is how nineteen-year-old Anton started a new discussion thread on *Români în UK* in the summer of 2008. His tale spoke of homelessness, alienation and unfulfilled dreams and its potency was derived from its rawness. This was a story that was not told through the filter of time by someone who had battled and prevailed; it was an unfolding drama. After Romania's EU accession in 2007, when a tourist visa was no longer required in the UK, many young Romanians tried their luck and remained in the country without the safety net of the coveted work permit. The gamble did not pay off for Anton and many more like him. After harsh experiences and desperation amplified by fierce backbiting among Romanians who found themselves in the same predicament, his decision to return to Romania had become almost final; and yet he came into the forum to tell his tale and invite pity, advice and even judgement.

Anton was not a frequent user of the message board, having posted only eighteen times previously. However, his tale sparked no less than 188 replies, an unusually long run for any topic. The arguments became so heated that the discussion thread was eventually locked by the webmaster upon his return from holidays, to prevent participants from further exchanging digital blows. During these few weeks, Anton himself had a good online scrap with another Romanian whom he had accused of pilfering and dishonesty and who then descended into the ring to do battle and to give his own version of the events. Other users intervened as well and often disagreed with one another on various issues like the success or failure of immigration, the (natural) ability that Romanians have to overcome difficulties, Romanians and their relationship with others, happiness and migration, pride and humility, and even the role of the online forum and its ability to deal with a heavy-going topic such as this one.

Among all these themes one in particular stood out: the participants attempted to assess the traits that created a successful émigré. They seemed to attribute to such a character a certain dose of accompanying pain, foolishness and even insanity; occasionally also strength and superhuman powers. Their views have inspired this chapter, which discusses emigration not only as a Romanian fixation derived from specific local experiences, but also as a process refuelled by the experiences and narratives of emigration. By the nature of the process, emigration creates new encounters and new feelings that feed a culture of interrogation and intermittent dissatisfaction. This underlying unhappiness leads to self-examination, reflexivity and protest. It becomes, therefore, political.

Judging from what migrants say in Anton's discussion thread, emigration attracts specific characters endowed with certain characteristics. Among these, courage, perhaps sometimes foolhardiness and resilience seem to be the key features that help migrants stick it out in difficult circumstances. One contributor to the discussion reflected, 'you need a lot of patience and courage' (Rada, *Români în UK*), while another told Anton: 'I don't advise you to stay in the UK if you do not have the balls' (Antonia, *Români în UK*). In the same contributor's view, it is the struggle that makes some thrive: 'Difficulties made many determined not to give up, to try for more, to break through'. Yet Antonia also cautioned against any foolhardy behaviour: 'Good people, don't plunge without a safety net; don't emigrate without a penny in your pockets and full of empty promises.' She later attributed Anton's mishaps to his young age and lack of experience and the fact that 'you went with the flow'. Antonia seemed to imply that some chose to emigrate because of the examples set by others, because of 'the flow', but any narratives or trends that entice migrants also leave them insufficiently prepared and too expectant. This is a theme echoed in other posts on diasporic websites, in which premigrants are always urged by settled migrants to use the sites to their full potential, obtain advice, research and prepare realistically for what awaits them.

Rising or not to the occasion appears to be the defining element of successful emigration. One participant explained:

I never imagined I would work this much, but I don't complain and I am not going home. When folk see you back home they say 'look at him, everybody makes it outside, only he is coming back like a coward with his tail between his legs'[;] it's hard, I know, grit your teeth and chin up. (Bogdan, *Români în UK*)

A similar thought is expressed by Rada: 'I gritted my teeth and carried on. . . . Romanians rarely manage to succeed in the first year. . . . Nobody gives you a desk job on the first day, you work your socks off, then you may reap the rewards' (Rada, *Români în UK*). In this view, migration is fuelled by the dream, by making it to the 'desk job', a metaphor for achievement that returns in other migrant stories.

Migration is also about the survival of the fittest – those who have 'the balls' – so it is ultimately about natural selection. As Iancu said, 'you need to have the perseverance to overcome, to make something from nothing! Natural selection' (Iancu, *Români în UK*), while another participant added that 'emigration is not for everybody, you need plenty of balls and cold blood' (Cătălin, *Români în UK*).

Anton's story and the subsequent reactions of the diaspora suggest several arguments for discussion, starting with the implication that migration produces severe forms of self-examination and reevaluation. As a result, diasporic websites become primarily spaces of perpetual assessment of the self and the relationship between the self and the other. This almost hypochondriac scrutiny explains how the desire to emigrate and then endure can be induced by an alluring narrative of self-enhancement, but the eventual migration success depends on certain qualities and abilities. The successful émigrés must also suffer from conditions which compel them to undergo extraordinary and almost masochistic tests.

Migrant Pathology

Online diasporic debates and my own interviews with members of the Romanian diaspora have revealed a preoccupation with illness, anxiety and dissatisfaction understood in a number of ways. One context in which the theme of abnormality appears is that of sick identity. A second context is the Romanian emigration phenomenon understood as a pandemic, as a suppurating wound. From some reflections it clearly transpires that Romanian emigration is not caused exclusively by financial difficulties, but is a sign of non-conformism and dissatisfaction. A third context in which illness or mental disturbance appears is in the description of migrants by migrants. Migrants appear to display unusual symptoms that range, as we have already seen, from fixations and unfulfilled desires to complexes of both inferiority and superiority. The implication is not only that some of these existing traits can be successfully deployed during migration and even enhanced, but also that new symptoms are added by the migration process itself. Migration, understood as a form of illness or pathology, can either kill the dream (as in Anton's case) or make the migrant stronger, almost a superhero (see, above, the views of Antonia, Bogdan, Cătălin, Iancu and Rada). The discussion presented here aims to give more nuance to the theory that the migrant body is usually regarded as foreign and 'incomprehensible' (Sayad 2004: 179), suffering from 'sinistrosis' (Sayad 2004: 184) and thus abnormal in some way.

I will start by discussing the preoccupation with a sick national identity or national stigma, which continues from the previous chapter. As we have already seen, auto-denigration has always been a Romanian tradition. Historian Sorin Mitu has even gathered a number of intellectual, historical writings peppered with Romanians who either entertained some form of hatred for their Romanian condition or were ashamed of being Romanian (Mitu 1997: 97). More recently, in the interviews and observations conducted by Rogers Brubaker's research team in the Transylvanian town of Cluj between 1995 and 2001, it also emerged that Romanianness became particularly problematic when, after 1989, Romanians came face to face with new legal restrictions for work or travel and began to compare their own 'inferior' citizenship with Europe's 'good citizenships' (Brubaker et al. 2006: 321–6). During this period, Romanianness came to be regarded as a 'stigmatized citizenship' (Brubaker et al. 2006: 321), as a 'spoiled identity' and tribal stigma (Goffman 1990: 14). As one of my interviewees told me, 'there are people on the forum who like to forget that they are Romanian – they think it is something inferior' (Mia, London, 27 September 2008).

The stigma arises from a discrepancy (Goffman 1990: 12) between what Romanians imagine their identity to be and how their identity is actually perceived or even discredited in encounters with 'others'. A social survey conducted in 2002 by a research team from the University of Cluj which comprised 222 respondents from Sibiu county in Transylvania revealed that although 70 per cent felt proud to be Romanian, 11.8 per cent believed it was a disadvantage and an additional 5.1 per cent felt frustration towards being Romanian. Taking into account the fact that most emigrants are in their twenties and thirties, it is interesting to note that 19.5 per cent of those under thirty-five years old thought that being Romanian was a disadvantage. Had the survey been conducted in an exclusively urban area, I suspect that the figure would have been even higher. Like in the previous chapter, we observe again a vacillation between pride – 30 per cent of the respondents thought that Romanians were talented, while 28.6 per cent thought that they were hospitable and other positive traits included: the respect for tradition and the past (19.7 per cent), being defenders of European history and civilization (15.6 per cent) and being united (6.1 per cent) – and complexes of inferiority which lead to collective anxiety. The second greatest sin after idleness was not caring about Romania's bad image abroad (21.9 per cent), followed by individualism, not being sufficiently involved with present social issues, being opportunistic and being xenophobic (Grancea and Ciobanu 2002: 375–8).

As Goffman explained, the stigmatized person often fluctuates between 'cowering and bravado' because of the anxiety felt during interactions with others (Goffman 1990: 29). In the case of national stigmas, the oscillation is between a patriotic complex of superiority, produced by the Romanian national education system, and the inferiority felt by tourists or migrants in real interactions with ethnic others in authority, while queuing for a visa and being turned down as undesirable, for example. Before the 2007 EU accession, queuing for a visa became a degrading trauma experienced by many young Romanians. Mia, a Romanian I interviewed in London and with whom I also exchanged several preparatory e-mails, summarized thus her experience of applying for an au-pair visa at the British Embassy in Bucharest:

> I queued and felt humiliated. The system was disorganized, lists were circulated in the park next to the embassy and entry numbers were being allocated. We were kept like cattle in a pen, behind metal fences. (Mia, e-mail, 15 July 2008)

Romanian migrants take the stigma with them when they emigrate and it tends to become worse, as more difficult encounters ensue once abroad. In a short piece published on a Romanian site, which is not included in this study, Mia, the same migrant I interviewed in London, explained that when she arrived in the UK, 'I thought that it was evident where I was coming from and people in the street were reading me like an open book' (Mia, *Click Romania*). In many other exchanges, migrants reflected upon their spoilt identity, the sickness that follows Romanians everywhere. One of the online participants created this self-portrait of Romanian migrants in Spain: model one 'comes from a poor area, usually rural, minimal education, no culture, he works in construction, she cleans or washes dishes in a restaurant, they speak Spanish with grammatical mistakes (they can't even speak Romanian correctly)'; model two is 'the youngster who has graduated but can't find a job[,] . . . comes abroad to work, usually menial jobs'; model three, 'the HUMAN DIRTBAG[,] comes to steal, to traffic prostitutes and beggars'; model four refers to 'the slaves of the human dirtbags – prostitutes, beggars etc.' (Marilena, *Spania românească*, emphasis in the original).

Another online participant with whom I exchanged several personal e-mails deployed the same sarcasm when she wrote:

> There are several categories of Romanians in Italy: many, very many girls and women who don't do much but have an Italian *fidanzato* or *marito* [fiancé or husband] who supports them financially; those who have no qualification or have it only on paper and want to work, so they accept any type of work and are happy; those with a degree but who also have a profession and do not accept just any job, so are unemployed or do not have the desired job and are unhappy; and the last category, but not the least important one . . . those who came here to thieve and are veeeeeery happy. (Sorina, e-mail, 1 July 2008)

The vanity fair of Romanian migration described here speaks of a traumatized personality, of a sick Romanian reality, which becomes even sicker once it is transposed into the sanitized realm of the 'civilized' world. The encounter with this world creates a new trauma. The migrant is displaced, their presence incomplete and immigration viewed as an internalized form of 'delinquency', of immorality (Sayad 2004: 283). As Sorina explained in an online discussion thread, 'wherever I go, the moment I open my mouth and they notice I am a foreigner, they start addressing me informally and treating me as if I had a mental handicap, asking me whether I do cleaning for some family ☹' (Sorina, *România Italia Net*). In another post she inferred that Romanian migrants are deserving of the stigma or the handicap bestowed on them: 'In Italy and the "Occident" it is OK for those who, for one reason or another, have never achieved anything whatsoever in Romania' (Sorina, *România Italia Net*). However, she also criticized those who accept being 'handicapped', those who 'give up the aspiration to work in their own profession, to make use of their degrees' (Sorina, *România Italia Net*). Other participants were more accepting of the inferior migrant condition:

> I left my pride aside and I did various jobs – cleaning, ironing – and now I work in a retirement home doing personal hygiene. It's not easy, but if you have a well defined goal in life, you can get used to anything. (Florin, *România Italia Net*)

In an online interview, Camil, who lives in Udine, Italy, complained that journalism jobs for a migrant were few and far between, but said:

I worked other jobs too; I did not feel ashamed. I grew up with the idea that work is healthy, at whatever level. It wasn't necessarily my life as a migrant that taught me this. But I started to be afraid of failure. (Camil, online interview, 6 September 2008)

Mia, in her post on *Click Romania*, also added: 'I was amazed that people were prepared to pay me to dust and hoover an already clean house. I had an issue with ironing boxer shorts, though. It wasn't the pattern or the suggestive cut, it was more the idea, but I dealt with it.' She added in an e-mail, 'I suddenly thought that instead of "cleaner" I should say I am an ambassador. I represent my country wherever I go. We are all ambassadors in the eyes of the foreigner' (Mia, e-mail, 15 July 2008).

The swing between failure and achievement that many migrants speak of reverberates with Anton's story and, as we have seen, is indicative of a sick or stigmatized identity. As a result, many migrants turn the complex of inferiority, the migrant condition, into an issue of pride, of achievement, as evidenced by the discussion following Anton's post. For some migrants the sickness, the stigmatizing *fleur-de-lis* that signals to others their difference, can become a badge of honour, a claim. As Gabriela observed, 'we adapt to difficult conditions (thanks to the warm up we enjoyed in communism); we work hard[;] . . . we are winners because we are still standing . . . [. W]e have the potential to win, but some of us "lose their way"' (Gabriela, *Italia România*). Such views become proof of the ambivalence that individuals come to feel in relation to their stigmatized identity (Goffman 1990: 51).

Natural Selection

In response to Anton's story, Iancu used the expression 'natural selection' to refer to the survival of the immigrant. This evolutionary metaphor offers a good starting point for discussing the other two contexts in which the suggestion of disturbing conditions or abnormality appear – migration as pandemic and migrant super-powers. This section will dwell only briefly on the issue of migration understood as a virus. The previous chapter explained at length the conditions under which Romanian emigration grew to become a significant phenomenon in the post-communist period. This section will focus on the 'natural' traits which migrants must have in order to complete their journey successfully, as well as the distinctive, almost abnormal characteristics they acquire as a result of the migration process.

With regards to migration as a symptom of a national illness, it is clear that the exodus that has been associated with Romania since the 1990s is the cumulative effect of a national psychosis induced by half a century of communism and dictatorship, followed by a lengthy and traumatic transition process. As an eastern German friend once remarked, Eastern Europeans are still ill and dealing with the consequences. Migration is one of the ways of appeasing the pain and can easily become a wave that sweeps people away. This would not be possible if people were not frustrated. Many Romanians attain good levels of education, but then the social and economic conditions prevent them from fully achieving their goals in their careers. As a consequence, their financial potential is also thwarted, leading to a degree of despair (Boia 2001: 181, 222). Mia explained to me:

> I started from zero in order to earn some money. In Romania, my last salary was 250 Euros per month as a marketing assistant in Târgu Mureş. . . . When I phoned my friends and family in Romania, I was ashamed to say that I am doing cleaning. Many judged me. Here I was, going to a foreign country to do cleaning, when they had careers in Romania. But I am putting money aside. In Romania I could not have done that. (Mia, London, 27 September 2008)

Despair is also fuelled by a lack of alternatives, an uncertain future and a general sense of pessimism. Political analyst Alina Mungiu-Pippidi infers that Romanian society is largely defined by pessimism and social envy. Pessimism is the consequence of being a traditional society: this type of society as a rule tends to be more pessimistic in its outlook. Social envy, on the other hand, is the outcome of the communist experience characterized by an acerbic competition for very few resources (Mungiu-Pippidi 2002: 82–5). When I interviewed the writer Adriana Vidroiu-Stanca she gave me this startling example:

> Something happens with some Romanians, you could say they succumb to a virus; they try to become what they are not. I asked the Romanians who renovated my house, 'What are you going to do with the money that you earn?' One of them said, 'I'm going to buy the most dangerous car and I will drive all around the village back home to make everybody envious'. So I asked him, 'Have you got a driving licence?' and he said, 'No, but I'll hire a driver to make them even more envious!' (Valencia, 2 September 2008)

Social envy has become a Romanian disease that most online participants and almost all of my interviewees mentioned. The Romanian phrase *Să moară şi capra vecinului*, which means roughly, 'If my goat dies, then the neighbour's should too', seems to have become a central Romanian trait. The following comment confirms it:

There is a 'virus' of emigration based on the old idea from the communist times that the West is the land of plenty. During communism the borders were closed so people were forever curious about what was on the other side. Romanians are innately curious, they want to explore and they are daring. However, the main reason for the mass emigration is more likely to be caused by the first wave of migrants who came back with their success stories. The poverty back home is not enough reason; emigration is not necessary. The main cause is the desire to have a car and a house that will cause envy. Some think less about themselves and more about what the neighbour is thinking. (Adriana Vidroiu-Stanca, Valencia, 2 September 2008)

This type of migrant, who saves money with difficulty but is ready to blow the lot back home, is one of the main causes of the immigration virus. In Adriana Vidroiu-Stanca's opinion:

This concept about life is totally wrong. Unfortunately, almost 90 per cent of Romanians think like this. I think this is the right justification for the mass emigration that we have witnessed. Many work here for a year to put aside a thousand Euros so they can go on holiday back in Romania. They start throwing the money around in restaurants, so that everyone in Romania begins to believe that here is the land of plenty. They begin to believe that the Romanians here have achieved a lot. It's a syndrome. They have to prove to those back home that they have emigrated successfully. People back home see this and want to achieve the same. They don't realise that these people live ten to a room; they are exploited. They eat basic, cheap meals in order to put aside these thousand Euros, especially the younger immigrant workers. (Valencia, 2 September 2008)

Anghel calls this display a '*mise en scène*' of success and wealth (Anghel 2008: 796) which redefines the difference in status between migrants and non-migrants (Anghel 2008: 798).

Social envy and emigration mythology appear to be rooted in a pervading sense of dissatisfaction. In a recent analysis of the online Romanian community in Ireland, Gloria Macri notes that many online participants believe that Romanians are unhappy as a nation and that unfortunate Romanian national characteristics and the situation back home have forced Romanians into exile (Macri 2010: 208). In some of the views I have found, many participants comment as well on the need for Romanians to lighten up. As Ionela advised in one of her online posts, 'Romanians have to leave behind the inhibitions, the squabbling (negativity)[;] they need to relax/have more fun + enjoy life and what the Romanian space and the "abroad" space offer. We need "national calm"' (Ionela, *Români Online UK*). In a discussion about whether Romanians are winners or losers, one participant explained the transition from the psychosis suffered in Romania to the normality of the West: 'Winners? Against whom?! At war all the time with the image in the mirror, maybe! Losers? Who fights against us?! . . . All of this infighting happens inside, not "outside". Outside Romanians become either normal, educated and integrated, or deported' (Luca, *Italia România*). To borrow again a term from Goffman (1990: 44), Romanians need 'normalization' and healing.

Natural selection is a powerful tool that compels some to move to a more suitable climate. It is time, therefore, to come to the third context in which allusions to some sort of abnormal or extraordinary features appear – among the migrants themselves. Natural selection suggests that, at first, a process of self-selection takes place leading to emigration, followed by a second selection operated by the circumstances that the migrant encounters. Only by surviving this second stage can the migrant claim superhero attributes. Based on statistical research data, Piracha and Vickerman (2003: 54) posit the interesting idea that migrants would have done better in any circumstances, either at home or abroad, because of their strong innate incentive to succeed. Migrants often exhibit more motivation than the native citizens in the host country. This view is shared by Cohen, who hypothesizes that diasporans have an 'advantageous occupational profile' and tend to be well represented in professions and self-employment (Cohen 2008: 149). The following view is a confirmation of this hypothesis: 'We foreigners, those who are still trying to make it[,] . . . will always work harder and will have more ambition to achieve a career, money, comfort. Many of us came here for a better life and are prepared to work hard for it' (Rus, *Români în UK*).

Some of the typical attributes of migrants have already been mentioned in the exchanges following Anton's story. Similar traits were mentioned by a number of other immigrants. They can be summarized as ambition, courage, flexibility and feistiness and are illustrated in the following examples. 'You have to be open and able to adapt in order to succeed and win against the homesickness that plagues you, at least in the beginning', Camil from Udine in Italy told me in an online interview (6 September 2008), while Iulia from Finland reflected, 'you need courage to leave with your husband and child and go into the unknown, abandoning everything and taking only two suitcases. You need to be a bit reckless to start on this thorny road' (online interview, 21 September 2008). A premigrant reflected lucidly on what is required: 'I have the ambition to succeed even if we are starting from the bottom. . . . I am not allowing myself to become emotional. I need to be tough for my family' (Filipa, *Români Online UK*). Enache also advised: 'take the bull by the horns' (*Marea unire, Spania*). Responding to one of my questions, Mia commented: 'What quality does an immigrant need? Courage. Courage is the special quality a migrant needs' (London, 27 September 2008). Mia's views were echoed in numerous posts: 'You need a massive dose of courage and a little madness to take a decision dictated by the heart' (Norina, *Realitatea din Italia*); 'You need courage in any situation . . . [. L]uckily, we Romanians do not lack it' (Roxana, *Realitatea din Italia*); 'I think it helps us survive any situation . . . [. W]hen we think we cannot anymore, we get up with even more strength and carry on!!' (Norina, *Realitatea din Italia*).

In one of the forums, a settled migrant gave this advice to a premigrant: 'Most recruitment agencies in the UK ask for professional experience here, but if you have good English, a strong CV, perseverance, ambition and a "can do, will do" attitude, you will succeed' (Olivia, *Români Online UK*). Putting oneself to the test seems to be a key component of the ability to emigrate successfully: 'I wanted to prove to myself that I can' (Mica, *Realitatea din Italia*). Lina, who was still in Romania, praised those who had left and thus proved themselves: 'YOU DARED TO WISH MORE AND YOU HAD THE POWER, THE CAPACITY to look for another country, another land where you found what you were looking for' (Lina, *Realitatea din Italia*, emphasis in the original).

Indira, a Romanian journalist living in Milan, with whom I briefly corresponded, reflected in an e-mail:

> The diaspora needs a lot of attention. It lacks care. We are a bit more fragile because we are not in our country, but at the same time we are stronger than those left at home. We are stronger because we had this courage; we assumed the risk of being a foreigner in another country. As a subject, we are more complex. (E-mail, 12 July 2008)

This view summarizes some of the contradictions encapsulated within 'natural selection'. The selection singles out individuals with extraordinary capabilities, deviating from the norm, able to survive when uprooted and transplanted into a new habitat. However, the selection must also claim its victims – people like Anton. Even for those who are apparently successful, migration comes at a price, which makes normalization difficult to achieve. This price has been termed elsewhere 'the Ulysses syndrome' (Dr. Joseba Achotegui, quoted in Agudelo-Suárez et al. 2009: 16). Migrants are at increased risk of suffering from stress, anxiety and emotional instability as the result of insecurity, discrimination, poor workplace conditions and poor quality of life in general (Agudelo-Suárez et al. 2009: 14).

Journeys of Accumulation

Migration may not induce 'national calm', but it gives migrants a sense of achievement. The acquisition of new cultural capital, the opportunity for new, self-revelatory experiences and the chance to prove oneself, empowers them. For this reason alone, migration becomes a self-regenerating phenomenon whereby migrants draw energy and the capacity to withstand from the process itself. As one interviewee eloquently explained:

> Now that I am in Spain, I am not the person that I used to be back in Romania. I am more complete – I have learned many things, but I preserve whatever I brought with me. I have added, I feel richer (spiritually richer). (Adriana Vidroiu-Stanca, Valencia, 2 September 2008)

The theme of 'richness' is echoed in most diasporic thinking. Camelia, whom I interviewed in Valencia, also said: 'Of course you have the media in Romania, you see and hear things, but it is not the same as learning about the world from your own experience. You become a richer person' (28 August 2008). Camelia transferred this newly discovered richness onto the second generation who will continue the process:

> My child, who will be born here, will of course be Spanish, but he, or she, will also have Romanian blood. The richness of a person depends on this mix; the ability, for example, to speak several languages, to understand several cultures at the same time. (Valencia, 28 August 2008)

According to various research projects conducted in the last five years by sociologist Dumitru Sandu and his team, which included surveys and interviews in both Romania and Spain, 50 per cent of migrants considered migration to be a good thing. Migrants highlighted, in particular, the way their thinking had become more mobile and modern as a result. Commitment to work, friends, leisure and politics was also higher among those with immigration experiences (Sandu 2010: 104). Migration becomes for some a necessary rite of passage, an exercise in transnationalism (Massey et al. 1994: 1500–1).

Diasporic transnationalism has been defined before by a number of theorists. Massey and colleagues analysed the importance of migrants' 'social capital', described as migrant networks and ties designed to minimize the risk of migration, access to institutions that intermediate migration and cumulative causation that helps develop a culture of migration (Massey et al. 1998: 42–50). Van Hear adapts Massey's terminology to talk about 'migratory cultural capital', which he sees as practical knowledge, allowing the migrant to operate successfully in the migration industry (Van Hear 1998: 51). Meinhof and Triandafyllidou adopt Bourdieu's terminology to define 'transcultural capital' as the 'strategic' use of 'knowledge skills and networks' acquired by migrants (Meinhof and Triandafyllidou 2006: 202). The concept encapsulates all Bourdieu's subcategories of 'capital', including economic, cultural and social capital.

In their ethnographic study of Francophone African musicians living in Europe, Meinhof and Triandafyllidou suggest that it is the capital acquired by migrants at the point of origin that is deployed to great effect in the new transnational contexts migrants find themselves in. They are right to infer that this capital is activated and serves migrants well in their new lives. Meinhof and Triandafyllidou's research also reveals the practice of up-skilling and acquiring new dualities, but because of the ethnic and professional nature of the diasporic groups studied, their work on transcultural capital remains focused on the relationship with the homeland and the values that are brought across and given new meaning. In her study of Romanian and Hungarian professionals in London, Krisztina Csedő, too, finds that a larger premigration capital leads to more opportunities for skill transfer. However, Csedő remarks that opportunities to make use of these transnational skills depend on the capacity to negotiate their value at the destination (Csedő 2008: 807).

I nonetheless would like to shift the focus to the migration process itself, to the journey that is the main source of transcultural capital for Romanian migrants. I do not suggest that experiences and capital acquired at home are not significant. On the contrary, I have placed so far great emphasis on the importance of communist and post-communist experiences for the new generations of Romanian migrants. Although migrants themselves often claim that 'I have started from scratch', 'I came with nothing', 'my life was in a suitcase' and deplore the fact that at least in the first few years after becoming an immigrant, they are not able to put their degrees or professional specializations to good use and more often work in low-status jobs, their lives and experiences in the homeland provide them with key resources. My interviewees, like Camelia, mentioned, for example, the quality of the Romanian education system, even during communism, and Adriana Vidroiu-Stanca explained movingly the role of her 'baggage' in her new start in life:

> The night that I left Romania with my daughter (it was during the time when one could go abroad as a tourist, but couldn't remain permanently legally; it wasn't like now, where you can come and go as you please), I had a feeling that I may not be able to return. We didn't know what we would need, so our suitcases were full of stuff. I said to my daughter, 'I am scared of starting from scratch'. I felt afraid to open my eyes and look around me. Every object in the house had its own history, every object was

a part of me, I was afraid to leave everything and start again. My daughter brought me two cups, two saucers and two spoons and she said, 'let's take these with us, that way we won't start from scratch'. We left with a bag of clothes and necessities and another bag that contained my daughter's cuddly toys. She told me she didn't want to leave her childhood behind. (Valencia, 2 September 2008)

It is clear that migrants do not start from scratch and as explained before, dissatisfaction, disillusionment and unhappiness are initial causes of migration and later incentives to succeed; however, transcultural capital acquires new value with the experience of migrating. The expression 'it opened my eyes/mind' is a recurring theme in the discourse of many diasporans.

I have been here eight or nine years now. I left home in order to struggle with life – to forge my own life. My mentality has changed as a result of this experience: as a country, as a people, as a nation we were blinkered. It opened my eyes to see things in a different way. I see life differently (human rights, for example). I am convinced that these things would have had a different meaning back home. (Camelia, Valencia, 28 August 2008)

As Brah observes, in the case of the diaspora we can speak of multiple journeys (Brah 1996: 181), which become a 'confluence of narratives' (Brah 1996: 183). According to Romanian diasporans, these are classic narrative forms that include rites of passage, which are transformed into symbolic power and capital.

Comparisons between the confined and bounded space of the homeland and the open spaces discovered during the journey form a constant theme in diasporic reflections:

My longing for home will never cease, but I don't regret it [the experience of moving abroad]. It 'opened my eyes'. I saw and lived in beautiful places, I made friendships, I acquired experiences. This would not have happened had I stayed at home. (Ramona, *Români Online UK*)

Migrants describe an odyssey during which they, of course, learn about others and other cultures, but find out primarily about themselves.

Romania is a good enough country for my standards. . . . I did not want to emigrate 'for good', but I love 'itinerating' and I don't think I'll ever get 'tired' . . . [. I]t seems a valid way of 'opening minds', in other words, education. (Ionela, *Români Online UK*)

Anca reiterated the same feelings:

> Luckily my mental capacity gave me the necessary psychological space to create a new life. I see the uprooting from the homeland, the years lived in a foreign country and finally the return to the origins, as a journey, a complex process which defined me, a proof of maturity. Today I can say that this journey was worth it[;] . . . what I brought with me in my luggage is important. (Anca, *Realitatea din Italia*)

Migrants accumulate transnational capital as a result of a complex expedition, during which they seem to grow in age, maturity and stature and transform a certain provincialism into a deeper understanding of the world and their place in it.

The odyssey also tests migrants' strength and ability to cope, transforming them into new beings, with special traits and abnormal powers, a theme that returns constantly in diasporic reflection, as in the following post:

> The experience I acquired in these three years in Italy made me stronger, helped me know my true limits and even develop new aptitudes . . . which is going to be an advantage when I go back home for good. . . . I am convinced that had I remained at home, all this would have stayed in my imagination. (Mica, *Realitatea din Italia*)

In the newer edition of his classic text on global diasporas, Robin Cohen uses the metaphor of the 'diasporic rope' to describe the different threads that contribute to diasporic strength (Cohen 2008: 160). He stresses the importance of diasporic 'awareness', which comes from this complex juxta-position of experiences and knowledge (Cohen 2008: 148). As we have seen, migrants are aware of this renewed strength and improved knowledge, which open up new opportunities. Ionela, for example, commented in great detail about the alternatives available as a result of diasporic experiences and she, once again, emphasized the importance of direct and immediate practice, rather than mediated experiences or learning about the world from an armchair:

> Let people leave Romania, so that their minds 'open' more (I should hope). It's an opportunity to improve life experiences and mentalities, damaged by the Romanian media. If they prefer it abroad, no problem, it's a step forward for them; if not, they will appreciate Romania more . . . [. M]aybe they will achieve financial success and send the money to Romania or open a Romanian business abroad or even open a business in Romania, inspired by what they have seen abroad . . . [. I]t is positive if people leave

for a while or for good because you can learn a lot through travelling[. A]s an English guy used to say, 'few things can be more enriching than travel' . . . [.] I tend to agree. (Ionela, *Români Online UK*)

For migrants like Ionela, the migration journey opens up the realm of possibilities, a complex diasporic rope that gives migrants the unusual power to make and remake their futures.

Some of these reflections also encapsulate the cosmopolitan theme, speaking of the same deep change:

I think I have evolved intellectually since I moved here. Visited museums, read books, learnt new things, plus [learned] good English. I have changed many of my points of view and renounced many preconceptions. By moving to another country my horizon was enlarged. . . . I'm in England, but I could have been in France, Spain, even America or Canada, same result. (Rus, *Români în UK*)

In a post extolling life in the UK, Zica explained that best of all she liked:

The cosmopolitanism one notices immediately, the multi-coloured world of Indians, Africans, Jamaicans, English, Polish, Turks etc. It gives you a good feeling; you feel at home, a home made up of all these different nations driven by the same ideal, to live a better and more tranquil life . . . [. A]nyway, my advice is, let's take utmost advantage of our life in the UK. (Zica, *Români în UK*)

Within the same thread Emil confirmed that 'diversity was one of the main motives for moving over here' (Emil, *Români în UK*).

Shedding preconceptions and acquiring new understandings are important changes in a people that are often described as isolated and provincial, not having had the opportunities ascribed to larger nations and greater cultures. A sense of empowerment permeates most diasporic thinking, transforming diasporans into extraordinary beings. At the beginning of the chapter, Anton's story asked the question, 'How is success to be measured in the case of migrants?' It is debatable that this is a valid question in a context in which, as migrants themselves consider, the mere fact of the departure and travel, let alone arrival, is a small miracle and a sign of unusual capabilities.

Despite these achievements, Anton and many others displayed a degree of unhappiness and disillusionment that prompted me to ask on several occasions whether some of these diasporans were truly happy. Some migrants took pride in their achievement and renewed strength. Mihai wrote:

I may be from Eastern Europe, I may be Romanian, but that does not mean I do not count . . . [.] I am above many here, those who have everything but, astonishingly, are more miserable than I am . . . [.] I am happy for what I am . . . [.] I have education, dignity and fuck anybody who 'crosses the line' with me, no matter what nationality they hold. (*Români Online UK*)

Yet most of the time the response was lukewarm.

I am contented, not happy. At the moment I am missing something in my life. I am settled. What does happiness mean? A state of spirit? We could talk about it endlessly. I can just say that I am contented. Happiness comes in moments, and it means something different to different people. It is easy to confuse happiness with other feelings, like satisfaction; there are many, many ingredients in happiness. (Camelia, Valencia, 28 August 2008)

I would argue that unhappiness is a powerful tool. It may range from Camelia's cautious response to the overt anger and bitterness echoing in Anton's words. Unhappiness is a source of strength. A spoiled identity, the suppurating wound of migration and abnormal individuals are capable of generating extraordinary feats. The stigma can be appropriated and turned into a badge (Sayad 2004: 253). Permanent dissatisfaction and internal conflicts can become a strong source for diasporic politics. As Myria Georgiou rightly observes, we should not be detracted from the potential that diasporic groups have for 'alternative' or 'subversive' politics by certain dissensions that erupt inside these collectives (Georgiou 2006: 49), which make them appear uneven and disunited at times. Conflicts, inner battles, confused and often opposing views inside the community are a sickness leading to acuity; they become the preparatory ground for diasporic reflexivity and eventual micropolitical action.

Conclusions: Returning to Anton's Story

The pathology of immigration acts as an evolutionary mechanism. Social envy and a spoiled identity can act as triggers for a process of acquiring capital leading to (political) self-reflexivity. Once acquired, the capital is readily imparted to a sceptical crowd of premigrants, who feel both enticed and repelled by the extraordinary feats of courage claimed by established migrants. This occasional boasting is all the more reason to fear and deny failure when failure occurs.

Migrant pathology provides an identity badge which is fiercely protected against external attacks. Anton was initially welcomed and offered advice, but when his diatribe turned against other Romanians in the UK, other users took a grim view of his opinions and threatened him with expulsion. Rareş complained that 'he [Anton] comes on a forum where he doesn't belong' and asked for the newcomer to be banned, threatening to leave if those 'offending Romania and Romanians in the UK' were not thus punished. When other users pointed out that he was overreacting, Rareş explained: 'I truly care about this forum; it has been, UNTIL TODAY, the only free and decent space within our colourful community. I WANT IT TO REMAIN LIKE THAT; I don't think that in our desire to attract more users we have to capitulate' (emphasis in the original). He added that the forum was his preferred choice because 'it lacks the dictatorship and anarchy of the other [rival] forum'.

Rareş's view represents a contradiction between the temptation to censor or impose rules and freedom of participation and expression. The tension between the openness of the online medium and the necessity for rules that define any organized group is evident here. When Anton continued to accuse other Romanians of various mishaps he had suffered while living in London, Bogdan told him, 'go home, people like you make me ashamed'. Lia intervened to propose that the thread be deleted, while Dorin commented, 'and send some toilet paper to the administrator, asking him to clean up'. The webmaster finally locked the thread upon his return from holidays.

In this case, flaming was resolved by the imposition of rules designed by a group already cognisant of its own identity. Bringing personal disputes into the forum was deemed a form of destabilization, which users found upsetting. The 'culprit' was symbolically punished and virtually excluded by the tyranny of majority power. However, the instance also shows a form of diasporic confidence, through which the group refuses to be 'messed about' and closes ranks against outsiders. It is proof that only the toughest survive in the process of natural selection.

The forum reveals itself as a place where the extraordinary migrant body is tested and judged to be fit or not. The toughness of the migratory journey is evident in the intolerance that meets those who have 'failed' the natural selection test and are judged to be 'unfit'. Online, a clear assignation of how successful one has been is received. In the absence of established or traditional social structures, it is only the achievement that counts and can earn the new migrant a rightful place at the top of the hierarchy dominated by settled or 'proven' migrants. Online, the performance of the migrant body, which in the physical world is so often judged to be incompatible with the body of the host, is turned into positive abnormality, one from which great powers can be derived.

PART II – ARRIVALS

'Bread Tastes Better at Home':
The (Il)liberal Paradox of
Western Societies

CHAPTER THREE

'Waking up among Strangers'

Translation, Adaptation, Participation

A few years ago, in an extended feature for the *Guardian*'s Saturday Review, Salman Rushdie drew an interesting parallel between artistic and cultural adaptations and concluded that the best adaptations were free, not rigid, 'a genuine transaction' between old and new. He warned that failure may await those who cling to the 'old text', wishing to preserve the old ways (Rushdie 2009: 2–4). His observations spoke about tensions and dilemmas, losses and gains, inherent in the process of cultural contact and cultural translation, which result in change, be it needed, wanted or resisted.

The previous two chapters of this book (Part 1) dealt with the fallout of the post-communist transition which compelled many to try to achieve social mobility through emigration. They also discussed the evolutionary nature of transnational capital accumulated through the journey of migration. This chapter takes into account not only the effects of the transition, but also the complexities of the emigration/immigration experience, to start to unravel various adaptation models negotiated in the process of cultural translation. The diasporic reflections of arrival and settlement elaborated online provide the first instances of diasporic politicization. Arrival and settlement occasion identity repositionings that ultimately decide who is in and who is out, with reference, of course, to the host majority, but also with reference to 'the other within': those who are in, but also out (this refers to the relationship between Romanians and Romany Gypsies, for example). Arrival and settlement kick start a diasporic identity-building process, which begins with an emotional awareness that is followed by rationalization and politicization.

This chapter combines online immigration stories with extracts from interviews carried out with diaspora representatives. While the first have a rather blunt and unforgiving quality, the latter attempt to conceptualize in a more refined way the transformative quality of cultural encounters. Both accounts confirm Rushdie's hypothesis that cultural encounters, translations and adaptations remain necessary, despite limited success and often failure. They remain a complex way through which the diasporic organism is forever making and remaking itself. As Georgiou reminds us, a diaspora is never bound or stable, but is defined instead by formations, connections, journeys and cultures in the plural (Georgiou 2006: 4). Taken-for-granted fixities and old attachments are challenged constantly and that is why we need to see the diaspora not as a 'bounded' entity, but as 'an idiom, a stance, a claim' (Brubaker 2005: 12).

The realities of immigration, as well as the elitist projections of the experience detailed bellow, indicate that the frictions and exclusions between groups and within groups can prepare the diaspora for political consciousness and activism (discussed in more detail in Chapters Five and Six). Diasporic racism and cannibalism may be two of the pitfalls of cultural translations, but adaptation struggles resulting equally in cultural wins and losses are an important part of diasporic reflexivity and action.

A Search for Terminology

Like Rushdie, Amersfoort and Doomernik remark that, for migrants, there is no escape from the inherent tension between preservation and adaptation, the negotiation between the familiar and the new, stability and change. Change must happen, because refusing it leads to marginalization, which is unacceptable for any community (Amersfoort and Doomernik 2002: 56). One of the Romanian contributors online warned newcomers: 'You must try to *understand* local culture, tradition[;] . . . it's essential if you *want to integrate*. Otherwise you risk remaining/becoming lonely and frustrated, rejected, suffering from protagonist obsessions' (Nicoleta, *România Italia Net*, emphasis in the original). Change is thus accepted as the by-product of immigration: 'It's incredible how we can reinvent ourselves starting from scratch, using resources we did not know we had, in order to adapt, to progress in Italian society! And how much it changes us!' reflected one diasporan (Lina, *Realitatea din Italia*).

Nicoleta uses the term 'to integrate', but adaptation through change seems to be subsumed. In other accounts, though, integration emerges as the ultimate hot potato of diasporic reflexivity. Change needs to have some limits, perhaps to avoid complete loss of identity, and integration has to be managed in some form, to avoid chaos and trauma. In other words, there should be some reflection about what needs to change and how, as well as what the basis for integration is, especially those crossovers that allow a rational adaptation.

In my interview with lawyer Giancarlo Germani, the president of the Party of Romanians in Italy (PIR), the term *integrazione* that he used referred to the successful cultural adaptation of Romanians, facilitated by the common Latin roots, which should prevent deep cultural fault lines. 'With other people, partly because of religious differences, we don't get along so well', he explained. He urged Romanians 'to understand the mentality of the host society' and advised the Romanian government to sponsor a media campaign that would educate would-be migrants about cultural differences and diasporic 'manners'. He added:

> Integration is essential, not just for Romanians or Italians, but for a Europe that contains twenty-seven nations. Italy's future depends on it. If, as Italians, we are not able to integrate the Romanian community, which is culturally closest to us, and is the biggest, then we will make a huge mistake for the future of our children. (Rome, 3 July 2008)

Germani is clearly an advocate of managed integration, a term that he uses quite loosely, and he places the responsibility on immigrants, home governments and host governments. This view is disputed. When I asked the president of another Romanian cultural organization in Rome about how he understood integration, he replied:

> Integration and adaptation are not appropriate terms. We do not need integration because we are well educated with manners and common sense. What Italians have in comparison to us is the socio-economic environment for which we have come. We are a bit more practical in certain areas than the Italians, we are gifted, we adapt, we know a bit of everything [in Romanian, 'ştim să facem de toate']. Why should we adapt? We just need to adopt their capitalist behaviour; learn their capitalist laws. We are already integrated and in many ways better behaved than them (for example, they don't cover their mouths when they yawn). Integration just means respecting the laws. (Mugur, Rome, 2 July 2008)

Mugur understood integration as a form of education and up-skilling, particularly picking up the capitalist know-how leading to economic prosperity. Like Germani, he refers to specific manners and behaviours, to a 'civilizing' aspect, but unlike Germani he insists that Romanians already share them and are even more adept than the Italians at practising them. According to him, Romanians are already 'Jacks of all trades' (ştim să facem de toate). From his patriotic viewpoint, integration into Italian society and European integration are part of the same phenomenon and since Romanians have a natural right to be part of Europe, societal or cultural integration is just a straightforward adoption of laws. As an Italian cultural insider, Germani may be more aware of the complexities of adaptation even in the case of communities which are culturally akin. The term 'integration' seems, therefore, to be an inadequate tool to define the various guises in which adaptation can occur.

Adriana Vidroiu-Stanca, the head of one of the Romanian cultural organizations in Spain, offered instead a critique of the term:

> In order for us not to stand out as immigrants anymore, we need to integrate, which is quite a complex term. In this context, to integrate means to fill in whatever is missing in Spain. Spain misses this part, which we can bring. I don't really like the word 'integration'. I used to use it in the beginning, but now as I understand better what is going on, I like to use the term 'participation'. I even correct the Spanish authorities when they use the term 'integration'. It's participation. Becoming part of this society means more than integration. (Valencia, 2 September 1998)

This opinion echoes her views on the personal enrichment of the migrant and on bringing together the best that the two cultures have to offer. She explained:

> Participation means constructing, to have the same values, to pay your taxes, to respect the rules. Integration would imply that you would forget who you are, and you become assimilated. But I am who I am and I participate in this society in whatever way I can. We should replace 'integration' with 'participation'. The word 'integration' started to be used as a reproach. The Spanish keep asking us to integrate, but it implies a separation, discrimination. That goes for both the words 'assimilation' and 'integration'. There is something xenophobic about them, but if you use 'participation' you make the migrant feel that he or she is useful, equal: it does not have racist connotations. Even Romanians should change their discourse to include this term. (Valencia, 2 September 2008)

Finding a term that can best describe the multiple negotiations between the old and the new and satisfies both the majority's desire for seamless transition into the host culture and the minority's need for acceptance and cultural recognition may seem impossible. Participation, adaptation and integration imply transformative acts; all require a translation, a cultural mediation, an understanding of both differences and similarities; and all attempt to avoid marginalization. As Ramona Mitrică, the director of the Romanian Cultural Centre in London (RCC) remarked:

> Our focus is the British audience and we consider that Romanians are part of that audience. So our activity is not just for the Romanian community. We work for integration, dialogue, participation, whatever you like to

call it and what we aim for is not to isolate Romanian culture. (Ramona Mitrică, London, 25 November 2008)

The difficulty of naming and defining processes results from the complexity of occurrences that these terms wish to describe. However inadequate, there is a common understanding of what adaptation entails emerging from the elite or 'official' discourse. Whether the same commonality emerges from the real life stories told by diasporans is less certain.

In their view of each other and also in their relationship with 'others', Romanians confirm Rushdie's hypothesis about the significance of adaptation choices, but display a much more uncompromising and one-sided stance. The relationships forced upon them by immigration are defined by power and authority, perceived superiority *vis-à-vis* other minorities and dislike of majorities who display an assumed authority. Imperfect negotiation, spoiled identities and adaptation aberrations can speak of course of loss and failure. However, I would like to propose that the phenomena encountered online and discussed in the remainder of this chapter are a natural rite of passage on a journey that remains difficult to manage and fraught with loss and failure. These imperfect negotiations between the old and the new are more true to current neo-globalizing phenomena than erstwhile theories, which treated the diaspora as a homogeneous entity and 'correct' adaptation as a necessity.

Romanians and their Significant Others

Migrants transform the national symbolic imaginary of their destinations. Bromley speaks, for example, of the 'active' transformation of the societies that migrants enter (Bromley 2000: 3), while Ignacio uses the term 'perpendicular' (Ignacio 2005: 9) to visually represent the interface between two or more culturally different worlds. Romanians are White, Christian and Latin, but these characteristics do not necessarily allow for a seamless transition into the host society, as desired by the elites on both sides. They allow nevertheless for a more insidious reflection elaborated from a position of difference that is based not so much on racial or even cultural differences, but on an 'awareness', as Cohen calls it, of the precarious immigrant situation (Cohen 2008: 148).

Exchanges about the host culture are often based on a sense of loss, especially loss of innocence. A migrant in the UK wrote: 'I was full of energy when I came here. . . . Slowly, my wings were clipped . . . [. O]ne pays a very high price. . . . England does not represent what it once did, an intangible myth' (Sever, *Români Online UK*). Other views are similarly defined by a difficult pairing between hope and dreams, on the one hand, and the realities encountered at the destination, on the other: 'I'm fed up with living among strangers

. . . [. W]hen I think about how I used to dream[,] . . . how impossible getting here seemed[,] . . . and now I can't wait to escape from this island. I feel empty here.' (Lara, *Români Online UK*) Some seem to find negotiating the pitfall of translation quite hard and the immediate fallback is the nostalgia for an elusive *Heimat*:

> I want to go back HOME, the only place where I belong, where I am not someone without a country [*patria*] . . . [. F]or better or worse it's mine and yours . . . in the same way the UK is theirs. I am looked at as a stranger here, everywhere I go, because I am a Stranger. (Romana, *Români Online UK*, emphasis and capital letter in the original)

Romana used the Romanian word *patria*, which does not have an exact translation in English. Like the derivative 'patriotism', *patria* embraces strong feelings for the homeland and an unswerving allegiance, not immediately denoted by the word 'country' or even 'homeland'. This online participant spoke eloquently of the inadequacy and alienation felt as a result of being treated as a 'Stranger' with a capital *s*; hostlands everywhere in Western Europe have been transformed by migration and have now devised certain reactions and treatments, which bring a renewed awareness of almost impossible translations.

In his article, Rushdie used the term 'loss' to warn against the dangers of negative feelings associated with migration. These feelings can quickly degenerate into building barricades rather than bridges. Awareness can lead to heightened powers of critique and reflection, but can also leave the migrant on the edge. In Italy, Sorina offered her usual incisive and blunt account of treatment at the hands of the host population:

> I don't believe that Italians respect migrants, even when these migrants have an exceptional degree in their pockets. Or they do respect them as long as they don't aspire to be more than *badante, operaio, donna pulizia* [in Italian: carer, labourer, cleaner]. They don't believe migrants are capable of other jobs, even though migrants are usually more capable than the Italians. (Sorina, *România Italia Net*)

Provoking statements like these are always neutralized by the calmer and more appreciative reflections of other migrants. Romica observed that she liked the Italians' love for their country and their appreciation for everything 'made in Italy'. She added: 'we could follow their example. I remember that at home we were always after imports, it didn't matter how expensive, thus putting our economy into disadvantage' (Romica, *Italia România*). In another forum, a debate ensued about the location of home, so Liliana said,

'I feel at home in Italy' (Liliana, *Realitatea din Italia*), but Aris replied, 'I, on the contrary, feel more and more a foreigner in this country – Italy' (Aris, *Realitatea din Italia*). To this Liliana reacted with, 'the way we feel is up to us' (Liliana, *Realitatea din Italia*). In a separate thread, Luna tried to grasp the views of those Italians who feel under siege: 'It's a bit strange, no? To be at home and feel estranged. . . . How would we feel? Difficult to imagine. . .' (Luna, *Realitatea din Italia*). Other contributors responded by praising Italy's diversity. We can see that at the meeting between the two worlds, insecurities give rise to conflicting feelings about the Romanians' relationships with their significant 'others'.

Some migrants try to offer an explanation for the way their migrant status is handled by the host society. This is how Mia justified it: 'They haven't got anything against us, they simply don't know. They don't know us, they haven't heard about us yet.' She continued to explain that migrants themselves have the tendency to cut themselves out of the host society:

> Initially, I thought I could only have Romanian friends. It's more difficult to build a friendship in the absence of a common language. A foreign language is charming, but it is difficult to build friendships without a common lingo. Humour, for example, is difficult to translate. (London, 27 September 2008)

Accordingly, many migrants start to feel 'lost in translation'.

However 'lost', migrants display a rich diversity of views, often related to whether the migrant is a newcomer or settled. In the summer of 2008, *Români în UK* online forum hosted a thread discussing regrets, but also appreciation, of choosing the UK. Whereas newcomers focused on negative aspects like the British weather, the quality of food, wealth–poverty divides, high prices, inaccessibility of certain jobs or social positions and the poor quality of schooling in the UK, established migrants talked about opportunities for varied cultural activities, travels and experiences, highlighting cosmopolitanism, free access to museums, the abundance of green spaces and the absence of stray dogs.

There were converging views as well. A newcomer, Sergiu, claimed to like the UK because of its 'order and discipline' (Sergiu, *Români Online UK*), while Alma, a more established contributor, said she loved 'life in the UK, with its simplicity and straightforwardness' (Alma, *Români Online UK*). These more optimistic migrants reminded others of Romania's own negative traits (like the abundance of stray dogs) and urged them to accept their chosen country, with its good and bad attributes. One contributor concluded: 'my recommendation for all of us is: extract maximum rewards from your presence in the UK!' (Zica, *Români în UK*). In a similar thread in one of the Italy-based forums, *Realitatea din Italia*, migrants wrote positively about museums, culture and architecture, cleanliness, warmth, diplomacy, Italian cuisine, proper treatment of women and love of green spaces. On *Italia România* in August 2008, participants also appreciated Italy for its cuisine, landscape, fashion and humour. Such positive views seem to belong to outsiders looking in with admiration. While in the subtext it is easy to detect an unfavourable comparison with Romanian culture, it also appears to be a joining of experiences and a cultural translation. However, admiration for host societies comes at the expense of the fear of being stereotyped and found to be not just a stranger, but a problematic one. 'Lately I have been avoiding confessing that I am Romanian, because the reaction is not great' (Bicu, *Români Online UK*) is an often encountered theme.

Throughout this research I found little evidence of overt racism towards Romanians, apart from the discourse of certain sections of the press and the political establishment, as well as policies and laws of dubious character to which I return in the following chapters. My inability to find specific instances may have to do with the type of migrants who congregate online and who are mostly settled, having already adapted to their host societies. As we have seen from Anton's story, newcomers often find themselves at the mercy of strangers and are therefore more likely to be discriminated against by both the host population and settled migrants, strangely enough. The migrant condition prevents many from seeking any legal or public redress, as some difference in treatment may be meekly accepted when migrants themselves feel 'foreign' and out of place. However, it is often the case that migrants fail to recognize events and behaviours as racist, because racism is usually understood as directed at non-White populations. Nonetheless, racism targeting Eastern Europeans remains racism, or 'xeno-racism' (Ambalavaner Sivanandan, quoted in Fekete 2009: 20). The racism of today is a 'racism without races', based not on biological, but on cultural differences (Balibar and Wallerstein 1991: 21), and so Eastern Europeans can easily become what Balibar calls 'white niggers' (Balibar and Wallerstein 1991: 34). Again paradoxically, this type of racism is internalized by many Romanians, who start accepting and championing the superiority of Western cultures, while displaying feelings of inadequacy. In addition, internalized racism produces empathy with the racist majority.

In the *Italia România* forum, a participant recounted that soon after moving into a new block of flats, she discovered a bag full of dog faeces on her balcony, a 'welcome' present from neighbours. By way of reply, other contributors opined that although some Italians may be racist at heart, they know how to separate their feelings from economic considerations and take advantage of a cheap, but well skilled workforce. In October 2008, in another thread dedicated exclusively to whether the Italians are racist or not, a conflict emerged between participants who were supporting different views, ranging from 'Italians are racists and snobbish because they feel superior' to 'they have the right to be racist', 'they have been scarred by the arrival of Eastern Europeans', 'racism helps Italian politicians obscure Italy's real problems', 'Romanians are more racist than anybody else' and 'it is human nature'.

In October 2008, almost two years after Romania's accession to the EU, a participant on *Români Online UK* complained that after initially being offered a contract at a Primark store in Oxford, she was then told that according to internal regulations, Romanians and Bulgarians were in fact banned from working for the retailer. She was directed to the Citizens Advice Bureau by online contributors who complained about the ignorance of bureaucracies.

An extensive study conducted in Spain, which included the Romanian diaspora among other immigrant communities, revealed instances of racism, mistreatment and precarious working conditions. The most common form of discrimination was the inaccessibility of jobs that were not in construction, tourism and agriculture (Agudelo-Suárez et al. 2009: 2). A similar phenomenon seems to be happening in Italy, where Eastern Europeans seem to be destined mainly for elderly care and tourism, by nature jobs that are temporary and rather isolating.

Giancarlo Germani, the president of the Party of Romanians in Italy, believes that Romanians' lack of unity, initiative and reaction invited a certain amount of bad treatment from the majority. He explained:

> Many Romanians are being taken advantage of, all over Italy. There is no one in Italy now who is less paid, less exploited and less enslaved than the Romanians. I feel a mixture of pity and anger. Their mistrust in unions and lawyers resulted in this. The Italians are great psychologists; they have understood these psychological difficulties that Romanians have and they keep them in this state of fear and uncertainty. (Rome, 3 July 2008)

He gave the example of the Filipino lobby, which ensured decent minimum wages for their workers, despite the community being less numerous than the Romanian one.

These examples show that the issue of discrimination is very much part of diasporic life, but only rarely events and behaviours can be construed as overtly racist or discriminatory. This results in the apparent inability of the Romanian diaspora to deal with the issue effectively. In interviews, migrants seem reluctant to elaborate on the topic. Like other diasporans, Camelia made excuses for the host population when she told me:

> There have been unpleasant experiences here in Spain as well. Racism, for example. I have had a couple of experiences of things like that. Racism is

rare, but it exists. I think it also depends on the image that you project. You are treated as well as you treat others. Of course many people here wonder, 'Why should I have an office job when such a job could belong to a Spaniard?' In the beginning, of course, they make you feel the difference. For them you are 'different'. But once they know the person you are, they settle down. (Valencia, 28 August 2008)

The rarity of planned, targeted and personal racist attacks does not prove that racism is absent. Rather, I suggest that racism is experienced as a subversive phenomenon, which adds to its insidiousness. Racism, with its emotional power, permeates diasporic reflection and, in turn, instigates discriminatory responses, a sign of the inability to deal collectively and rationally with the issue. Frustrations are thus directed at either the indigenous population or non-White migrant groups. The following diatribe against the deficiencies of British society is a good example:

Life in the UK is a 'mix' of prosperity (if you're lucky), stupidity, nonsense, illegality, disinterest, lack of culture, [and] incompetence, even worse than Romania sometimes . . . [. F]or me, England is a country with a '?' I often try to find logical explanations for their laws, for what happens in this country, but the only answer I get is 'British style', a weird lifestyle, a society difficult to 'penetrate', to understand and live in[,] . . . and I wonder again why we Romanians need to swallow someone else's porridge??? Only because we chose the UK??? Why do we have to punish ourselves when, like any nation and any individual, we have the right to a better life[?] . . . [W]hy do we piss ourselves when it comes to fighting for our rights, rights that nobody can take away[?] (Mihai, *Români Online UK*)

The thread Mihai contributed to was initiated in the autumn of 2007, a few months after Romania's accession to the EU. By then Romanians had endured a year of negative portrayals in the British press, which had been dominated by a language of 'fears, threats, floods, tides and invasions' (Light and Young 2009: 291). Previously, Romanian immigration to the UK had been limited by visa requirements and typified by those able to secure it: students, professionals and those in mixed marriages. 2007 was the first year when Romanians could enter the UK without a visa, resulting in speculative labour immigration. However, Romanians felt aggrieved by the treatment that A2 (Romania and Bulgaria) countries received in comparison to the A8, which joined the EU in 2004 and were given free access to the EU labour markets (Light and Young 2009: 285). By contrast, Romanians and Bulgarians have since been subjected to work permit quotas in Britain and other EU countries, a form of institutionalized and nation-based discrimination.

On *Români Online UK* Mihai vented his anger and frustration in unambiguous terms when he continued:

> We prefer to be laughed at, humiliated, made a joke of by some degenerates who know nothing else but 'SHREK', pubs, sex, drugs, violence and bad language . . . or by some mentally disturbed person who looks like they have been electrocuted, hit by a train . . . this 'superior nation', why superior??? . . . Can't see it myself . . . [. O]ur problem is that we love playing the victim, complaining and bemoaning, but we don't realize we are wasting our time. (Mihai, *Români Online UK*)

Behind the frustration, there is a valid discourse about equality of rights and a necessary redress that could be achieved through collective action. While derogatory and discriminatory discourses have to be condemned, at the heart of flaming incidents are real concerns about the subaltern position and lack of power that define diasporic life. However, diasporic activism needs a rationalization and mainstreaming of frustrations. Arnold thus observed: 'I agree, but let's not forget that nobody forced us to come here, we chose this country and we have to respect their traditions, culture etc.' (Arnold, *Români Online UK*). In another forum, Daiana's posting: 'At the end of the day, who are the English, are they not human? You only need to respect them for their unswerving stupidity, that's all!' (Daiana, *Români în UK*) was also answered calmly with 'we are no better or worse, only culturally different, different in the way we see life' (Rareş, *Români în UK*).

The process through which fear, rejection and frustration are rationalized can become the basis for diasporic action. The discussion thread featuring the exchange between Mihai and Arnold became a call to rally against the unfair treatment that Romanians received in the British press. In the period during which this project was conducted, two similar instances sparked initiatives to combat media discrimination. In June 2008 two *Români în UK* users wrote to Virgin Media to complain about the images that accompanied Romania's televisual introduction to the Euro 2008 football competition. Most team introductions had been facilitated by images of cultural landmarks, apart from Romania, represented by colourful images of Gypsies, dilapidated villages, carts and horses. As a result of this complaint and the later official protest of the Romanian Embassy in the UK, the clip was retracted. In the online forum the webmaster praised the 'mobilization' and initiative of the two members.

The second instance is the establishment of the *reAct!* website, set up by members of *Români Online UK* and aiming to 'counter and respond to factually distorted news coverage about Romanians in Britain' (*Reactgroup.org*, accessed 24 April 2010). The website was first publicized in October 2007 on *Români Online UK*, but its activity remained sparse. By April 2010, it had officially reacted to only two news stories: one in the *Daily Mail* and one in the *Express*. While *reAct!*'s external success remained negligible, internally it served as a mobilizing tool. In October 2008, its founder, Olivia, was still receiving messages in support of the call to 'stand up and speak out!' These two cases show that discriminatory treatment in the hostland can cause disparaging remarks, but equally can elicit positive forms of diasporic action aimed at reversing the discrimination. While racism clearly breeds acceptance, self-flagellation and othering, it equally leads to refusal, reversion and action.

Intradiasporic Racism

The examples mentioned above are positive though not always successful attempts to raise the profile of the minority and tackle discrimination. This, however, remains a marginal outcome of online debates, which are still dominated by anger venting and blaming. We have seen that excuses are made for majority racism especially by those displaying inferiority complexes. Feelings of shame and inferiority are often resolved by disjointing strategies. The body of the in-group is examined and the parts that are found to be 'infected' are symbolically excised. Racism breads racism and so once racism is internalized, it can easily be enacted against scapegoats. The ethnic body is purged and the blame of any ill treatment shifted, usually onto the Roma community. Ionela's view is an example of how the minority transfers negative experiences onto the minority within the minority:

> I never hid the fact that I am Romanian, on the contrary I spoke at length about Romania, I was never affected by what other Romanians do here. Discriminated? Not really. Personally I didn't even care when I saw Gypsies begging in Harrods[;] . . . each to their own. I will never allow my destiny to be decided by those around me. (Ionela, *Români Online UK*)

Although the complex of inferiority is denied, it is in fact subsumed in the denial. The distancing performed here is caused by the fear of being tainted and of rejection. Other posts are even more unforgiving:

> We invaded Rome like the barbarians, we exported the worst, first of all IDIOCY, THEN criminals, thieves, whores, pimps, mentally disturbed, *manelari* [*manele* fans], Gypsies, dogs . . . [and] occasionally someone honest who is now suffering because of the rest of the herd. . . . One day they will have to change the name of the country from Romania into Romani-a. (Patriciu, *Români în UK*, capitals in the original)

Patriciu provided a vivid exemplification of the theme of strategic disjointing. He clearly distanced himself from those Romanians who contribute to Romania's bad image in Italy. He also wished to separate himself from the Roma community, whom he blamed for the bad reputation Romanians suffer, due to the 'undeserved' confusion between 'Romanian' and 'Romany'. The strategies of blaming, othering and distanciation are customary in the process of diasporic adaptation, and they are enacted through flaming by expressing xenophobic and racist attitudes.

Hard as it is to accept such prejudiced attitudes, they are an intrinsic part of diasporic adaptation. Loss, inadequacy, inferiority and homesickness are feelings that are abundantly talked about in diasporic literature. However, diasporic xenophobia and racism, which are often the result of all the above feelings, are not. Habitually racism is blamed on indigenous bigots and right-wing groups. Nonetheless, racism and xenophobia are an important part of the way diasporic groups negotiate the pitfalls of cultural translation. A statement such as, 'as my father used to say, in 50 years all the English are going to be coloured (laugh)' (Patriciu, *Români în UK*), shows that Romanian racism is the consequence of internalizing the migrant status, adopting an already existing racist discourse against non-white others and reacting to perceived threats, like Romania's bad image and the amalgamation of all Romanian migrants under one label.

Romanian racism against ethnic Gypsies has three main causes. Primarily, it is the result of the specific historical context that has shaped the relationship between the Romanian majority and the Roma minority and has written the Gypsies out of official history. After the Gypsy liberation from enslavement in the 1840s and unsuccessful reinsertion into the social hierarchy, the imaginary of the Gypsies became hostile. Their exoticism was rewritten as delinquency and their somatic and physical characteristics like skin colour, physiognomy and lifestyle gained in importance (Grancea 2002: 66–7). As in other examples of racism, psychological and somatic features both real and imagined have helped create an almost fictional racial identity (Balibar and Wallerstein 1991: 99). This is used to justify the attacks that the Roma have been subjected to in the aftermath of communism (Fonseca 1996: 140–7).

In a small survey conducted in 2002 with 222 respondents, Romanians showed hostility towards any type of relationship with the Gypsies, apart from in public and professional contexts (Grancea and Ciobanu 2002: 377–8). Contact with members of the Roma is only acceptable to Romanians when it takes place in 'institutional, highly formalized contexts' and as much as two-thirds of Romanians dislike the Gypsies (Popescu 1999: 52). Romanians seem to have developed a type of psychosis against the Roma which the historian Lucian Boia attributes to the rapid demographic growth of the ethnic minority and its increased economic power, as well as the racist discourse of the press

(Boia 1997: 200). The result is that at best the Gypsies are leniently offered the acknowledgement of their musical and sentimental inclinations, nullified, though, by accusations of deserved poverty (Mihăilescu 1999: 117).

Anti-Roma attitudes also stem from the specificities of Romanian culture, which has repeatedly displayed a fear of culturally unfamiliar groups. After the forced communist project of national homogenization, ethnic segregations resurfaced after 1989 (Gallagher 2004: 375). Anti-Gypsy attitudes emerged under the belief that it was impossible to socially 'manage' this minority (Cesereanu 2003: 11). Cesereanu observes that since the 1800s, the linguistic expression of the Romanian press and intellectuals has always been defined by several registers feeding into an 'imaginary of violence' – registers that can be defined as: racist, subhuman, criminal, libidinous, excremental, funerary or bestiary. These registers, together with the religious register, which calls for the satanization of the minority and for social hygienization (Cesereanu 2003: 8–11), amount to an extraordinary discursive inventory that becomes naturalized through repeated use. As we shall see, many of these registers reappear in the diasporic discourse, such has been their omnipresence.

Finally, racism is the result of the diasporic condition, where the racist discourse of the majority is internalized and directed against other immigrant groups, usually non-white and of a non-European extraction, seen as even more dispossessed and lowlier. As Georgiou explains, though with reference to Greek Cypriots in the United States, whiteness and Europeanism are often deployed by migrants who wish to distance themselves from 'Third World' immigrants and are aspiring to get ahead and achieve success in the host society (Georgiou 2006: 159). The Roma are thus identified as the 'other' within the minority and when the minority feels discriminated against, the blame is passed onto this 'other' using various registers of violence. The stigmatized, Goffman explains, tend to treat those more 'evidently' stigmatized with the same attitudes that the 'normals' use against them (Goffman 1990: 130–1). The Roma represent the ideal target for another reason: they are the 'outcast' or the 'suitable enemy' for many Westerners as well (Fekete 2009: 5) and we only have to look as far as the Gypsy backlashes in Ireland in 1998 and 2008, the UK in 2000–2001, Italy since 2007 and France in 2010.

The Roma become 'a certain category of strangers who must remain strangers' (Mihăilescu 1999: 122), even when Romanians and Gypsies are brought together by the experience of migration. It may also be useful to note that while in Romania the Gypsies do not provide significant labour or class competition (although this is slowly changing), because the state does a 'good job' in ghettoizing this minority, abroad class differences are erased and the competition for labour is open. All of the above phenomena coalesce into an anti-Gypsy discourse that attempts to remove the gangrenous limb from the ethnic body and cleanse the wound. Hygienization, and I am using the term with the full weight of its historical and political connotations, is supposed to repair a spoilt identity.

The following examples are as illuminating as they are disturbing. The broadcasting of the BBC documentary *Gypsy Child Thieves* in September 2009 as part of the *This World* series provoked both an attack against its Romanian director, Liviu Tipurita – 'Who is he?' a forum participant asked – and the Gypsy community, who once again were tarnishing Romania's image abroad. Instead of viewing the trafficked Gypsy children as victims, many *Români în UK* contributors chose instead to focus on the Roma traffickers and the Gypsy migrant community in general. One participant remarked that 'they will continue to pose as victims, they will continue to dishonour our name ROMANIA[;] . . . they will continue to destroy wherever they go' (Patriciu, *Români în UK*, emphasis in the original). Under a patriotic guise Patriciu reproduced familiar topoi: Gypsy slyness to extract maximum benefit, ruinous tendencies and the tarnishing of the country's image. He also voiced the usual complaint about Romanian officials: 'In Romania, you've guessed, they d. . . give a f. . . about nothing. . . . Gypsies did it to us again' (Patriciu, *Români în UK*, elisions in the original).

This theme was also picked by another contributor, who wrote: 'We Romanians are condemned to feel ashamed whenever we are identified as criminal Gypsies because Romanian officials do not react. They are idiots, intellectually impotent and lacking a spinal cord' (Sorin, *Români în UK*). Sorin alluded to the irksome confusion between Romanians and Roma, which is voiced by many diasporans, unhappy with the West's inability to differentiate between 'good' and 'spoilt' Romanians. Like other Romanians, he suggests the inauthenticity of citizenship when performed by ethnic Roma.

As an aside, I would like to briefly refer to an episode I experienced while working as a self-employed interpreter. It was 2000 and I arrived one evening in the sleepy town of Didcot in Oxfordshire. At the police station I found a Romanian Gypsy male who had been detained for trespassing. The duty sergeant gave me a worried look and asked, 'Are you sure you can speak the same language? He looks different from you, more Indian like.' Reactions such as these can only reassure Romanians of their right to discriminate – 'if he does not even look like me, how can he or she be Romanian, or even a human being?' The following anecdote is also true. In a private e-mail exchange with Radu, a Romanian who now lives in Bologna, I was told that when he was working in a restaurant in Perugia, his colleague once remarked, 'you are the most decent Gypsy I have ever met'. Radu then told me:

> I had to explain to him who we are, who our ancestors are. It is not debasing to be Romany (Gypsy), but I would prefer not to be confused with

a Gypsy due to the image they have in the world, which they themselves have contributed to. (E-mail, 28 June 2008)

Similar anti-Gypsy attitudes merge with other familiar racisms in the following post:

> You do not have to be a genius to see the resemblance between local Indians and our Gypsy castes, a clear proof that ours come from the same place. But at least the Indians have been colonized by the English and it shows in their civilization and culture. (Grigore, *Români în UK*)

Grigore brought together his two experiences, as a Romanian and as a diasporan, to marry his old anti-Gypsy racism with a newly acquired anti-Indian racism derived from popular British imperialist discourses. He was able to do it because he could match up the Romanian stereotype that the Gypsies are uncivilized with the Romanian belief in the West's civilizing mission.

As mentioned above, concerns about image are obsessively reiterated in many diasporic discourses. In a thread discussing the benefits of migrating to Scotland, Lupu observed:

> Our 'bronzed compatriots' have not arrived in Scotland yet, at least not in such great numbers that our name is tarnished. As a result, the Scots have a better opinion of Romanians than the English. If in Austria they ate swans, here they would for sure kill hare and grouse. (Lupu, *Români Online UK*)

The euphemism *bronzat*, which means bronzed or tanned, is derogative in the Romanian language. Lupu confirms the usual view of Gypsies as a scourge, but also picks up on another cliché inherited from popular press mythology: Gypsies as swan eaters, as destructive pests. To some extent it is obvious that intradiasporic racism is the result of media representations. Since 2007 media coverage of Romanians in the UK has included, to give just a handful of examples, Fagin-style Romanian gangs trafficking Gypsy children in Slough (Kelly and Reid, *Daily Mail*, 25 January 2008), Roma who had suffered racist intimidation in Belfast and returned 'home' to less than enraptured greetings (Edemariam, *Guardian*, 26 June 2009), Roma who indulged in benefit fraud in the UK in order to build luxury homes in Romania (Ungoed-Thomas, *Sunday Times*, 23 August 2009) and Romanians (read: Romanian Gypsies) who 'stole' (read: abusively occupied) people's homes in Northampton (Reynolds, *Daily Express*, 23 March 2010).

Migrants appropriate the discourse of the popular press, although paradoxically it is the same press that demonizes their own presence in the host country. An interesting case of ethnic dissociation takes place, where

Romanians attempt to read any Romanian crime as a Gypsy crime. Heterostereotypes achieved by constructing others as an undifferentiated mass are thus overwhelmingly negative in the case of the Roma, providing a clear polarization with the autostereotypes that Romanians construct for themselves (Popescu 1999). This is paradoxical once more, since the inability to differentiate between Romanians and Roma is a custom that Romanians deplore in Westerners. As Rogers Brubaker and colleagues explain, the sharp contrast between Romania's ethnic groups, like the distinction between Romanians and Gypsies, essential for the construction of Romanianness, is undistinguishable when abroad (Brubaker et al. 2006: 324). Migrants attempt to redress the situation by vilifying the minority within the minority.

The hygienization theme thus returns in the following two posts: 'Wherever I went, I felt how the Gypsy curse was following us. . . . Wasn't this the reason for leaving Romania? To escape the putrefaction of Romanian society?', complained Ilie (*Români în UK*). Milena wrote: 'They bring no benefit to the country or community. They don't work, don't pay taxes, have no religion (at least 99 per cent). They only like to rob and party. I can't see the difference between them and a virus' (Milena, *Realitatea din Italia*). The 'virus' is just another reference to the infection that needs to be dealt with, the illness that needs to be excised, the foreign body that needs purging.

Bogdan's story, on the other hand, brings to the fore another strategy:

> We are perceived as what we are, as what the publicity about us is. I was in a restaurant when Romania joined the EU and all they showed on the telly were Gypsies in their carts, some old women with headscarves in front of a village gate and a shepherd with his sheep, that's all. So some nigger, I will never forget, asked me whether that was back in my homeland and everybody started to stare[. O]h God, how I felt[!] (Bogdan, *Români în UK*)

Bogdan expressed the shame of being Romanian, a condition he resolved by deploying othering strategies in the case of the Roma and distanciation strategies in the case of other non-whites. By using the term 'nigger', Bogdan established a hierarchy that assuaged his sense of shame and dissociated him from inferior 'others', thus restoring his social credibility.

In this book I have tried thus far to show that online diasporic communities are inherently dynamic and able to construct a language of political claims often forged through conflict and emotional debate. Although I have found diasporic racism to be an all-enveloping feature of the way Romanians treat the Roma in online forums under the mask of anonymity, there is some diversity of opinion. Contradiction remains a feature of the online forum. After reiterating the usual clichés about image, Lorelei remarked, 'Spain "wants" to see us as Gypsies' (Lorelei, *Spania românească*), while Vlad commented that 'the ignorant sees us as Gypsies, the fascist as slaves[;] many do not see us at all. . .' (Vlad, *Spania românească*). These two participants transferred some of the blame to the ignorance of Western societies.

Other attempts to steer the conversation away from irate ramblings resulted in more reasonable interventions such as: 'It's difficult to find a solution for them, so that they can work in a modern society, but maintain their traditions at the same time' (Sorin, *Români în UK*) or 'Stop blaming the Gypsies. Roma, Romanians, Hungarians etc., if they've got a Romanian passport, they are Romanian citizens and that's that' (Dorin, *Români în UK*). Ceanu also pointed out: 'How racist and naive we are! The Gypsies who live in our country are Romanian! The way they are is our own fault and we need to assume this guilt. These are our Gypsies. Let's not wash our hands' (Ceanu, *Italia România*). Responding to another participant Pintilie declared: 'You must have been refused a job simply because you were Romanian [in Italy]. Consider the fact that Gypsies get the same treatment in both Romania and Italy. Add the lack of education and respect we and others give them . . . ghettoising an ethnic minority means neither help nor integration' (Pintilie, *Realitatea din Italia*).

These are among very few comments showing the degree of openness we have come to expect from at least some sections of the diaspora. Such views need to be separated from the hypocrisy of liberal mimicry such as this naïve comment:

> All world governments should unite and take some decisions about them, settle them somewhere, educate them. . . . I am sad to write these things. At the end of the day, they are PEOPLE TOO and some of them even excel on stage as singers and dancers. In Bucharest I went to see Joaquín Cortés' show. (Doina, *Spania românească*, emphasis in the original)

Strong feelings, expressed with emotion, about the 'nature' of the Roma community, can be seen as an important factor in the process of adaptation. Nothing can justify discrimination, but diasporic racism is an indication of dissatisfaction, inability to cope and emotional disturbance that diasporans cannot or do not know how to channel into rational expressions. These characteristics can, under the right conditions, be rerouted into appropriate forms of activism. A process of (self-)education needs to take place in parallel. One would also presume that the deeper the immersion of migrants into the host society, the better the chance for racism to be expelled.

In a thread encouraging Romanians to get involved and react to the bad image projected by others, Mihai alluded to the post-1989 national anthem, an 1848 revolutionary song entitled '*Deşteaptă-te, române*' (Awaken,

Romanian!) whose main refrain is 'Awaken, Romanian, from your deadly sleep!'. He wrote:

> let us show them that Romanians are super, we are not Gypsies, we don't steal other people's chickens ... [. W]e Romanians work very hard to achieve something in life so we deserve to live better, we deserve to rise from 'THE DEADLY SLEEP' AND FIGHT to have like other nations a united community, who has something to say, [and] we can. (Mihai, *Români Online UK*, emphasis in the original)

This post may be reproachable for a number of reasons, but it also shows a pent up frustration that was ready to be converted into something more positive.

We have seen that on many occasions diasporans describe their migratory experiences as an opening, as a learning experience and as a rite of passage. However, many are not willing to embark on a process of adaptation that challenges beliefs which have been inherited early on and are buried underneath those received truths with a shorter shelf life. While diasporans are ready to learn local customs that define their host's culture, they refuse to apply the new ways to their own culture, because they see themselves as experts in how Romanianness should be performed. Romanians are keen to maintain social distance vis-à-vis the Roma and this is achieved by inculcating the minority within the minority with inferiority traits and deploying a register of violence. However, Goffman warns that stigmatizing is a form of 'sickness' (Goffman 1990: 155) that has both political and psychiatric implications (Goffman 1990: 149). Romanians would, in theory, need to cure themselves of racist attitudes against others and against themselves, in order to develop valid political projects.

Diasporic Cannibalism

In October 2008, *Români Online UK* forum was avidly debating a newspaper article. The conflict that crept up midway had nothing to do with the article's topic. It started from Zoe's complaint that in Romania, customer service delivered by shop assistants, waiters, nurses and receptionists was abysmal. This was not surprising, she seemed to imply, because these were 'lowly jobs'. Several participants took issue with this view, pointing out that these were decent jobs, executed by hard-working people. Some used irony to attack Zoe – 'your posts continue to be an excellent source of fun, please carry on' (Dan), until Zoe's rebuttal – 'receptionist or nurse is not such a big deal here [in the UK]. One mostly sees Nigerian nurses or other women from who knows where. Nobody wants a job like that', which opened the season for personal attacks.

Mardare pointed out: 'Zoe, you remind me of the Nazis and their Aryan theories', while Filipa said, 'Are you human or a devil with a human face? You emanate so much hate and arrogance it makes me sick . . . [. Y]ou think you know everything now that you are married to an English guy.' Zoe complained of persecution, the proof being the attacks she was subjected to whenever she contributed opinions, and called Filipa 'a Gypsy'. Filipa retorted with, 'you're sick . . . [. Y]ou must be one of those girls who prostituted themselves until managing to bag an English . . . stupid idiot.' The moderator, Severin, had to intervene and warn Filipa for breaching rule 2.7 of the forum, which required that contributors respected other people's opinions and any polemics were carried on in a decent manner. Zoe, but not Filipa, apologized with a long explanatory post and eventually the discussion moved on.

This was a normal day in the life of Romanian diasporic forums, where personal conflicts abound. This is not unusual, since diasporic spaces are defined by heterogeneity and contestation, but yet manage to concomitantly construct a collective identity (Brah 1996: 184). In her study of Somali and Afghani websites, Brinkerhoff noted similar types of infighting (Brinkerhoff 2009: 113). Cohesion splinters are the normal result of various historical contexts of migratory waves, differences in origin and generation and different degrees of identification and assimilation (Lowe 2003: 137). Online participants have little opportunity to choose whom they socialize with. Like in any migratory context, a great variety of personalities are thrown together as Romanians, not necessarily as like-minded people. In this instance, we can see that Zoe speaks with the confidence of someone who has escaped economic precariousness and enjoys social acceptance (she has an English husband), exactly the type of support that other diasporans lack or crave. This example also shows the way power is configured to differentiate members within the same diaspora (Brah 2006: 183). Zoe was empowered by her social status, but lost out when the community regrouped to attack her posts. Participants like Filipa who are quick to flare assume power by throwing accusations while claiming to talk in the name of the community. It is also important to note the ability of the community to regulate its own existence and establish a mode of interacting that includes corrections whenever necessary. The discord is resolved at the expense of isolating one member and forum rules prevail eventually.

With conflicts a daily occurrence, a gloomy atmosphere can often descend on the online community. Most participants complain about the tendency that Romanians have for conflict and mistrust: 'It makes me sick . . . [that] we aren't able to support ourselves as a community in a foreign country' (Selina,

Români Online UK); 'We are Romanians and we are in a foreign country. We could be more united, like back home. Instead, envy keeps us apart' (Enache, *Marea unire, Spania*). Some fuel the general mistrust, as in the case of Filipa and Zoe, by talking about stark differences between subgroups within the community:

> Red necks who came to 'make money', who don't think twice about the UK system, don't want to integrate, complain 110% that the UK is shit, unlike some backward village back home[:] . . . those Romanians are not like me and therefore I would never want to interact with them. (Otilia, *Români în UK*)

Dana's view includes similar accusations in a more moderate tone:

> I am fed up with Romanians who left Romania barely six months ago and criticize other Romanians and the country, as if blue blood is coursing through their veins. . . . Romanians always wish to stand out, lording it over their brothers. (Dana, *Romanian Community of Ireland*)

Despite perceived differences, it is important to note the passion with which the group discusses the need for unity, an illusory necessity. 'If we discriminate against one another, what hope do we have for the British to accept us?'(Webmaster, *Români în UK*), was the opening statement of another thread in 2009. The webmaster was referring to a user who had complained about list messages from the website, informing users of events and meetings. The user declared that he avoided Romanians and was not interested in such announcements. The webmaster granted his request and deleted the account, but in a post on the forum, could not help but criticize those Romanians who, like the ex-user, made a point of avoiding other Romanians. The usual heated discussion ensued, until another user reacted:

> Please delete my *romani.co.uk* account and all my private details. A site that is publicly ridiculing its users and does not respect confidentiality does not have permission to have my details. (Dorel, *Români în UK*)

Dorel's initial opinion had been, 'if you are born in Romania, it does not mean that you need to follow a Romanian lifestyle. At the end of the day, all of us have abandoned our country in search of a different lifestyle, most often superior' (Dorel, *Români în UK*), with which the webmaster took issue. While Dorel's wish to exit the online community was at the extreme end of the spectrum, some participants simply expressed concern about mistrust, lack of unity and perpetual conflict online:

I'm no friend of the Webmaster, but you should see other Romanian sites in other countries, some even endorsed by our Webmaster. Horrible attitudes, swears and threats just because I wanted to say hello. They thought I was suspicious, a KGB or CIA agent; privately I was told to fuck off because they were just interested in jobs and rentals. (Felicia, *Români în UK*)

This was not my experience, as usually I was well treated and welcomed on all the sites I researched and posted to, but the themes raised by Felicia are valid concerns, shared by other online diasporic groups. Grigore's view was similar:

The changes over the past few months speak volumes about the relations between Romanians (old members don't post anymore). Ambitions/ wounded pride/public accusations/private indecent messages. Is this typical for Romanians only? My personal experience suggests that it is, at least for some of us. (Grigore, *Români în UK*)

Participants seem obsessed with the lack of trust in one another. Before a research visit to Spain, I had asked in one of my posts on the forum for volunteers to meet me and talk about their experiences. Enache replied by advising me, 'it's preferable to meet Romanians online, that's the only way to avoid their shortcomings rubbing off on you' (Enache, *Marea unire, Spania*). Initially I interpreted such views as an indication of the nature of online environments. Clashing personalities and anonymity create mistrust. However, mistrust remains a feature of most physically based Romanian communities I have encountered and it seems that the Internet is only allowing mistrust to be more obviously revealed. After the 2011 Romanian Christmas party in the north west of England, an annual event, one of the participants posted some disparaging remarks about the community on her personal blog. One of her readers reacted by disseminating her posting to the whole e-mail list and an e-mail exchange ensued on the topic of trust and manners. So mistrust always remains an issue even in the 'real' world and it is the online medium that allows it to be shown and discussed. Although some egos might be bruised as a result, it also allows tensions to be resolved openly.

Unity, or lack of it, is a key topic with regard to the future of the community. Diasporans wonder whether migration changes 'innate' Romanian characteristics, like infighting and mistrust, and whether Romanians abroad can show more unity than Romanians back home. The conclusion is often pessimistic: 'Romanians are never united at home, even less so abroad' (Gugui, *Români în UK*); 'we, Romanians, have never been and will never be united' (Ceanu, *Italia România*); 'we are unable to support the development of a community when abroad (see all the conflicts online), let alone change mentalities back home. . . . Maybe our children's children. . .' (Selina, *Români Online UK*); 'In order to get involved in community work, you need a community. This means something soldered, coagulated, crystallized. Let's say we would like to do something for a community. But . . . [t]here is no such thing. And [there] won't be' (Cucu, *Români în UK*). Iorgu seemed to give the definitive answer to the question, 'Can diasporans perform unity better than Romanians back home?' when he posted the following assessment:

> I haven't made any Romanian friends in eight years. It's better this way. If I need friends, I go to Romania. Let me tell you, the worst race is the Romanian one. I regret being born in that shithole, Romania. (Iorgu, *Marea unire, Spania*)

Iorgu thought that abroad things could get even worse, but that the causes lay with the situation back home, which has shaped Romanians in certain ways.

The overarching assessment could be, 'Romanians are always unsatisfied and negative' (Ionela, *Români Online UK*), which reiterates the idea that Romanians suffer from a degree of dissatisfaction and critical awareness of their own status and situation. This awareness leads to acute observations about what the group needs to do in the face of certain dangers, such as, 'We shouldn't be afraid or ashamed to say we are Romanian. This is what everybody would like, [for us] to quarrel amongst ourselves and lack unity because then they could choose for us, rather than let us choose for ourselves' (Mihnea, *Realitatea din Italia*). In the same vein, Monica offered a critical account of the diaspora's status:

> Tomorrow we will be a nation of complacent diasporans, a people dependent on *manele* and luxury vehicles, disinterested in a history manipulated for so long that it is difficult to make sense of anything. (Monica, *Italia România*)

A diaspora burdened by conflict, mistrust and a lot of prior 'baggage' is the picture emerging from diasporic accounts, which is confirmed in most of my interviews, where I had the opportunity to ask for more in-depth assessments. Gianfranco Germani told me this anecdote, depicting the typical Romanian attitude: 'a Romanian is drowning in the sea. Another chap comes along in a boat trying to save him. The Romanian, instead of getting into the boat, wonders, "Why is he here? What's in it for him?"' Germani complained that he, too, had to fight Romanian racism. As an Italian at the head of a Romanian party, he is often challenged. He told me: 'There are many Romanians who are wolves in sheep's clothing – when they go online, they become very nationalistic, they become little extremists.' He gave the example of the Italian diaspora who thrived by helping one another:

> When we Italians migrated to America, we always lived with a friend or relative and there was a network of help for the new arrivals. Romanians lack that solidarity. . . . Italians who used to cheat other Italians in the 1900s ended up in cement. Romanians lack the consciousness of a common good. . . . We cannot accept that a people in a foreign land cannot be united. When we see that Romanians are the first to exploit each other, to argue amongst themselves, we cannot believe it. (Rome, 3 July 2008)

Adriana Vidroiu-Stanca gave a similar account:

> Romanians are difficult to unite, we don't trust each other. Everyone wants to do things individually. Sometimes envy is constructive, but ours is a destructive one. It makes it difficult to group together towards the same objective. (Valencia, 2 September 2008)

These bleak opinions show that the same traits displayed by Romanians online plague the community in everyday life. The diasporic forum just makes them more apparent, with the advantage of them being openly acknowledged and deplored. We have to wonder whether this initial individualism and the current online debates can one day become an active communalism, once migrants have fully settled in the host societies and have rationalized their own adaptation tensions. Some researchers already note examples of migration and labour networks being established on the basis of common provenance and kinship (Anghel 2008; Boswell and Ciobanu 2009), as well as successful professional networks (Nedelcu 2009), which means that Romanianness can spark community formation and action. It may be that diasporic cannibalism is a necessary stage in the process of translation and adaptation.

Conclusion: Loss, Revelation and Rationalization

The question that confronts us is whether conflicts weaken or empower the group as a whole. As we have seen in both this and the previous chapter, many diasporic voices complain about the lack of group cohesion, which appears to be a Romanian trait preventing diasporans from achieving political goals. However, we could also consider the possibility that conflict is a natural way to explore diasporic transformations and, like Stuart Hall, wonder about 'what we have become' (Hall 2003: 236). Internal conflicts and the reconfiguration of diasporic power and diasporic hierarchy may be a preparation for what Hall calls 'positioning' (Hall 2003: 237) and Brah 'situatedness' (Brah 1996: 182). Conflicts such as those between Zoe and Filipa and between the webmaster and Dorel are important because they show the group where allegiances are, who speaks and who is silent, and what their weaknesses and strengths are. Conflicts crack the community open: they are a revelation inviting an examination by others, but also stringent self-examination of losses and gains. Sometimes asking questions becomes more important than announcing agendas (Brinkerhoff 2009: 167).

Solidarity may take time to achieve, but just months into their journey of emigration-immigration, online participants are able to show an acute awareness of their immigrant position. This allows them to develop a sophisticated critique of the diasporic condition and the future of the community. Even as conflict and mistrust envelop many discussions, we can see unity emerging as a paradoxical consequence. Rarely do participants log off, never to return. Far from removing themselves from the group, diasporans continue to stick together and debate their failures and achievement as a diaspora. It becomes a process of rationalization. Unfortunately, in-group solidarity is also achieved at the expense of exclusions. Romanian diasporic identity is built by racializing the Roma and performing an act of distanciation.

Going back to Rushdie's words, quoted at the beginning of the chapter, we could easily interpret the behaviour of the diaspora online as an indication of unsuccessful adaptation, a failure that leads to frustration and loss. However, we need to acknowledge the impossibility of talking about absolute success or failure within the complexity of migratory journeys. As Sayad reminds us, when compared to rules of behaviour in the host society, which always constitute the 'norm', migrants will always seem 'deviant' (Sayad 2004: 29). We also need to understand diasporas as groups defined by fluidity, by various states of being, in the process of becoming. Despite conflicts, racism and difficult relationships with others and each other, Romanian diasporans are on the way to articulate views and ideas which may be interpreted as prepolitical and leading to more structured forms of micropolitics.

Chapter Four

'Nobody Wants to Know Me'

Immigration Controls and Diasporic Associative Models

Since the Treaty of Rome in 1957, free movement has been at the heart of the European Union's common market (Geddes 2003: 129). However, EU interventions in the field of migration policy have shifted from minimal involvement to more formal intergovernmental cooperation and, since the Treaty of Amsterdam in 1997, increased communitarization. However, because migration policies remain focused on immigration controls (Geddes 2003; Faist and Ette 2007), some academics argue that Europeanization has had little impact on the national politics of immigration (Faist and Ette 2007: 25). Whichever view you take, it is clear that since the 1980s Western democracies have come to be defined by the 'liberal paradox' (Hollifield 2004) of increased labour demands, paired and in tension with political exclusions (see Massey et al. 1998). In addition, since immigration policies in Europe remain in the tight grip of nation states, another inconsistency arises, according to Geddes (2003: 24), who observes that the double crisis of the nation and of the welfare state in Europe raises questions about state capability to resolve social integration (see also Schierup et al. 2006). We could call this a social justice paradox, where a growing number of 'non-citizens' remain disenfranchised, their basic political rights trampled on and their voice not represented in the European public sphere (Schuster 2005: 769). Some are non-EU citizens with work, but no political rights, and some are EU citizens who lack either work or political rights while in another EU member state.

Throughout the past two decades Romanian migrants have remained caught in both the liberal paradox, which, because of ongoing legal work restrictions, will continue to create exclusions until at least 2014, and the social justice paradox that helps maintain illegal work networks and prevents work migrants from accessing basic rights. This chapter analyses the legal basis laid at the foundation of Romanian diasporic organization and activism development, before returning to online micropolitics in the following chapter. It is important to do so for three reasons. First, because the situation of non-EU work migrants and the predicament of mainly Romanians and Bulgarians among EU migrants remind us of Bourdieu's warning that it is imperative to rethink the way we legitimate the imposition of frontiers, the curtailment of free movement and the treatment of foreigners in modern democracies (Bourdieu 1998: 17).

Second, because Eastern European work migrants rip open not just Western multicultural and anti-racist claims, but also the existing class system forged in relation to labour markets. Eastern Europeans are a relatively well educated, culturally undifferentiated, hard-working and white workforce. They are largely preferred by Western politicians and industries and Hartman is right to claim that Europeans manage to carve out a strategic, exceptional space in the labour market, not available to those without European passports and physiognomies (Hartman 2008: 498). However, as Massey and colleagues observe correctly, in accordance with segmented labour-market theory, Western employers seem to need only people who can enter low-level and low-paid jobs, with no aspirations for social status (Massey et al. 1998: 29). As a result, for the last two decades, most of this workforce has been relegated to the informal economy, shaped by illegality and insecurity, at the mercy of legislation crafted by politicians aiming to please a hysterical press and an increasingly anxious public. This reveals Western democracies as illiberal, xenophobic and class entrenched, while frustrations are also building on the side of settled migrants, desiring social mobility.

This brings us to a third reason for which discussing legal arrangements is necessary: instability and frustrations have also had a positive effect and that is the appearance of new types of diasporic political expressions. As Garapich observes, east–west labour migration has enlarged European civil society with migrants who are socially and politically aware (Garapich 2008: 740). It is understandable then why the study of east–west migration can provide, as Adrian Favell points out in the introduction to a whole issue dedicated to the topic by the *Journal of Ethnic and Migration Studies*, a rival theoretical corpus to the one developed by American scholars studying Mexican migration (Favell 2008: 706). Attempting to contribute to this new theoretical corpus, the following chapter offers a comparative analysis of the paradoxes emerging from the study of Romanian migration to Spain, Italy and the United Kingdom, together with resulting diasporic associative patterns.

East–West Migration (Spain and Italy)

Italy and Spain are new countries of immigration and therefore have taken special steps in the last two decades to improve their once rudimentary legal arrangements. After joining the EU, Spain has passed several versions of the Law on Foreigners. Some of the initial versions made attempts to control but also integrate migrants, while latter versions focussed on facilitating expulsions (González Enríquez 2007: 321–2). Romanians started arriving in Spain as immigration laws were becoming tougher, but they were still able to benefit from a string of regularization processes. Seasonal work could easily be arranged though brokers, particularly in agriculture, picking strawberries and oranges. Like in Italy, labour arrangements in Spain were characterized by 'economic informality' (Geddes 2003: 152). This less regulated, more nepotistic and clientelistic system (Schierup et al. 2006: 177–8) allowed Romanians to settle legally or illegally and benefit from a booming economy between 1996 and 2005, in time for regularization and EU citizenship after 2005 and 2007.

All regularization attempts have taken place within the last decade and these multiple chances of switching to a legal status made Spain very attractive to Romanians. The 'normalization' process implemented in 2005, which was aimed at immigrants who had arrived in the country before 8 August 2004, became the most important and comprehensive amnesty for Romanians, before Romania's accession to the EU in 2007. It recognized that irregular and illegal migrants were already part of the labour market (Fauser 2007: 148; Elrick and Ciobanu 2009: 104) and Romanians hastened to Spain to benefit (Elrick and Ciobanu 2009: 107). Overall, 573,270 residence and work permits were approved (González Enríquez 2007: 323), 110,000 of them belonging to Romanians (Baldwin-Edwards 2007: 9), the second largest immigrant group to be legalized after the Ecuadorians (Culic 2008: 156). After 2007, the number of Romanians in Spain continued to rise, particularly within the construction industry. In 2006, with a population of almost 400,000, Romanians were the third-largest migrant group, after Moroccans and Ecuadorians (González Enríquez 2007: 326); by March 2008, 664,900 Romanians had registered in Spain, thus representing the second-largest migrant group (15.9 per cent; the largest being Moroccans) (Elrick and Ciobanu 2009: 101). More recent figures in 2008 attest to the presence of 729,000 Romanians in Spain (Elrick and Ciobanu 2009: 112).

Work restrictions imposed after 2007 resulted in the inability of already present migrants to regularise their status and pay taxes (Favell 2008: 704). As a result, in 2009 the Spanish government acknowledged that due to the economic crisis and rising unemployment, Romanians would find more job opportunities back home and thus it was illogical to maintain restrictions.

From 1 January 2009, Spain, unlike the United Kingdom and Italy, lifted all work permit restrictions, which together with another fifteen EU members it had imposed on Romanians and Bulgarians in 2007. However, this decision was reversed in July 2011, when restrictions were again introduced, in the context of the prolonged economic crisis and twenty per cent unemployment figures. Until then, access to welfare in the absence of labour restrictions made it easier for Romanians who were already in Spain to wait out the storm. As a result, the mass return of the 'strawberry pickers' predicted by the Romanian press in 2008 and 2009 did not materialize. However, as a result of the 2011 restrictions, at the beginning of 2012, the Romanian diasporic press reported a significant movement of Romanians from Spain to the UK, with as yet inconclusive consequences.

Overall, Romanians found Spain to be a welcoming and lucrative choice, the common Latin roots enabling an easier cultural and linguistic insertion into society. This commonality was expressed by both Spain and Romania after the Madrid terrorist attack on 11 March 2004, which killed 191, among which were sixteen Romanians, the highest number of casualties among any ethnic minority. The Spanish state granted indefinite leave to remain to all Romanians injured and the families of the deceased (Trandafoiu 2006: 137). Paradoxically, an ultimate sacrifice was needed in order for Spain to recognize migrant rights for a handful of families. In general, Spain's treatment of the Romanian diaspora has been regarded as fairer than Italy's. The public protest of a Romanian man who set himself alight in Madrid in September 2007 in order to complain against the poverty affecting his family was regarded as unfortunate and uncharacteristic. A survey conducted in Spain by the Romanian Agency for Government Strategy in March–April 2008, which replicated the survey conducted with Romanians in Italy in November–December 2007, showed that the life of the Romanian diaspora in Spain was characterized by more home ownership, less homelessness, better salaries and more elevated career aspirations than in Italy.

Initially, Italy was as appealing to Romanians as Spain, if not more so. Romanians were attracted by the linguistic and geographic proximity, the established migration networks and Italy's institutionalized incapacity to control migration (Culic 2008: 155). However, like Spain, Italy had just ceased to be a country of emigration and was fast becoming a country of immigration (see also Schuster 2005: 758). This shift within a single generation required, as Daniele Mancini, then Italy's ambassador to Romania, explained in a roundtable organized in 2007, a huge cultural change, which demanded Italians to adapt faster than they were prepared to (*22 Revista Grupului Pentru Dialog Social*, December 2007).

Like Spain, Italy adapted its immigration legislation late into the twentieth century and therefore in frequent instalments, each more restrictive than the one before. After some changes to the immigration-related legal regime in the 1990s, a period during which Italy had to deal primarily with the *mani pulite* (clean hands) corruption scandal, the new political class that emerged in its aftermath seemed much more decided on controlling what was fast becoming a contested issue. Things became even more tense after Berlusconi's coalition came to power in 2001, both the post-Fascist Alleanza Nazionale and the populist Lega Nord being immigration hardliners (Geddes 2003: 157). For Romanians, whose migration to Italy was rapidly gaining pace, the *contratto di soggiorno* introduced in 2001 (a residence permit depending on a contract of employment) became an important, sought-after goal.

The liberal paradox caused by the tension between work permit quotas and the demand for foreign labour in the service and agricultural economies led to the inevitable regularizations (Kosic and Triandafyllidou 2007: 188), from which Romanians benefited in increasing numbers. The so-called Bossi-Fini Law (*Legge* 89/02), which came into force in July 2002, may have initiated a more restrictive period in Italian immigrant legislation, but the regularization programme that followed did grant 600,000 permits. It is estimated that there were 143,000 Romanian applicants, the leading national group in terms of applications (Baldwin-Edwards 2007: 9), of which 134,000 were successful (Einaudi 2007: 369). This was a huge increase from the eleven thousand Romanians who were granted residency in the 1995 amnesty. From my interviews in Valencia I understood that some Romanians who did not manage to regularize their presence in Italy at this time moved on to Spain to take advantage of the Spanish 'normalization' programme in 2005.

After Schengen visas were lifted in 2002, tourism became the preferred route to feed the informal economy (Einaudi 2007: 370), thus circumventing some of the more restrictive legal developments. The rapid growth of the Romanian community in Italy also continued after Romania's accession to the EU. While at the beginning of 2007 there were 342,000 Romanians legally registered in Italy, a year later the number was almost double, growing to 640,000 (ISTAT quoted in *Financiarul*, 21 June 2008). This is a conservative estimate, since many Romanians are still not able to legalize their presence. Like many other EU countries, in July 2006, Italy announced transitory restrictions on some categories of workers from Bulgaria and Romania, although these restrictions do not apply to agriculture, tourism, domestic and care services, construction, engineering, managerial or highly skilled work. Media speculations put the real number of Romanians in Italy at somewhere between one million and 1.5 million. We know though that by 2005 Romanians became the largest immigrant community, making up 11.9 per cent of the population (Miglietta and Tartaglia 2009: 50), and that, according to Caritas statistics discussed on *Realitatea din Italia* forum, in June 2008 there were just over one million Romanians in Italy.

Romanian migration to Italy tends to be young, with 60 per cent of Romanians under the age of forty-four (Bonifazi 2007: 136). This explains the forty thousand Romanian children now growing up in Italy (according to Ambassador Mancini, *22 Revista Grupului Pentru Dialog Social*, December 2007), raising questions about their future integration as 'Italians' in the Italian society. More than 70 per cent of Romanian migrants are educated to secondary or degree level, with one-half working in industry, one-quarter in construction and the rest, mainly women, in the care and domestic sectors. This resembles the immigration to Spain and even the immigration to the UK (after 2007 only), when relatively well educated Romanians chose to accept menial jobs, usually avoided by the host population.

As in the case of the United Kingdom, in the face of increasing legal restrictions, self-employment became a preferred route to regularization and conservative estimates put the number of Romanian small businesses in Italy at twenty-three thousand. Self-employment and business migration mirrors the opposite move, with Italians becoming the largest foreign group in Romania on the basis of twenty-five thousand businesses (according to Ambassador Mancini, *22 Revista Grupului Pentru Dialog Social*, December 2007). Nonetheless, Italian businesses in Romania (shoes and clothing industries) are larger than Romanian businesses in Italy, employing around eighty thousand people. These reciprocal business interests set Italy apart among the three countries studied here. They require a closer relationship between the Romanian and Italian governments and an additional incentive to iron out any tensions. As we shall see, this proved to be a crucial aspect during the 2007–2008 'Mailat crisis'. In order to contextualize this event and its aftermath, it is important to understand why Italy has had a harder time integrating Eastern Europeans than Spain or the UK, even though the two peoples share the same Latin roots.

In Italy the lack of differentiation between the different categories of immigrants became institutionalized and immigration started to be talked about as a source of social conflict in the 1990s (Colombo and Sciortino 2004: 209). While in the 1980s Italy found labour immigration to be more manageable, asylum immigration became increasingly difficult to integrate (Einaudi 2007: 239), so by 1999, more than 70 per cent of Italians believed that immigration caused a growth in delinquency (Einaudi 2007: 240). This belief was also cultivated by the increased sensitivity caused by globalization anxiety and terrorism fears (Bonifazi 2007: 179). Although these developments would not have been much different from similar evolutions in other EU member states, in Italy the two 'Albanian crises' of 1991 and 1997 (see Einaudi 2007), which involved trafficking scandals, navy blockades and sunken vessels, not only helped the popularity of the Lega Nord separatists (see Favell 2008: 703), but also established a more pronounced false association between immigration and criminality (Einaudi 2007: 235).

While it is true that over the years the number of foreigners arrested and sentenced in Italy has steadily grown (Bonifazi 2007: 225), it is also the case that numbers can easily be interpreted to suit particular frames, in this case, immigration seen as deviance or criminality. The 'threat' discourse (see Huysmans 2006) has moralized migration and migrants (Sayad 2004: 137) and has 'mainstreamed' the 'foreigner/criminal equation' (Fekete 2009: 4) in most Western countries. In comparison to other countries, the Italian media seems to have bought these discourses much more easily, paralleled by the incredible political success of right-wing extremist parties, with a tight control on broadcasting.

The Mailat Case

On 30 October 2007, Romulus Mailat, a Romanian citizen of Roma origin, attacked, raped and killed Giovanna Reggiani, an admiral's wife. The case became the flying kite for public concern about security and immigration in Italy's capital. Very early on, there were signs that this was not a run of the mill murder, due to the high profile of the victim and the opportunity of the media to pounce on the favourite topic of illegal 'nomad' camps (*campi nomadi*). Although Italy has a native Roma population, most of these camps were established by Roma from Eastern Europe and especially Romania. Like all numbers, the estimates are shaky, but around one hundred thousand Romanian Roma may have been temporarily settled in Italy in makeshift camps in urban locations and therefore quite visible. Hours after Reggiani's murder, Rome's local council announced an extraordinary meeting in the vicinity of the murder (Tor di Quinto Station). Although Mailat was quickly arrested thanks to a tip off from another Romanian citizen, in less than twenty-four hours the police had descended on the Gypsy camp at Tor di Quinto and arrested seventeen Roma. Romania reacted by sending three police officers to help Italian colleagues with the investigation, thanks to a bilateral accord signed in July that year.

Legal changes quickly followed. After bilateral discussions about curtailing crime on Italy's territory, Italy scheduled for 2007 and 2008 the expulsion of hundreds of incarcerated Romanians, based on another agreement signed in 2003. On 2 November 2007, an urgent decree allowing the government to send back to the country of origin EU citizens who committed acts of violence in Italy was instated. This gave the green light to abuses all over Italy. The prefect of Milan approved several removal orders for Romanian Roma on the basis of possible 'social threat' and 'inability to integrate'. Controls and censuses took place in several illegal Roma camps (fifteen of them in Rome), as did the forced closure of camps and vigilante attacks. Thorough border controls were implemented. A mass fingerprinting programme for the Roma (including the fingerprinting of children) was proposed in June 2008. The interior minister Roberto Maroni justified the new decree by the need to find an antidote for criminal activity and the Bossi-Fini Law of 2002 had already paved the way to fingerprinting, which became necessary for those renewing their residency permit, *permesso di soggiorno* (Bonifazi 2007: 189). Despite EU pressure, sparked by the concern about legislation that was clearly targeting an ethnic minority and trampling on children's rights, Italy carried out its finger-printing programme.

Italy used the Mailat case to solve its 'Gypsy problem' (*problema zingari*) and finally intervene, undemocratically one might say, where it had tolerated marginalization and injustice for a long time. On a trip to Italy in 2003, I was shocked to come across a Roma makeshift camp outside Naples train station, with no running water or toilet facilities, making one wonder why Naples council chose to ignore it. The visibility of such camps in busy urban locations was a recipe for adverse public opinion. Calling the Roma *nomadi* (nomads) indicates the decision taken by the Italian government to treat the Roma as culturally alien and as a problem, thus legitimizing their marginalization (Sigona 2005: 746). Illegal Roma camps had sprung up in many Italian regions, inviting media coverage focused on 'emergencies', order, security and control (Sigona 2005: 749). Some were later legalized and some facilities were brought in, but they remained under constant security surveillance, while local authorities preferred to eventually push them out of sight, on the margins of towns and cities. Sigona suggests that the ghettoization of the Roma has denied them a space for conflict and eventual resolution (Sigona 2005: 753) and thus managed only temporarily to stop the inevitable public unrest. The alien cultural values and the 'deviant' lifestyle of the Roma were instead used to justify racist measures like compulsory fingerprinting (Fekete 2009: 13). An additional interesting fact is that in Italian courts, deviance and normality are assessed by several factors, including the ability to hold down a normal job (Geddes 2003: 170). By not conforming socially and culturally, the Roma were easily assigned to the world of deviance and crime.

Worried about the image of Romanians in Italy in the aftermath of the Reggiani murder, the Romanian government supplemented its consular staff in Rome, Turin and Milan and proposed three new consulates in Trieste, Bologna and Cosenza. In October 2008 Romania and Italy signed the Rome Declaration regarding judicial collaboration between the two states. The total number of Romanian police officers in Italy grew from fifteen to thirty, five being of Roma origin. The Romanian Government also launched a publicity campaign aimed at improving Romania's image. Throughout the 'crisis' the Romanian government responded less to the concerns of the Romanian diaspora and its day-to-day life in Italy in the aftermath of the media and political attacks, and more to the demands of the Italian government, the question of Romania's image abroad and the possible effects on bilateral business interests. Only in 2009 was this passivity of the Romanian government redressed at the level of political discourse by concerns about the rights and dignity of Romanian citizens resident in Italy. Gianfranco Germani, president of one of the Romanian political parties in Italy, explained:

> Unfortunately Romania has been the target of an intensely negative media campaign from both the left and the right of the political spectrum. The Romanian government didn't understand straight away how it needed to act. Romanian politicians have treated Veltroni [then the mayor of Rome] as a friend, whereas he has now proved that he is not a friend to the Romanian people. When this media campaign started, the community wasn't organised – Romanians only had the Romanian League, which has now virtually disappeared. (Rome, 3 July 2008)

Acknowledging the effects of the Mailat case on the Romanian diaspora came after months of complaints by Romanian migrants about the inability of the Romanian government to act on their behalf. The Romanian Agency for Government Strategy conducted a survey between November and December 2007 among Romanians in Italy, which revealed that 63 per cent considered that the Italian media coverage of the Mailat case was biased and 72 per cent thought that their image as Romanians had suffered as a result.

At a first glance and taking into account cultural considerations one would expect Romanians to be the preferred minority (see also Favell 2008: 712). As Germani explained:

> If tomorrow a million Romanians leave and they are replaced by a million Chinese or a million Arabs, for me as an Italian it is worse. Romanian culture has the same Latin roots that we do. These are practical issues – we can easily achieve an understanding between Romanians and Italians. We discuss; we quarrel; we have the same roots. Apart from the recent problems, due to the media campaign, there has always been a good integration of Romanians in Italy and of Italians in Romania.

However these views are not shared by the majority of Italians. As Hollifield reports, those less skilled and those in greater numbers provoke more political resistance even when their labour is needed (Hollifield 2004: 902). There is also the added consideration of the Roma minority. Despite centuries of discrimination, or maybe due to it, the Roma have never conformed, a strategy that the European Union, despite its liberal discourse, has found hard to tolerate. They are used to living on the edge, surviving at all costs and preserving a culture that has always been under attack (Fonseca 1996). This non-conformism is the key of their survival and integrating would equate to self-genocide. Endemic Roma racism, characterizing many European countries today, explains why the racism suffered by this minority in Romania was not just replicated but even greater in Italy, whose inability to deal effectively with socialization challenges, weak policing and a bureaucratic court system maintained illegality at the heart of immigration.

Media reactions show that Italy's status as an emigration country is embedded in its national consciousness. Its relatively recent transformation into a country of immigration has induced a certain cultural inability to deal with the change at a psychological level. An informal economy that harbours a large number of illegal immigrants, as well as Italy's weak immigration laws and inefficient administration, have transformed immigration into a security threat, a job threat and a cultural threat (Kosic and Triandafyllidou 2007: 194).

The government's emergency decree allowed the immediate expulsion of EU citizens who posed a threat to public order or public security and thus allowed Italian authorities to refuse entry or execute quick deportations, contravening one of the EU's four main freedoms – mobility. It also created a dangerous precedent, as became obvious in France in the summer of 2010. Franco Frattini, the then EU commissioner in charge of security and justice, supported the initiative, despite the backlash that included numerous Gypsy camps being burnt or vandalized. In his turn, Romano Prodi, then still Italy's prime minister, asked for new EU rules that would tackle criminality by EU migrants. Romania first responded with accusations of xenophobia, but ultimately conceded to double the numbers of Romanian police officers working in Italy. The Romanian government also proposed 'voluntary repatriation' for people with an 'integration problem', as reported by the Romanian national daily *Evenimentul Zilei* on 6 November 2007. These legal battles were a sign of 'differentialist racism' (Étienne Balibar quoted in Brah 1996: 186) stemming from incompatibilities and from the 'insurmountability of cultural differences' (Brah 1996: 186).

Fierce debates followed on Romanian diasporic websites based in Italy. In a thread discussing the expulsion of the first EU citizens (all Romanian) on *România Italia Net* in November 2007, users posted no less than 243 messages in short succession. Contributors lamented the confusion made between ethnic Romanians and Romanian citizens of Gypsy origin, complained about the inability of Romanian authorities to stop 'undesirables' from travelling abroad, accused Italian mayors who wanted to capitalize politically on the events and expressed fear about their future in Italy. There were calls for the two governments to solve the crisis and calls to adopt matching laws in Romania, all interspersed with fragmented quotes from the new legislation and Italian media reports. Most views were also ferociously anti-Gypsy:

In Romania, Gypsy supremacy has been created as a result of their aggressiveness and people's FEAR. . . . We need more drastic measures, because we've reached boiling point, but as you can see, if we ask for tougher measures against Gypsies, we are accused of racism. (Floricica, *România Italia Net*)

Romanian Hour, based in Turin, started to gather online signatures in support of the 'Campaign to remove all Romanian criminals – United Against Crime!' initiated on 10 October 2007. The campaign soon gathered 273 signatures (mainly Romanian, but a few were Italian) despite its clear anti-Gypsy tone:

With this protest we ask both Romanian and Italian governments to send back home all criminals who transgress Italian laws, so that they are prosecuted and punished. We consider that Italian laws are too permissive and inefficient for these hardened criminals who tarnish our image. There is no reason why Romanian citizens who respect the law should suffer because of these dregs of society! We can't ignore their abuses and carelessness any longer! Sign now for them to be returned and locked up in Romania!

The Mailat case gave the right-wing Italian government the opportunity to address deep-rooted public fears while making political gains. It also contributed to the deepening of the ethnic fault line between Romanians and the Roma. The diaspora was split and rendered inefficient by the paradox of having to fight against Italian media attacks and political discrimination, while at the same time siding with the policies of the Italian government in order to distance itself from the Roma. The Romanian government was equally inefficient, bound by its obligations to all Romanian citizens, but hampered by anti-Roma public opinion. The online arena offered the opportunity for the expression of all these dissensions and occasional mobilization, though practical resolutions were never achieved. One can spot a glaring absence: that of the Roma, whose lack of political mobilization off- and online invites further abuse. They have become the ultimate 'other' *in absentia*.

East–West Migration (the United Kingdom)

Unlike Spain and Italy, the UK has been a longstanding country of immigration, but even here, once-liberal policies have been replaced over the last few decades with some of the most restrictive policies in Europe. Since 1962 public opinion has played a crucial role in shaping immigration policies (Geddes 2003: 32), which are generally defined by the interplay between promoting legal labour routes and curtailing illegal migration (Düvell 2007: 349). Analysts like Geddes or Düvell also point out that in the UK case, economic growth and immigration remain clearly entwined. However, the same academics notice the 'dualism' that defines UK immigration policies, which are trying to fulfil economic demands under the pressure of social anxiety about the threat to public services (Düvell 2007: 357). In this respect, the first Eastern European enlargement in 2004 represented a significant moment, when arrivals from the eight Eastern European accession countries doubled between 2003 (677,000) and 2004 (1.29 million), according to Düvell (2007: 350).

Due to its specific geographic situation, the UK has always been in a position to enforce its own border controls, while the controversial 'reception centres' established more than a decade ago represented a more structured and severe attempt to deter illegal migration than the approaches we have seen in the Italian case. Labour controls were also strictly implemented until 2011 through the Worker Registration Scheme, to which Romanians had to adhere, even after the 2007 accession. There have been no official regularization processes, apart from a small number of compassionate and family reunification cases, and the idea of any kind of amnesty was again dismissed in the general election of 2010.

Because of the six-month limit imposed through the work permit scheme, Blanchflower and Shadforth were of the opinion that A10 workers (from countries who joined the EU in 2004) should not be considered immigrants, but commuters (2009: F136). These limitations should therefore be seen as an additional attempt by the UK government to curtail permanent settlement. However, while this was clearly the intention of the UK government, Boswell and Ciobanu dispute the idea that Romanian immigration to the UK is defined by circularity. They used a comparative approach analysing Romanian migration to Italy and the UK and focused on a small community in northern Transylvania. By studying its immigration patterns they found that in the UK Romanian immigration tended to be more individualistic, defined by formalized social and economic systems and by the relationship with non-Romanians, while in Italy informal social and economic structures meant much more reliance on Romanian kinship networks (Boswell and Ciobanu 2009: 1361). As a result, their research suggests that while in Italy Romanian migration is much more circular, in the UK it has become more permanent (Boswell and Ciobanu 2009: 1356). The geography and the cost of travelling to the UK, as well as the cultural distance requiring more commitment, particularly linguistically, have always encouraged professional migration and long-term migration projects.

Since April 2011, Romanians can apply for an accession worker card or for the right to work under the Seasonal Agricultural Workers Scheme (SAWS) and the Sectors Based Scheme, which recruits for the food manufacturing sector. Under the European Union Association Agreement, Romanians have also been allowed to remain in the UK if self-employed or running their own company. As in the case of Polish migrants (see Garapich 2008), this became a favourite route for migration to the UK, further encouraging longer-term settlement. Work rights since 2007 remain limited for Romanians and Bulgarians (so-called A2 workers), largely dependent on qualifications and experience (those highly skilled are assessed through a points system) and also on what jobs British citizens are unwilling to do (seasonal agricultural work, for example). Restrictions will remain in place until 1 January 2014. Accession statistics show that up to March 2008, almost nine thousand Romanians had been granted a work permit and an additional twenty thousand had been registered as students, highly skilled workers, self-employed (about one-half of the total) and family dependents (Blanchflower and Shadforth 2009: F149). Since October 2009 under the Workers Authorization Scheme and since April 2011 under the accession worker card system, children and dependents of those who already have the right to work in the UK need not apply for authorization. According to Cristina Irimie, editor in chief of *Români în UK* monthly newsletter, the BBC puts the total number of Romanians in the UK at 97,000, 27,000 of which are self-employed (figures valid for September 2012). However, Irimie's personal expertise leads her to conclude that these numbers could be doubled in order to provide a more accurate picture. What official figures omit, Irimie points out, are those whose applications for a work card have been rejected. Many of those are still living and working in the UK (e-mailed newsletter received from Irimie on 9 October 2012). What we have therefore in the UK context is an official, highly skilled and permanent migration, as well as a large number of illegal workers who travel as tourists and then stay at the mercy of the economic context, but without being able to access basic services and rights. They, too, seem to settle for longer than a few months, due to the high investment required in the migration project.

A Continuing Paradox

Over the last decades, in Spain, Italy and the United Kingdom, migration policies have gradually become part of 'high politics' (Castles 2004: 857), having moved away from the technical realm of political economy and into the symbolic realm of diasporic identities that can destabilize national identities (Favell 2001: 24). Like in the three cases described here, most European nation-states have redrafted their immigration policies in an attempt to 'reorganize and reimagine' symbolic boundaries (Geddes 2003: 23) and reinterpret national identities and European citizenship under the pressure of social, political and demographic changes (Bonifazi 2007: 183). Although France is not the object of the present research, it has become nevertheless an important and more recent example of the perpetuation of institutionalized racism towards fellow European Union members. Right-wing governments coming into power over the last decade in a number of EU member states have aggravated the liberal paradox and have strengthened the populist, anti-immigration discourse.

The resulting legislation addressing the status of economic migrants has racialized the labour markets (Schierup et al. 2006: 5), creating social dumping and making xeno-racism acceptable (Fekete 2009: 20). As a result of the political and historical context encountered, Romanian migration became adaptable and opportunistic, permanent migration co-existing with circular shuttle migration and urban professionals making way for rural, unskilled labour (Horváth 2008: 772). Often migrants shifted between statuses (illegal then regularized, with or without professional contracts, within or outside permit quotas), supported by an increasingly buoyant migrant economy of brokerage, kinship and professional networks. Many analysts continue to see Eastern European migration as transient but beneficial in making the labour market more dynamic and efficient (see for example IPPR 2006; Blanchflower and Shadforth 2009), but it is imperative to note that as migrants settle long-term and gain employment and welfare rights, it is wrong to continue to see them as temporary outsiders (Castles 2004: 869).

The dependency on precarious, unfavourable and ultimately unfair legislation has made many diasporans more aware of their condition and the resulting identity politics remains mainly non-institutionalized micropolitics, occasionally conducted online, with rare incursions into the main social and political fields. Over the period studied here, Romanians have lived through an important status change, from highly regulated to free to move. It is to be expected that this shift from instability to stability will result in more coherent political strategies, although Schuster argues that in the case of Italy, security for some categories of migrants did not necessarily lead to greater political involvement (Schuster 2005: 771). This is because work permit regularizations are being undermined by culturally and racially inspired policies which create a volatile political context.

Romanian migrant communities remain fragmented due to ethnic fault lines, which make protests like the ones organized in the UK by the black community several decades ago unlikely (Schuster 2005: 769). Community leaders are often viewed as unrepresentative by the community and once individuals acquire some standing, they tend to focus on personal lives and interests (Schuster 2005: 770). Romanians interpret EU citizenship as the right to travel and work and when that is achieved or semi-achieved, a certain inability to understand ensuing cultural and political responsibilities lingers. The result is the incapacity to deal with public backlashes of the Mailat type, which are rooted in xenophobia and widespread social fears, for example of unemployment (Massey et al. 1998: 121). Nonetheless, with political affiliations in more than one nation-state (see Vertovec 2004), diasporans have the capacity to compare and reflect upon their status both in the host society and back home. Within this framework, the analysis of diasporic associative models and political activism gives hope for the future.

Diasporic Associative Models

The institutionalization of the Romanian diaspora shows how Romanians adapted to the various political contexts, creating associative models that range from the culturally populist model in Spain, politically representative in Italy and culturally organizational in the UK.

The preferred method in Spain has been the establishment of cultural associations, which aim to promote the integration of Romanians into Spanish society and, in parallel, represent and preserve Romanian culture in Spain at a popular level. This associative model, which I call culturally populist, is well suited to the Spanish context, which has been more tolerant of Romanians and recognized a certain cultural *voisinage*. The Federation of Associations for Romanian Immigrants in Spain (FEDROM) is the umbrella association established in Madrid on 24 July 2004 to cater for the five hundred thousand Romanians present in Spain at that time, one hundred thousand of them living in the Madrid area, and high numbers around the Henares corridor, Alcala, San Fernando, Coslada, Torrejon and Arganda del Rey. At the beginning of 2010 the FEDROM website counted 106 Romanian associations in Spain, of which twenty-eight were members of FEDROM and four were founding members (in March 2012, FEDROM numbered twenty-two members). FEDROM established the practice of annual diasporic congresses, with the first one taking place in 2006, attended by forty Romanian associations. The participants discussed two main aims of the Romanian community in Spain: integration into Spanish society including the creation of state support structures for new migrants and the maintenance of linguistic and cultural identity. The participants asked for optional Romanian specialist classes in the Spanish schools with a high proportion of Romanian students. The subsequent media exposure, paired with the Spanish government's recognition of the Romanian diaspora as a significant one, paved the way for the introduction of classes in Romanian language and culture from autumn 2007. Spanish regional ministers for integration and citizenship now work closely with the associations to provide appropriate language and employment support through job fairs and other similar schemes.

Following the same model of numerous small-scale associations gathered under the banner of 'federation', usually regionally based and often family run, who meet annually to discuss the status of the community, the Federation of

Romanian Associations in Europe (FADERE) is also based in Spain. The culturally populist model receives the approval of the Romanian government, as evidenced by the presence of Romania's President Traian Băsescu at the 2008 FADERE congress. With guests from the United States and Canada, the congress aimed to represent the Romanian diaspora globally and its moderate success prompted another large-scale congress in France in 2009 and one in Bucharest in 2010.

These annual diasporic congresses have the endorsement of the Romanian government's Department for Relations with Romanians Living Abroad, which seems to prefer associations promoting cultural representation rather than political aims, but only receive lukewarm responses online and among some sections of the diasporic community. Due to the localized nature of associative activities, many associations lack the active online presence that would foster widespread diasporic activism. On the one hand, in the context of everyday life in Spain, some of these associations play a vital role. They provide a focal point for new arrivals, offer information and help with legal matters and organize events at key points in the year. On the other hand, many of them work on a contextual and opportunistic basis and lack individuality and a professional approach to fund raising, event organizing and cultural promotion.

I visited AROVA, the Romanian Association in Valencia, in August 2008. It was a Sunday and part of the Romanian community had gathered at the Romanian Orthodox Church in Calle Rosales. After church, in a nearby street, the AROVA headquarters welcomed new arrivals. Several Romanians were looking at the newly advertised jobs and asking about legal counselling available later in the week. AROVA was founded on 20 May 2005 on the initiative of the wife of the Orthodox priest with the aim of promoting Romanian identity, protecting the rights of Romanian migrants and providing opportunities for education, information and event organizing. Maria Simona Toadere has remained the association's president ever since and together with the association's secretary, Iuliana Șchiopu, she showed me around and told me about various activities. At the time, 127,750 Romanians were living in the whole of the Valencia region and AROVA was providing legal counselling, Spanish language classes, charity work, musical groups, various cultural events and a football team (the Valencia Star).

During a visit to the same Romanian Orthodox Church in August 2008, Rafael Blasco, the minister for immigration and citizenship in Valencia's regional government, had heralded Romanians as an example of integration and AROVA was keen to continue the process, improving the image of Romanians in Spain. The association proffered that it was politically neutral and happy to collaborate with both Socialists and Populars in the Spanish political context, but was also keen to improve the relationship with the press and increase community visibility. A key concern at the time was getting all

Romanians registered on electoral lists, which had become a condition for obtaining an identity card.

AROVA is one of the associations that provide a key service to the daily lives of Romanians in Spain. AROVA's cultural events were clearly motivated by a desire to not only resocialize the community, but also open it up to a Spanish audience and enhance its image, with the overall aim of integration into the Spanish society. However, Adriana Vidroiu-Stanca, the founder of the *Nou Orizont* (New Horizon) Romanian Cultural Association and the magazine with the same name, claimed that the myriad of associations could not all provide a professional service. Her opinion was:

> If they don't have the money and professionals available, then all these Romanian associations should just organise private events. But when important festivals are being organised that represent Romania's image, we have to be a bit more responsible and professional. (Valencia, 2 September 2008)

Vidroiu-Stanca, whose association is also based in Valencia, preferred a model that would entail fewer but more representative associations, ideally better funded and both run by and showcasing Romanian professionals, intellectuals and artists. As a result, her association is the more elitist version, but it remains anchored by cultural aims, primarily making Romanian culture more visible in Spanish society.

> Some associations have this desire of protagonism; they want to see their names in the newspaper. This harms Romania's image. We cannot all represent Romania, but we can choose the few who can do it well. Patriotism is still alive; let's show the best Romania has to offer. There are enough xenophobes and racists in the world, let's not feed their hate towards Romania. We need to show some valour in order to gain these peoples' respect. If we don't respect ourselves, how can we expect others to respect us? If we don't show them who we are, then how are they going to know us?

Apart from the populist but amateurish approach to mainly folkloric and Christmas festivals favoured by many associations, she also pointed to other associative pitfalls. The changing nature of the political context and a climate in which funds were hard to come by put many associations at risk of becoming politically subservient.

> Because these associations are lacking funds, they need to adapt according to the opportunities that arise in order to obtain the necessary funds available. Unfortunately, there is not much difference between Romanian

and Spanish political parties. There is a lot of corruption. So a lot of Romanian associations are being used by some parties as pawns for their own political gain.

Both AROVA and *Nou Orizont* are staffed by volunteers, although embassy support is occasionally available for large events and the Romanian government's Department for Relations with Romanians Abroad has also sponsored certain initiatives, such as a discussion forum in Madrid in 2008 attended by twenty-one Romanian journalists working for diasporic publications in Europe. The ideal solution would nonetheless be, in Vidroiu-Stanca's opinion, the creation of a proper diasporic political party: 'We would have a stronger voice if we had an organization which could function as a political party, with a statute that clearly designated this party as the voice of the Romanian diaspora.' Such small parties already exist, but they are usually either localized or unrepresentative and due to size and funding issues they are only viable when in alliance with larger Spanish political parties. For example, Partidul Românilor din Castellon (The Party of Romanians in Castellon) supported Izquierda Unida, the communist United Left in the 2007 local elections, by proposing twenty-seven candidates across the whole region. However, such alliances are dictated by opportunity rather than ideology and can discredit a political organization, which means that the parties remain small, unpopular and unrepresentative. In turn, this leads to a lack of recognition by Spanish politicians of the political power of the diaspora.

While major Spanish political parties have nonetheless courted the diasporic vote to a certain extent and invited Romanian candidates to join their lists, a fully representative, nation-wide Romanian party is still a desire on the part of the community. Partidul Iberic al Românilor (The Party of Romanians in Spain, PIRUM) was launched in June 2009 in Catalonia. PIRUM's main activity so far has been to initiate a series of informal meetings in Barcelona in October 2009, attended by representatives of diasporic organizations in Europe, with the aim of establishing a permanent dialogue and, in time, collaborative projects and coordination at a European level. The most interesting thing that PIRUM talked about on this occasion was the establishment of a brand for the Romanian diaspora. It is not clear whether this should be a political brand and how it would work in practice. Through a series of online video clips, PIRUM also tried to convince Romanians in Spain to register and vote for the party in the May 2011 municipal elections, billing itself as 'the first party to represent foreigners' (it failed in its attempt). In July 2011, the party also protested against the government's plans to introduce work restrictions for Romanians in the context of the economic crisis. PIRUM does not represent the whole of the Romanian diaspora in Spain and remains an association like all others, albeit with a clearer political mission. Like many other diasporic parties, its ideological stance is undefined and although it has been talked about in the Romanian press, its online presence remains sparse.

The cultural approach taken by many associations means that there is little incentive, even for diasporans who would be entitled to vote in the Spanish local elections, to get involved with political issues. Many associations are simply linking their fund-raising activities with event organization and fail to recognize the more political aspects of diasporic representation. In a way, this reaction is understandable in the context of the conflictual, disorganized and unprofessional nature of Romanian politics and also in relation to many migrants' desire for immediate economic gratification, rather than long-term political and cultural goals. In 2007 only 66,000 Romanians in Spain registered to vote in the local elections, although 420,000 Romanians would have been entitled to. This was largely due to the failure of Romanian associations to mobilize Romanian interests, the mistrust for official politics and the threat of the confrontational Romanian political style being imported by Romanian candidates. As a result, candidates like the ex-footballer Gică Craioveanu, who attempted to become a councillor in Getafe on the list of the largest Centre Right Spanish party, Partido Popular (People's Party), failed to be elected. However, the presence of Romanian candidates on the lists of the main Spanish political parties and the alliances forged by the local Romanian parties show signs that the community is starting to be recognized as a modest political player, at least.

The cultural populist model preferred in Spain is replicated at more modest levels in Italy. Similar coagulations have been attempted there, when the number of small and local cultural associations became too vast. On 28 September 2008 in Rome, sixteen Romanian associations constituted Federația Asociațiilor Românilor din Italia (The Federation of Romanian Associations in Italy, F.A.R.I.). In Italy, nevertheless, due to an uncomplicated process of setting up political parties and the better defined political and conflictual context in which the diaspora exists, institutionalized political representation has become necessary. This politically representative model is illustrated by the first Romanian political party to be founded in Italy, Partito Identità Romena (the Romanian Identity Party), which was founded on 6 November 2006 and has now changed its name to the Party of Romanians in Italy (PIR). It is led by Gianfranco Germani, who is an Italian lawyer married to a Romanian.

The party has proposed Romanian candidates in local and national elections through alliances made with other Italian parties. It had initially been an associate of the Greens, di Pietro's L'Italia dei Valori and the Christian Democratic Party (Unione Democratici per l'Europa, UEDUR), because, as President Germani explained: 'in our statute the only ideological claim we make is our support of Christian values. Our aim is to help the integration of Romanians in Italy and the integration of Italians in Romania. We are the only community party who has as its main aim the creation of a bridge between two nations' (Rome, 3 July 2008). However, once again this leads to opportunistic associations and, in turn, contestation by many Romanians. The big question remains: can a diasporic party be ideologically defined or does it have to be politically diluted by its very nature? Either way, its success is problematic.

In the 2007 elections, PIR had twenty Romanian candidates on UEDUR lists, but there was little success because

> [t]he Romanian community doesn't go out to vote: firstly, because they don't know how – it's a particular procedure; secondly, because they don't understand what benefit voting brings to them. I'm sure that once they understand its importance, they will go and vote *en masse*, but somebody needs to go and explain it to them. (G. Germani, Rome, 3 July 2008)

While setting up a new party in Italy is fairly easy, bureaucratic difficulties appear in the exercising of political rights. Lack of information and adequate infrastructure when registering for elections and voting in Italy has repeatedly dented the chances of the Romanian minority in Italy to make a political difference. According to government estimates, 560,000 Romanians might have acquired the right to vote for the first time in the May–June 2007 regional and local elections, but only 240,000 were officially registered as residents.

PIR switched allegiance to Berlusconi's right-wing coalition, Popolo della Libertà (PdL), in June 2008. Germani explained rather unconvincingly that:

> Before the elections this year we were invited for discussions together with the Bulgarian party because together we have a million potential votes, and they decided that they wanted to invest in us. Because PdL is an ally of Lega Nord, who have clear anti-Romanian sentiments, we decided that it is better if we are inside the coalition to be able to change this. Berlusconi told us that we could only stop Bossi if we told him that the coalition would lose a million votes. There are another two Romanian parties in Italy, but we are the only one that is credited with this potential.

The 2008 elections did not prove to be any more successful either. Of the thirty-five thousand Romanians who had the right to vote in Rome, only eight registered on the electoral lists. According to Germani, the fault was partly with Italian officials and partly with the Romanians themselves:

> The communications office responsible for electoral procedures responded that they had provided the relevant information thirty days prior to the elections. Too bad that the electoral law says that a resident needs to sign up to vote thirty-five days before the elections! This makes things very

difficult because the Romanian labourers who come here don't have time for all this bureaucracy. Romanians are also used to Romanian politics, so they ask themselves what they might gain by voting. In my opinion they have a lot to gain, but for this to happen, Romanians have to be together. They perhaps have a glimpse of the potential, but they prefer to remain as they are.

On 8 February 2008 PIR made a complaint to the National Office for Racial Antidiscrimination about the lack of information surrounding the right of Romanians to vote in the local elections. However, the complaint did not change the outcome.

For Germani, the political force and potential of the Romanian diaspora is clear. However, apart from structural and bureaucratic issues, there is plenty of mistrust in official politics, a habit inherited from Romania, and an inability to trust other Romanians (see previous chapter). This makes forging alliances with Italian parties very difficult and keeps diasporic parties, like PIR, small and unrepresentative. Germani would like to see the community better organized and more united.

The other minority communities are enraged by the fact that they have to fight so hard in order to obtain the right to vote and they see that Romanians have that right, but they don't use it. A local councillor is elected with fifteen hundred votes; you can imagine how far fifty-five thousand votes in Rome could go. Even the Mayor of Rome could be Romanian one day, holding a budget of three hundred million Euros. It is an enormous force, which has not been utilized yet.

Some minor successes have been registered, but these are disproportionate to the size of the community. *Realitatea din Italia* website has publicized, for instance, the political success of six Romanians, who have been elected as local councillors in Italy, either as independents or on various Italian party lists. One of the Romanians, who is now a local councillor in Padua and was elected on a list belonging to a Centre Left coalition, explained that she received 330 votes (there would have been 7,000 Romanians with the right to vote in Padua), but she estimated that only around 200 of these were Romanian (a total of 450 Romanians were inscribed on the electoral lists). Her success had been determined, in her opinion, by a combination of discriminatory discourses by Lega Nord and the economic crisis that hit migrants first of all. Germani is right to think that Romanians are suspicious not only of official politics, but also of other Romanians or Romanian parties. As we shall see in the next chapter, this suspicion is exercised against most diasporic associations and representatives.

In 2008 PIR became a member of Assoforum Roma, a consultative and collaborative body that brings together 750 associations, ten of them Romanian, under the patronage of the mayor of Rome. This allows PIR to widen its activity and increase its networking opportunities. A first, small success was the president of Assoforum expressing his opposition to the fingerprinting of Gypsy children. While this was a useful intervention, the tense ethnic situation culminating in the Mailat case and its aftermath took much of the attention and effort away from much more practical matters, such as work restrictions. These were due to be lifted in 2011, four years after Romania's EU integration, but were not. The invitation to join the Assoforum, which was extended to a total of ten Romanian parties and associations, received online praise from PIR supporters. One user expressed the undisputed recognition that 'we need Italian support if we want to show tolerance, manners and the wish to live side by side in their country' (Pintilie, *Realitatea din Italia*).

PIR has a lively online presence, through the *Identitatea românească* website whose forum serves as an incubator for diasporic activism, such as the organization of street protests during the Mailat case, the anti-Romanian attacks of the Italian media and the discriminatory governmental laws directed at the Roma community and Romanians in general. *Realitatea din Italia* is its sister blog, which is heavily edited by PIR's president, Gianfranco Germani. The discussion forum hosted by *Identitatea românească*, on the other hand, provides a free space for mobilization and contestation (Germani himself has been challenged many times). The public protest meeting on 15 June 2008 in Rome, designed to combat discrimination, was prepared for by a long forum debate from April to June. Also in June 2008, a number of users challenged the political decisions of PIR's leaders regarding the alliances made with other parties and claimed support for a 'virtual Romanian party'.

Italy represents the most advanced model of diasporic associative activity for Romanians in Europe, due to the legal context that permits the setting up of political parties with relative ease, the size of the diaspora and Italy's special political circumstances (a right-wing government hard on immigration for much of the last decade, a subservient media and the Mailat case itself), which allowed the diaspora to express its radicalization through institutionalizing its political activity.

In comparison, the United Kingdom provides us with a culturally organizational model, which is less political, less tolerant of ad hoc cultural manifestations, more attentive to quality and more regimented. It has avoided the myriad associations we encounter in Spain and the populist approach to event organizing, but it also lacks the political visibility of Italian organizations, due to specific circumstances. The Romanian diaspora in the UK is smaller, numbering between seventy thousand and one hundred thousand people. The diaspora is made up of the old diaspora who settled after the Second World

War, some anti-communist defectors who arrived in the 1970s and 1980s and a group of professionals who have acquired either citizenship or residency since the 1990s. According to the Institute for Public Policy Research (IPPR), in the 2001 census there were only 7,500 Romanians officially residing in the UK, but since then the community has grown considerably, with over 40 per cent of all Romanians in the UK by 2006 having arrived between 2001 and 2004 (IPPR et al. 2006).

The intermarriage rate is high, as is the integration into British society. The numbers were kept down by the UK's restrictive immigration policies and since 2007 by work permit caps, which still favour the better-skilled migrants. The newspaper *Diaspora românească* (Romanian Diaspora) reported that in 2010 out of the 51,000 requests for work permits received before July 2010, only 5,000 were successful. Romanian workers who have been allowed entry in these smaller numbers since 2007, together with those arriving as au-pairs, those arriving through the Seasonal Agricultural Workers Scheme, the self-employed, students and also the overstayers and illegal workers, have started to change the skilled and professional demographics to a certain extent. Most of the Romanian diaspora is clustered in London and Birmingham, with smaller pockets scattered around the north of England and in Scotland.

The demographics influence the volume of online activities, much higher in the UK than in Spain or Italy when compared to the size of the diaspora. The main diasporic websites are *Români Online UK* and *Români în UK*, based in London, and the on- and offline activity of the Romanian Cultural Society in Oxford, together with the frequent events and information bulletins of the RCC and the Romanian Cultural Institute, answer most of the cultural needs. Diasporic publications like the weekly *Diaspora românească* and the monthly *Român în UK* (Romanian in the UK) also contribute in large measure to the circulation of cultural information. A specificity of these organizations and publications is that they are active both on- and offline, often creating a bridge between the two and thus managing to capture a great proportion of the diaspora. There are also a few other smaller cultural organizations, but many events in the UK are coordinated or funded by official institutions like the Romanian Embassy and its Romanian Cultural Institute, which allows for a professional and more regimented approach, mainly showcasing Romanian high culture or its traditional folklore to the British public.

The different approach taken by the UK government in the case of the A2 countries, Romania and Bulgaria, in comparison to the A8 Eastern European countries who became EU members in 2004 and whose workers were allowed to work in the UK without restrictions, has prompted the only consistent political reaction from Romanian organizations. Two petitions were organized by the *Români în UK* website and *Român în UK*, its sister monthly newspaper in 2007 and 2008, asking for equal rights to the labour market. Although unsuccessful in terms of governmental policy, this action attracted the support of the *Romanian Community of Ireland* forum, an unusual example of transnational mobilization and common action. In 2007 the campaign obtained the support of 2,052 signatories and 4,257 in 2008, more than double. The petition in 2008 gained the endorsement of Greg Hands, Conservative MP for the then constituency of Hammersmith and Fulham (now Chelsea and Fulham), a specialist in Eastern Europe as part of his foreign affairs remit, who nevertheless made no mention of this campaign on his website. The two petitions triggered the standard, non-committal response from the Prime Minister's Office and restrictions have constantly been renewed since, with the prospect of being finally lifted in 2014.

The different approach taken in Britain in comparison to Spain was confirmed by the former director of the RCC, Ramona Mitrică. The RCC has carved out a distinctive space among diasporic organizations. It is an independent and voluntary association, set up with the help of the Rațiu Family Foundation in 1994. Most of its work is in the fields of visual arts, film and music. The RCC organizes an annual Romanian Film Festival in London, which in 2012 held its nineth edition, has set up a School of Romanian Culture and Tradition, offers a prize for translating European literary works and provides support for residencies, mobility grants for film-makers and higher education scholarships, and organizes events and workshops. Instead of being exclusively aimed at Romanians, the RCC aims instead to capture in equal measure a British audience. As Ramona Mitrică explained, just before Romania's accession to the EU, there had been a renewed interest in Romania:

> We operate in a specific environment; we need to have a good knowledge of British culture, identify the gaps, needs and interests and assess where we fit in. I go to lots of festivals and shows and try to establish connections. . . . It is about placing Romania in the minds of the British. . . . We have something to promote, it's *how* we do it: we have to write the story. (London, 25 November 2008)

Organizations like the RCC are more in line with Adriana Vidroiu-Stanca's view of how cultural needs could be met and cultural promotion conducted, with quality and professionalism and away from populist events with amateur entertainers, cheap food and beer. Some may claim elitism, but Ramona Mitrică has a clear view of her target audience:

> We have ten years of experience in Britain. There have been different migration waves; it's not a fragmented community, but there are several layers, trends. Some have complained about [us] not supporting everybody, but this is a cliché; there are complaints like these in any community.

Particularly newcomers experience hardship and tough beginnings, so we tried to provide a lot of online information about practical issues and also cultural issues. But newcomers are not interested in culture and we have not got a community centre like other diasporas. There are supportive church activities, but our aim is to focus on culture. We have grants for researchers, students and artists, and we also offer support for reintegration in Romania. We aim to keep alive this connection with Romania, through sponsorship and various activities around big events, like, for example, elections.

The cultural organizational model observed here has developed in line with the needs of a smaller, more established, largely professional and better educated diaspora. It also responds to certain conditions in the hostland, like cultural opportunities in a city like London, the awareness that the British have, according to Ramona Mitrică, of Romanian people and Romanian culture, and the highly rated universities, attended by 2,500 Romanian students. Together with the culturally populist and politically representative models, it offers an example of how the Romanian diaspora has grown culturally and politically in the three countries studied and has attempted to change its non-citizenship condition. Associative models also offer a good framework for discussing specific online political activities. It is therefore time to turn again, in the next chapter, towards online micropolitics and discuss it in relation to the political context encountered in the three countries and the diasporic associative models already analysed.

Conclusions: To Mobilize, to Lobby, to Protest

Online diasporic communities evolve in relation to the host country's political context, as well as the individual members' personal experiences of life in the diaspora. As we have seen in the examples discussed in this chapter, the first instances of diasporic mobilization involved pertinent reflections and lobbying of officials and institutions, followed by organizing protests and public demonstrations. Diasporans have used the online forums to galvanize the community and give it a common purpose, helped by the concerted attack that Romanians in Italy, especially, have suffered at the hands of media and politicians. Although some of these political manifestations have also involved diasporic racism and diasporic cannibalism, they have also paved the way for more mature manifestations that take online debates into the public arena and lead to the institutionalization of the diaspora in parties and associations with both cultural and political missions. The online diasporic forums thus represent a key link in the coming of age of the Romanian diaspora.

PART III – POLITICS

'Diasporans Unite':
Identity Politics and the
Romanian Diaspora

CHAPTER FIVE

'Brothers, We Need to Do Something!'

Online Activism and the Politicization of the Diaspora

After outlining the legal challenges faced by Romanian migrants in the European Union and exemplifying three associative diasporic models, it is time to return to examples of online politics. Diasporic cyber-politics can be best understood within the contexts outlined in the previous chapter. In particular, this chapter aims to highlight how legal migratory frameworks shape migrant demographics and, in turn, diasporic micropolitics and how the deficiencies of diasporic associative models are being addressed online, where opportunities exist to supplement and give new impulse to political activities.

Here Come the 'Strawberry Pickers'

Spain has generally provided a more hospitable habitat for Romanians than Italy or the UK. By and large, most Romanians have managed to regularize their presence, have seen work restrictions lifted (at least for a time) and have not encountered major socio-ethnic tensions. The legal context has allowed family reunifications and circular migration, as well as the maintenance of links with the original home for, among other things, possible future return. The culturally populist approach to diasporic associations has also ensured a more mundane but helpful and continuous strategy for both integration and diasporic communitarianism. Diasporic online structures are therefore geared primarily towards imparting and circulating information, including recurrent e-mails from associations, online publications and diasporic discussion forums. As a result, between 2006 and 2008, there were few debates about troubling political issues on Spain-based websites.

Although the first congress of the Romanian community in Spain was widely publicized in December 2006 on *Spania românească,* there was little online appetite for cultural politics. At the time, forty associations met in Coslada, near Madrid, to discuss integration into Spanish society and the maintenance of linguistic and cultural identities. However, several online forum users felt that the abundance of associations did not necessarily reflect a good relationship between these diasporic structures and the community, in terms of representation, activity and impact on Spanish society. Alexandru commented that 'many associations went there to be seen, but have no activity ☺', whereas Raluca added, 'chances are small for anything to change (significantly)'.

This complaint was heard in the Italian context as well, as will be discussed. Despite the number of associations, the diversity of the diaspora, especially as the diaspora is particularly large, means that the online space offers better alternatives and opportunities for expression than offline, where migrants feel unrepresented or pressurized by strict rules. However, associations do receive praise when they act on behalf of diasporans, whenever unfair treatment is highlighted. Because there have been few ethnic tensions in Spain itself and the diaspora there is able to maintain close links with Romania, diasporans have taken issue instead with the way the Romanian media represent migrants and emigration. *Spania românească* forum publicized the initiative of diasporic representatives at the Conference for Romanian Communities in Europe (organized in Bucharest in October 2006) to protest against the label *căpşunari* (strawberry pickers), frequently used by the Romanian media, politicians and public opinion to refer to work migrants in Spain. Alexandru posted several news stories containing this label from the main national media, inviting other users' opprobrium. Olimpia called it 'a generalisation both absurd and stupid' and blamed not only the media, but also migrants whose behaviour, she said, proves that 'we are not a nation that shows solidarity' (*Spania românească*). Gorgana blamed it on both the unprofessional media and migrants who suffer labelling without complaint. She said: 'the *căpşunari* never complained to the media. I am sorry to see the Romanian media sunk so low'. In this instance the online diaspora attempted to enter in a dialogue with the Romanian media, unequal as it may be, in order to respond to derogatory labelling.

The label *căpşunari* poses a problem because of the uncertain nature of identity for Romanians in Spain. On the one hand, they feel better integrated and acknowledged culturally than their Italian or British counterparts; on the other, the ability to return to Romania on an annual basis reconnects them with the original home, preventing them from forming firm emotional bonds in Spain. Romanians in Spain are therefore less politically radicalized and hence their collective identity as diaspora is diluted, whereas their treatment as 'foreigners' back home paradoxically manages to strengthen their migrant and diasporic identity. Being labelled 'strawberry pickers' assigned them an unwanted identity from the bottom of the labour ladder and alluded to a precarious and temporary condition which, in the wake of work permit regularizations, was not applicable any more.

On 4 September 2008, a petition to the Romanian parliament was posted on *Petition Online*. It aimed to attract support for officially changing the name 'Roma/Romany' to 'Gypsy' or the linguistic original, 'Dom', in order to prevent, as the author said, 'a confusion that could prove fatal for the European future of the Romanian people' (*Petition Online*, accessed 4 November 2008). Conceived by a Romanian citizen living in Romania and endorsed by several Romanian newspapers (among them the national daily *Jurnalul Naţional*), the petition was also publicized on *Marea unire, Spania*, one of the main Romanian diasporic sites in Spain. By 1 May 2010 the petition had attracted a total of 28,879 signatures. Although a homeland initiative, the petition was endorsed by at least some users on *Marea unire, Spania*, as it chimed in with the anti-Roma sentiment, which was resurging in the aftermath of the Mailat case and was causing waves throughout all Romanian diasporic communities. This represented a rather marginal online intervention clearly linked to the Italian context, rather than a main concern for Romanians in Spain.

The Mailat Case and Diasporic Micropolitics Online and Offline

One of the main instances of online diasporic radicalization appeared in Italy, where the hostile political environment and the right wing's political preponderance prompted many more diasporic sites and users to get involved in online activism. In the immediate aftermath of Mailat's alleged crime and the political and media backlash, a protest manifestation was organized by PIR on 3 October 2007, supported by users of *România Italia Net* both online and offline. The public manifestation and the preceding online discussions were directed against Walter Veltroni, at the time the mayor of Rome, who had described Romanians as 'the most violent, dangerous and arrogant race'. Mayor Veltroni had claimed, as quoted by users, that 75 per cent of all arrests in Rome between January and August 2007 had been of Romanian citizens. More generally, Romanians felt they needed to protest against the xenophobia of the Italian media and also against the Romanian authorities, for 'not being supportive of us, when they should have been our first line of defence' (Daniel, *România Italia Net*).

Daniel commented on the declaration issued by the Romanian community, which called the protest 'a tough battle for legality and dignity', and wrote towards the end of his post: 'I am asking the forum administrators to consider this thread a social and not a political thread'. His words are an indication that political threads are not encouraged. Rather, webmasters and forum users are more inclined to treat diasporic issues as cultural or social. There is some reluctance on the part of webmasters to encourage political activism and an inclination on the part of Romanian diasporans to treat politics as a dirty word, determined possibly by their experience of Romanian-style politics, defined by partisanship and infighting. Cyber-communities thus prefer to see themselves as impartial cultural and social outlets, which dents their ability to properly coordinate any political involvement.

The Mailat case prompted, nevertheless, several websites to discard this approach in favour of broaching long-standing but previously ignored diasporic issues. In May 2008 Associazione Italia Romania Futuro Insieme (Italy Romania a Future Together Association, IRFI), an association militating for the integration of Romanians in the Italian society, promoted on *Realitatea din Italia* its proposal for a 'Charter of the Roma People', which asked for the official recognition of the identity and rights of the Roma. The president of the association interceded in the online discussion by asking polemically, 'Who intervenes to ensure that their rights are respected? Who has ever helped them to live a normal life here?' Anti-Roma sentiments were evident in some of the replies. Aris replied with, 'Why should they have more rights than us?' while Mihu commented that 'most Gypsies do not want to be "integrated", they would consider it an assimilation, their group identity would be lost, especially as they do not have the chance of ever having their own nation-state'. Contributors seemed split between strong calls to protect the rights and reputation of Romanians before the rights of the Roma were even considered and complaints about the reaction against the Roma in Italy. It shows that the community tends to victimize itself both when their Romanianness is on display and when there is an involuntary or malicious association between Romanians and Roma.

In another post, Mica promoted and supported the initiative of academics from several universities in Italy to demonstrate together with the Roma association Them Romano against the 'cultural genocide' of the community on 1 June 2008 in Rome. Although some participants reacted to this post with the usual anti-Gypsy racism, some noted the marginalisation of the Roma and Liliana observed, 'we are one step away from Auschwitz'.

The Mailat case continued to prompt numerous posts in the *Realitatea din Italia* forum from April to August 2009, where, apart from updates from the court case itself, which was ongoing at the time but was not discussed in great detail, participants took the opportunity to virtually and symbolically counter Italian public opinion. Users posted numerous stories about criminal acts committed by Italian citizens. Aris remarked that 'their criminals are no different from ours'; Roxana opinionated, 'media reporting of shameful acts committed by Italian citizens is always local and they are willingly underplayed'; and Norina commented that 'among Italians there are many good intelligent people, who do not allow themselves to be influenced by the flaming strategy practised by the media'.

Participants in the *România Italia Net* forum, on the other hand, followed the judicial case closely, posting many articles from the Italian press. Though these posts were read by numerous users for gist and information, few ventured any comments. Floricica also posted the text of the new law dealing specifically with sexual violence, in the context of which users expressed their hope that it would have a calming effect on both Romanians and Italians. Some participants interpreted the law as illiberal, claiming it was a return to a legal regime similar to the fascist one. Finally, Emilia opinionated that 'many Romanians arrested in Italy in the last few months are being indicted under media and public pressure'.

In the *Italia România* forum, a similar opinion emerged. In a thread from February 2009 participants talked of a 'campaign against Romanians' and the media exaggerations aimed at 'creating panic'. Ceanu bluntly said: 'Berlusconi profits from popular vulnerability during this crisis[:] . . . instead of focusing on the economic crisis he can talk about security.' Ceanu blamed the media and the right-wing political groups for the situation Romanians found themselves in. Users posted stories about statistical manipulations by Italian authorities and Romanians who avoided speaking their language in public. Ceanu asked the forum administrator, 'shouldn't we write to the papers? We should pool our forces with other associations and do something.' Although this suggestion was not taken up, though the administrator promised to represent the forum views in any national initiative, many participants conducted a good analysis of the causes that have led to public hostility, among which they cited the opportunism of the political class, the inefficient juridical system, insufficient police and the tabloidization of the press. Mircea also added:

> It's an exaggeration to talk about a setup, secret services etc. . . . Romanians have contributed too, they work on the black market accepting minimal wages, prostitutes discount their tariffs, the Romanians state says nothing because they know Romanian migrants send millions of euro home and want nothing in return.

Another contributor blamed both the Romanian and the Italian press for their similar strategy of exaggeration and emphasis on scandal and criminality. In the same forum (*Italia România*), Romanians were invited to sign various open letters. Mircea returned to the thread to make the point: 'it's clear that we need to organise ourselves, to react somehow, to separate ourselves from the riff-raff, but I don't know how'. Grecu responded by saying that 'the letter *Cara Italia* [Dear Italy, a letter originating from the offices of the Romanian Orthodox Church in Italy] is making an impact . . . [. W]e need to cooperate like before . . . [. I]t's not impossible[:] . . . we just need the will'. Other participants complained that Romanian representatives were inexperienced on the national stage and their profile not visible enough.

A culture of blaming permeated online discussions, but these threads also showed the ability to recognize the threat to the community and the willingness to get involved and address the injustice. Diasporans managed to perform a correct analysis of the political and media systems, but lacked the ability to act clearly and consistently either because they did not have a voice within Italian society or because they were represented by an inefficient home government and diasporic organizations lacking a public profile. Users continually point out in various contexts that the politically representative associative model is in fact unrepresentative and weak, with diasporic parties and associations disregarded by Italian public opinion and the political system. A precedent has nevertheless been set for a rehearsed and more efficient reaction in the future.

Politics continued to reenter various other fields, making it impossible for diasporic online communities to move away from the highly charged political context. When the Romanian film *Francesca* premiered at the Venice Film Festival in 2009, the politician Alessandra Mussolini inferred that the physical violence exhibited by the Romanians in Italy was clearly a national characteristic, since the film was also defined by bad and violent language. Mussolini was reacting to one of the dialogues in the film, in which she and other Italian politicians were being accused of extremist remarks against Romanians in Italy. Her complaint prompted the suspension of screenings during the festival. Alina Harja, a journalist and the president of the association Amici della Romania (Friends of Romania), reacted with an open letter on a number of media blogs and diasporic forums, including *Realitatea din Italia*. In it, she counteracted Mussolini's claims, pointing out that only 0.1 per cent of Romanians in Italy had committed any crimes. Her post prompted support from some contributors, while others, like Mica, recommended that all Romanian parties and associations in Italy should speak with one voice. She also lamented the tendency of diasporic politicians to be very active whenever it is a case of distributing leadership posts, but less so when the community is incriminated as a whole. Other participants mentioned the necessity of not just one voice, but also a brand, a name that would represent all Romanians in Italy.

As mentioned previously, most contributors to diasporic online forums in Italy, radicalized by the legal measures and public backlash unleashed in the aftermath of the Mailat case, have used the occasion to conduct a critical analysis of associative activities. In July 2008 in the *România Italia Net* forum Adi criticized the activity of a Romanian association fighting for the rights of Romanian labourers in Rome, claiming that the association had no political activities, but served only to build up the image of its president. Adi also criticized the attitude of different political representatives who swapped politics for culture. In his view, cultural gatherings were important for Romania's image, but most associations lacked political action. In the discussion that followed some contributors condemned the tendency of Romanian politicians to use the diaspora as pawns, considering that by supporting Romanian associations in Italy, these politicians aimed to gather votes rather than benefit the diaspora. The contributors referred particularly to the four deputies and two senators that have represented the diaspora in the Romanian parliament since 30 November 2008. The heated online polemic that criticized diasporic politics and the lack of representation of various diasporic politicians prompted Ştefan to exclaim, 'I am fed up with Romanian politics and Romanian "associationism"!' (Ştefan, *România Italia Net*).

In another thread posted in the Virtual Hyde Park section of *Realitatea din Italia*, the European Party of Romanians (established on 28 October 2007) came under fire on several occasions. The general secretary of the party was the first target and was accused of setting up several Romanian associations and leagues in Alessandria, all supposedly non-political, but then participating in the local elections on Lega Nord lists. When his wife was elected councillor on the PdL list, several commentators raised questions about the opportunistic political practices of Romanians in Italy.

A similar polemic in the *Realitatea din Italia* forum in June 2008 prompted participants to talk about the 'cannibalism' of Romanian associations, clearly displayed by diasporic politicians who behave selfishly and individualistically. Vic, a high-ranking member of PIR, nevertheless applauded 'the reinstatement of the Virtual Party of Romanians' and considered the online debate to be healthy for the community. He opinionated that 'a purely ethnic party had no chance in Italy' and that the path chosen by PIR, which has an Italian president, helped the party gain a more prominent place on the Italian political map. In the same forum Răzvan posted his view of what diasporic politics should entail: active participation in social and political life (voting); information points to help diasporans with instances of discrimination, legal documents, health and social security; and national representatives who can react promptly to the attacks of the Italian media and the Italian political class. He called for collaboration and unity instead of the typical infighting of the Romanian community.

These instances reveal the importance of online debates: they provide information and analysis of the political context; they mobilize the diaspora around key political issues; they position the diaspora within a complex field that includes diasporic associations and parties, mainstream parties and official public figures, politicians and the government back home; they provide several stages of radicalization leading to action. Unfortunately, the discrediting of politics under the communist regime and the 'dirty' politics of the transition meant that many were, and still are, reluctant to get actively engaged and prefer to discuss and criticize instead.

After October 2007, online debates crossed the threshold into the realm of political action, with many demonstrations being organized online. In April 2008 several members of the *Realitatea din Italia* forum discussed organizing a series of demonstrations to show unity and support for Romanians unjustly tainted by Italian public opinion. Mica thought that 'everything must start with education. We need to learn how to organize ourselves'. Mihu considered that Romanians lacked an all-encompassing organization to react promptly and efficiently and added: 'autoghettoization and forming a separate group away from the locals is not the most intelligent way of saving Romanian identity'. Aris, on the other hand, insisted: 'let's show that we are a force, different from the ones who give us a bad name. . . . We are a people, we have DIGNITY' (emphasis in the original). This exchange marked the initial stages of organizing public demonstrations and shows the ability of the online community to act politically.

There were also signs that the diaspora was increasingly acquiring a sense of its own abilities and position. In June 2008 *Realitatea din Italia* users reacted to a website entitled *SOS for Romanians in Italy*, a Romanian initiative of the Intact Media Group, owners of the Romanian television station *Antena 2* and a string of publications based in Romania. Luna posted a call to unity: 'The only ones who can do something are US, but there is no US, only ME, YOU, HIM and HER!!!! Unfortunately we Romanians forgot that "strength is doubled in pairs"' (emphasis in the original). More cynically, Pintilie observed: 'until yesterday we were *căpșunari* [strawberry pickers] and *macaronari* [macaroni eaters]: it's a bit late in the day'. In the same way diasporans are wary of diasporic associations, they are aware of media attempts to use them for commercial and political purposes.

In anticipation of a meeting in Rome on 15 June 2008, the discussion continued on *Realitatea din Italia*, spread over several threads, which debated the practicalities of banners, T-shirts and slogans. However, some voices remained sceptical about the group's ability to act as a force. Pintilie observed that the discussion always took place among ten or fifteen users, with many others unwilling to contribute. He added dejectedly: 'we don't care about proposals that aim to change something. . . . "There is no hope!" We deserve every spit and kick up the arse'. Galina, on the other hand, made the point that there was a difference between freedom of expression in online discussions and 'community tactics, which need certain rules'. The outcome of the 15

June 2008 meeting between various Romanian parties and associations in Italy was therefore eagerly discussed online. Contributors appreciated the success of the meeting and the improved openness and desire to collaborate in comparison with the previous meeting held in Milan. They observed the widespread geographic and ethnic participation, which included some representatives of the Roma (such as Queen Lucica). The meeting recommended 'small steps' and 'consolidation' based on commonality of interests, but online forum users also called for greater efficiency.

Users on all diasporic websites reacted in a similar fashion to the media, politicians and public opinion in Italy, manifesting a clear unity of spirit, replicated afterwards in the discourse of several parties and associations. The websites also created the space for protests and open letters to circulate, preparing for the implementation of dissenting and critical actions. In addition, the online community reacted against the establishment, providing a fierce critique of politicians (Romanian and Italian), journalists and governmental institutions. This indicates the development of a specific diasporic discourse, which is elaborated online independently of official organizations and structures, which are biased due to their partisanship and individual interests. Instead, online, a more all-encompassing spirit emerges, that aims to fight injustice with very few resources and plenty of idealistic notions, such as unity and commonality of interest. It is also useful to note that instances of anti-Gypsy discrimination and racism were significantly reduced in the latter stages of the Mailat case. This may be due to the fact that the whole of the community was criminalized, but it may be also linked with a new understanding of the diasporic position, as a minority under attack. Diasporic cannibalism therefore subsided to a certain degree.

Work Rights and Campaigning on Behalf of Others

Majority politics and its various injustices can become an important catalyst for diasporic mobilization. This was evident when the British government decided to impose and then maintain work restrictions for Romanians and Bulgarians after the 2007 enlargement. When in 2006 it became apparent that a stringent cap would be implemented, the *Români Online UK* forum started debating modes of protest under the thread 'Romanians of the world UNITE!' A subsequent meeting at the Romanian restaurant Rustic in London and a live Yahoo Messenger discussion on the evening of the August Bank Holiday (28 August 2006) produced several initiatives: open letters to the media, public demonstrations, an alliance with the Bulgarian community and a European syndicate for all migrants (though most did not materialize in the end). Bicu was of the opinion that:

The majority think that we are too small to change anything, but I would feel ashamed if we didn't try to do something ... [. W]e are not just talking about the right to work, but about Romania's image, my image, the way I feel when I say I am Romanian, [and] the equal treatment of European citizens.

What finally emerged was the 2007 petition 'Stop Discrimination! We ask for the right to work!', organized with the support of the *Român în UK* monthly newspaper. 2,052 signatures were gathered. A similar initiative in 2008, the petition entitled 'Romanians in the UK – equal citizens of the European Union – we ask for restrictions to be lifted!', garnered 4,257 signatures – more than double. The campaign ran between 2 September and 15 October 2008, and was organized again by the website and newspaper.

The 2007 petition prompted the Ireland-based website *Romanian Community of Ireland* to launch a forum thread entitled 'Romanians in the UK need our help', which was an invitation to sign it. Traian wrote: 'Can't you see that the British are doing the same thing as the Irish? Let's help them over there with our signatures, maybe something will come out of it.' Dinu replied:

Brothers, we need to do something about Ireland as well[;] we want honest work[;] stop this discrimination. . . . Are we building a united Europe or are we building a Europe with first- and second-class citizens? Brothers, we aren't all Gypsies and thieves. We need to make them see that.

Lucian added: 'in order to be noticed, we need to make ourselves heard. Come out of anonymity. If we don't do it, nobody will on our behalf.' Although links to other diasporic groups across the globe are a feature of most websites and many diasporans sign up to chat groups and forums based in other countries, while others move from cyberspace to cyberspace as a result of physically moving from one country to another, this was the first instance when one Romanian diasporic group took action on behalf of another (a forum based in Italy also posted encouraging messages). The UK-based petitions were unusual, in that the initiative, the web support and the signatures came almost entirely from Romanians already settled in the UK, who enjoyed the right to work. It was a rare instance in which the community acted on behalf of future and would-be migrants working illegally. However, the relatively low number of signatures indicated disinterest in supporting what was seen as someone else's cause or even a futile cause.

In the *Români Online UK* forum some users took, therefore, a more critical attitude towards both the initiators and the community as a whole. They thought that the petition was poorly worded and that Romanians were unable to sustain a concerted effort. In Ionela's opinion, the relatively small number of signatures was due to many Romanians feeling that 'it's not representing them. . . . Bulgarians should also be informed so that they can sign[:] . . . it's in their interest too'. Referring to the number of signatures doubling from 2007 to 2008, Zoe wrote, in English, 'it made me feel good to see there are many signatures! That's a huge improvement to the lower numbers who signed the other petition before. Well done everyone, but it's not enough!' Filipa urged Romanians, 'we should have the same rights like the other EU states'. Their encouragements had a snowballing effect, prompting many people to sign up, despite a certain degree of pessimism regarding the outcome.

The attitude of Romanian officials became a point of contention. In May 2008 on *Români Online UK* Selina commented positively on the BBC documentary series *Meet the Immigrants*, considering that it was significantly improving migrants' image. She concluded, 'this broadcaster is doing more than Romania's embassy in London. For them, SLEEP is more important, when they should at least provide some moral support' (emphasis in the original). The delayed reaction from Romanian institutions seemed indeed conspicuous, mirroring the sluggishness observed in the case of similar institutions in Italy.

In July 2008 the topic of work rights returned in another thread initiated by a researcher at the University of Essex, who invited users to comment on the work restrictions. Relu replied: 'Work restrictions that have been imposed on Romanians and Bulgarians after the EU integration are unfair and discriminatory. The most affected are the honest ones who want to find work legally.' He also observed Romania's population to be one-third of that of Poland and a 'deluge' unlikely. Mina, however, pointed out: 'I don't think anybody has anything against Romanians[:] . . . it's purely political'.

Anger against the imposition of work restrictions considered to be unfair and undeserved became almost unanimous. When Marina posted her unique opinion that work rights should be even tougher and visas should be reintroduced, users reacted angrily. Ionela replied with: 'this [is] from someone who has already received the blue card and has forgotten the stress and waiting before the "magic envelope" comes . . . [. M]any illegal acts are committed by Romanians because the labour market isn't "open" . . . [. W]hy are Romanians and Bulgarians "worse" than Baltic and other people?' Other participants ganged up on Marina using the information she had provided (her husband was British) and reminded her that she was still Romanian and she should not have disrespected Romanians who came to the UK after 2007. This exchange was indicative of the UK demographic context, split between pre-2007, already settled migrants and new, post-2007 migrants, whose position remains frail due to the legal context.

Work rights issues provided a catalyst for discussions and petitions, allowing diasporans to express their feelings on an issue that was not just practical and real, but also symbolic with regard to the way the European Union chose to differentiate between accession countries. The community acted as a diaspora, campaigning on behalf of co-nationals lacking the opportunity to speak or protest. Although most of the signatories would have already had the right to work in the UK, the campaign was aiming to help future workers.

The right to work was by far the most popular topic with a political relevance debated throughout 2007 and 2008, but other 'softer', more culturally related issues also brought the group to a consensus. The few examples included: Carmina organizing a letter of protest to Ofcom for the inaccuracies contained in the ITV documentary, broadcast on 6 November 2008, 'Duchess and Daughters: Their Secret Mission', featuring Sarah Ferguson on a trip to Romania to observe progress in childcare; Nelu protesting in February 2009 about the Romanian embassy's lack of services on Sundays; *Români în UK* users being urged in 2009 to vote for the Romanian sculptor Brâncuşi in *The Times* and Saatchi top two hundred artists of the twentieth century list (Brâncuşi came in at number sixteen, with 14,224 votes); and in December 2008, prior to the Chelsea versus CFR-Cluj game taking place in the UEFA Champions League, the *Români în UK* webmaster offering users the opportunity to download the CFR-Cluj hymn onto their mobile phones prior to playing it simultaneously during the game. These examples show attempts to bring the group together around more or less serious issues, which help the community become a diaspora and act as one on a more permanent basis. It also showed a certain sense of national pride emerging.

Cyber-alliances: Diasporans Unite!

Increasingly, changes in the sophistication, individualization and globalization of online diasporic networks are linked to critical mass – demographic, economic and temporal. The proliferation of people moving to the West, the economic prosperity acquired during their stay and the rise in permanent or semi-permanent settlements have led to the emergence of various models in the way Romanian diasporas conduct themselves online. The steep professionalization in the look and content of sites that took place after 2000 was followed by the emergence of sites with specific aims and flavours. More recently, a third important phenomenon has emerged: attempting to link the group into a larger matrix, primarily with the homeland and Romanian institutions abroad, but also increasingly with other diasporic groups. While it is still too early to talk about well defined cyber-alliances, the phenomenon is indicative of a constantly changing and improving terrain.

Collaborations and collective action have been prepared for by the rise of hyperlinking, cyber-connectivity and informal exchanges. The backing offered by the *Romanian Community of Ireland* website to the petition initiated by *Români Online UK* in support of lifting work restrictions in the UK provided an illuminating insight into the commonality of interests shared by migrant groups and raised the question of the likelihood of global action. Once support is received, reciprocity emerges. In October 2008, the administrator of *România Italia Net* invited users to 'give a helping hand' to Romanians in the UK and sign the online petition for the right to work without restriction since 'these restrictions "affect" all of us wherever we live'. In February 2009 the webmaster of *Români în UK* commented on an Italian senator's statement about the criminality of the Romanian community and their undeserved entry in the EU. Users complained about the lack of reaction of Romanian authorities and many deplored the situation that Romanians in Italy had to go through. They also criticized the mushrooming of inefficient Romanian associations.

Similar transnational dialogues have been slowly increasing. *Realitatea din Italia* publishes news from other communities on its website, taken from *Gazeta românească*, a diasporic newspaper printed in different versions in various European countries. To give just one example, in July 2009 it featured the Romanian Women's Society, established in 2005 in Fulham (now called Românca Society). There was an interview with its president and a description of its activities, including open letters to Tony Blair and Gordon Brown about equal rights to work and events such as Romania's National Day.

The Oxford Romanian Cultural Society has offered moral support to the Moldovan diasporic website *Acum* (Now), based in the UK, in view of the difficult political transition and regime change in the Republic of Moldova. However, the relationship never became official or permanent and it was mainly determined by historical and cultural affinity, as well as the much proclaimed brotherhood between Romanians and Moldovans. In April 2007 on *Români în UK* Patriciu proposed that other users join 'our brothers' from the Republic of Moldova for a demonstration in Trafalgar Square. The webmaster posted an invitation from the Moldovans to join the anti-communist revolution that had started back home. Some users showed themselves eager to join, others complained about the early start of the demonstration, while a few posted the reminder that Moldovans had not supported Romania's own revolution in 1989. Afterwards Patriciu shared pictures and videos and confirmed an attendance of forty Romanians. Adina responded to the sceptics by pointing out the worse status that Moldovans have in comparison to Romanians, mentioning human rights abuses and the absence of EU membership, which also meant the lack of freedom to travel without visas.

Increasingly though, some sites are trying to establish more permanent links with other online diasporic groups. *Români în UK* is just one site that provides a list of diasporic websites peppered around the world. *Romanian*

Portal US, on the other hand, has aimed from the outset to become a global website and has hyperlinks to the largest Romanian communities in Europe and North America. Although it is actively inviting collaborations from other diasporic websites, its forum remains anchored in American realities for now. Similarly, *Koolro* defines itself as 'the first social network of Romanians abroad', but it mainly focuses on the younger diasporic demographics in the United States. More promising is *Străinătate* (Abroad), the 'site for the true Romanian', which was created in December 2007. Although it only has 2,300 users (as of October 2012), it aims to provide a unique discussion space for Romanians anywhere. The forum has plenty of visitors, but the posts and replies are few and far between; it is too early to call it a global diasporic website.

Marea Unire (the Great Union) is a banner under which several countries' branches of one online initiative have been set up. It functions in the UK, Spain, France and several other European countries. In theory, it is a global network, anchored in a number of countries. In reality, it is a bunch of websites that have little to do with one another, apart from the name. Users, too, seemed confused by its purpose. Its Spanish branch, *Marea unire, Spania*, had a reasonably active forum but decayed when some users moved to the more specific *Spania românească*. A similar initiative is *E-migrant*, a website which had over 7,100 members (in March 2012), hosted in the US. It aimed to put migrants in touch with other Romanian migrants around the world and provide links to other online diasporic groups, but its search facilities remained rather basic and it closed down in the summer of 2012.

Even when official collaborations between sites are established, the beginnings can be strained. *Realitatea din Italia* (based in Italy) and *Străinătate* (based in Germany) have established such a collaboration because Danny, the initiator of *Străinătate*, envisaged a network of sites that would unify Romanians in the diaspora. He invited users on *Realitatea din Italia* to visit the site and contribute opinions. Users reacted positively, signing up to the new site. However, a few days later, *Realitatea din Italia* deleted the link to *Străinătate*. Although the administrator claimed it was a technical mistake (the site was being redesigned to give more prominent space to advertising banners), *Străinătate* decided to proceed reciprocally. Danny even accused Aris, the webmaster of *Realitatea din Italia*, of disinterest. Aris responded, 'I'd like to collaborate, but you never sent me anything, you guys never post on our site. What do we gain? We have exclusive material, which we sent to you. There is a link on the opening page, what else would you like?' The two webmasters decided in the end to continue the collaboration whenever possible and make each other 'site partner'.

Consolidations like the partnership between *Români Online UK*, *Radio Români Online* and the diasporic newspaper *Ziarul românesc*, whose UK edition prints seven thousand weekly copies in London since 2008 and twenty thousand monthly copies for the whole of the UK since September 2009, aim to reach as many Romanians in the UK as possible, through various formats, and especially establish an efficient network of information and exchange. Hyperlinking can be another indication of how a site positions itself in the diasporic global network. Most sites hyperlink with diasporic publications, online diasporic broadcasting, media in Romania, embassies and cultural centres and institutes, churches, YouTube, Facebook and Twitter, immigration services and official host institutions, solicitors, airlines and other customer services. This gallimaufry is common to all diasporic sites, but none transcends the concerns with settling in one specific country only. Sites remain firmly anchored into host realities, though initiatives like *Romanian Portal US*, *E-migrant* and *Străinatate* seem to allude to a new phase in the expansion of diasporic online networks.

There were several examples of the emergence of a transnational diasporan who navigates with ease between sites based in the US, Spain or the UK, in preparation for a move or in search of news from other communities. As one of these itinerant migrants explained: 'During the last ten years I was "temporary" in Spain and Germany; I am now in England! Life threw me this way, mainly due to financial difficulties' (Arnold, *Români Online UK*). In July 2009 *Realitatea din Italia* and the publication *Gazeta românească* featured an interview with a Romanian who moved from Italy, 'where we were "shitty Romanians"', to London, 'where we are humans'. The interviewee praised the benefits of working and living in the UK, including job security, more money, and respect, as well as cleanliness and a higher level of education (read better manners). A discussion thread on *Marea Unire, Spania* in October and November 2007 revealed that many contributors had been moving between Romania, Italy, Spain and the UK and those with such experiences were proud of their 'transcultural capital' and felt comfortable adapting to new surroundings. This type of migrant, who chooses to migrate between countries in search of a better cultural fit or under pressure from changing financial circumstances, may not themselves establish permanent links between the communities but creates a sense of a fluid, transnational space in which migrants move, making diasporic site-hopping an enjoyable and educative experience.

Sometimes users are too committed to a specific group and this can lead to competitive attitudes, as observed between *Români în UK* and *Români Online UK*, where online posts occasionally disparage the activities of the other forum. One cause resides in the discriminatory tendencies observed in many migrants and the autocratic inclinations of webmasters. Another cause is the lack of 'interactors' or 'networkers' capable of working outside their own network, of which some forums may have a few, but never enough (Kozinets

2009: 34). This hampers the desired collective action. The administrator of
Români Online UK explained that his site was set up in 2004 as an alternative
to *Români în UK*. Collaboration between the sites was turned down by
Români în UK, so the *Români Online UK* administrator conceded he had used
'less orthodox measures' to attract some of the *Români în UK* users to the new
site. In his view, *Români Online UK* provided a more structured website and
a more user-friendly forum than the 'disorganized' rival.

Competition between sites can occasionally descend into bitter acrimony.
A rumour circulated on *Români în UK* in September 2009 that *Marea unire,
UK* was going to be closed down. The webmaster denied the rumour and at
the same time warned users that his name had been denigrated on another
Romanian site in the UK (presumably *Marea unire, UK*). In addition, certain
dubious e-mails and phone calls had been used to advance harmful rumours.
Nelu, one of the users, made the most of the occasion:

> ☺))) it would be great if it closed down[;] the police should also inter-
> vene because of the racism, paedophilia, and identity and card thefts
> perpetuated on the site. I have personally complained online about what
> is happening. The webmaster should behave more responsibly.

This example shows that diasporic rivalry can degenerate into slanderous
accusations of cyber-crime, perpetrated by users from behind the veil of anonymity. Rivalry contributes to diasporic fragmentation and is an indication of
the infancy of 'cyber-alliances' (Braziel and Mannur 2003).

A positive development has been the improvement observed in the relation between diasporic websites, news websites and institutions based in
Romania. While many migrants harbour some rancour against the Romanian
political and economic system, back in Romania, the propaganda of right-
wing political groups and even the unhelpful discourse of some of the
Romanian media have included accusations of treason made against migrants.
The Romanian media, in particular, was instrumental in initially labelling all
migrants *căpşunari* (strawberry pickers), *macaronari* (macaroni eaters) or
stranieri (foreigners). Whether the online activities of the Romanian diaspora
have had any impact in changing this view is unclear. However, a new understanding of the diaspora's economic role through remittances has emerged in
recent years. The diaspora is also surfacing as an important political actor. Its
role in the 2009 presidential elections, when diasporic votes seemed to have
sealed the outcome of the decisive second tour, was heartily, though not
always favourably, discussed in Romania by politicians and journalists alike.
With the diaspora also electing parliamentary members to represent its interests in the Romanian parliament, it is easier to see the impact of the diasporic
voice, which initially emerged online and was continued through the work of

associations and pressure groups. Changing perceptions and attaining changes, even from a distance, are good preliminary signs that announce possible further involvements and alliances with the home, and, in time, fewer inferiority complexes and less envy.

Conclusions: Diasporic Micropolitics

Online activism on Romanian diasporic websites is defined by political selectivity. While lobbying, petitioning and negotiating have become part of the banal everyday in the life of the online community, many online activities stop short of constructing permanent political structures and operating by organizational rules. Online hierarchies are too fluid and destabilizing to give continuity to political initiatives. The occasional illegality that defines the lives of Romanian diasporans also hampers migrants' ability to establish relationships and formalize their presence (Garapich 2008: 747) outside online networks. Informality and insecurity regarding status and economic stability can cause mistrust inside the community, but as previous research with the Polish community has revealed, once migrants pass from the grey economy into the formal one, tensions are eased and public participation and formalized actions take shape (Garapich 2008: 743). It is to be hoped that after 2014, when work restrictions for Romanians are lifted throughout Europe, this will be the case with Romanian migrants, who will begin to feel less like immigrants and more like European citizens.

Siapera describes the work of the refugee websites she studied as 'prepolitical' (2005: 500). However, in my observation of Romanian online diasporic activism, this prepolitical stage has been surpassed. Diasporic deliberative democracy entails, according to Siapera, stating reasons, justifying claims, a public and direct dialogue, and problem resolution (2005: 509). Despite an inability to function professionally and consistently at all times, Romanian diasporic websites are fulfilling some of these functions and many more. It is probably unrealistic to think that what is by definition a boundless and chaotic medium will create the same rules of interaction as other more established forms of activism. On the contrary, paradoxes, conflicts and tensions need to continue online because it is through criticism and challenges to any form of authority that online micropolitics can evolve as an alternative and viable form. These may be heterogeneous and contested spaces, but all the while they are also aiming to construct 'a common "we"' (Brah 1996: 184).

The success of various incursions into the traditional political field may be limited at the moment, but it would be inappropriate to measure online political activism by the criteria we generally use within the social political field. New criteria are needed. It would also be a mistake to consider that

diasporic websites function in isolation. Any politics is simultaneously micro-
and macropolitics (Deleuze and Guattari 1987: 213). While the existence of
the social group depends on usually unnoticed changes at a 'molecular' level,
it is also true that diasporic micropolitics thrive in relation to larger societal
phenomena. Diasporic micropolitics may operate more at a 'tactile' level – the
level of feelings, emotions and opinions – but successful micropolitics is not
about size; it is instead about the nature of these activities. We must also
remind ourselves that both marginalization and pride lead to 'psychological
empowerment' (Brinkerhoff 2009: 41). Most notably, like other diasporas,
Romanians abroad show an increased ability to become assertive and active
and thus ensure diasporic continuity (Sheffer 2003: 248). This process is
enhanced by a developing diasporic public sphere (Laguerre 2006: 114), supported online though diasporic media (online newspapers and radio), multi-
layered debates and more informal gossip, the outcomes of which are easily
translated offline. The online and the offline are feeding off one another in
the same way the local and the global are mutually enforcing. This is the
uniqueness of the diasporic public sphere.

It is clear that diasporic websites host a diverse range of political activities
that are different but not dissimilar to mainstream politics. Online micropolitics are about contestation, negotiation, mobilization, decision-making and
activism, as well as self-publicity and public performance through which users
achieve status (often the role of thread initiators or even moderators).
Hierarchies of power emerge, clearly identified through the system of points
or labels attached to avatars that reward users for longevity and amount of
contributions. Discrimination and conflict are self-regulated, with the occasional intervention of webmasters and moderators, who have the ability to
police and punish, so there can be consequences. The most important characteristic is the identity politics expressed by debates asking what it means to be
Romanian and migrant in Italy, the UK or Spain; how diasporic identity can
be performed effectively; and which canons of identity performance are
adequate and acceptable. For all these reasons, online diasporic websites
become political.

CHAPTER SIX

'Languishing in Purgatory'

The Politics of Location and Homeland

Diasporic theory has always been eager to discuss homeness and belonging, possibly because questions such as 'Where are you from?' and 'Where is home?' become an intrinsic part of life in the diaspora. Such basic questions lead to reexamining self-identity, the precursor to getting involved in diasporic micropolitics. Moreover, the same questions in relation to additional concerns such as location, boundary, distance and other spatial configurations become key elements in macropolitics: they define the relationship between the diaspora and its homeland, which is increasingly eager to include diasporas in strategic political games.

This chapter begins by explaining Dante's Purgatory metaphor, which teaches us about the 'no place' that we find often discussed in diasporic texts. The metaphor is then used to analyse the positioning of the diaspora vis-à-vis the homeland, which is now shaping a number of political initiatives. If previous chapters discussed the relationship forged by the diaspora with the place of arrival and settlement, this chapter looks back towards the home left behind, but also forward, towards a new type of relationship with the mother country.

Inferno Lost, Paradise Still to Be Gained

Adopting Plato's concept of placelessness Bourdieu observes that migrants are 'atopos' because they exist in a 'bastard place' at the 'frontier between being and social non-being' (Bourdieu, quoted in Sayad 2004: xiv). This recalls Dante's description of the no man's land he encounters between Hell and Paradise; like Dante at the foot of Purgatory's first incline, the migrant may feel disorientation and insecurity. Dante explains that he felt like a '*peregrin*' (in modern Italian, *pellegrino*), a travelling stranger tired by the roughness and steepness of the road behind and apprehensive of the mountain that still remained to be climbed, in search of knowledge and spiritual achievement. However, Dante and his guide, Virgil, witness the splendour of the dawn together with other travelling souls, meet a friend and become optimistic about the road ahead, hopeful about Dante's progressive ascent towards Paradise (Alighieri 1993: 242–5).

To me, Dante's second canto of the *Purgatorio* speaks about the limbo migrants find themselves in (let us not forget that Dante himself died in exile) after arriving 'nowhere' and finding that the journey is in fact a never ending search for new meanings. Such considerations are often replicated in diasporic literature. As Gilroy explains in one of his most influential texts, 'routes' are more appropriate than the homonym 'roots' (Gilroy 1993: 19) when describing the everlasting diasporic journey of self-discovery and identity renegotiation. Roots, however, remain important, if only to provide a point of reference, a comparative yardstick and an introduction to the route forming ahead.

So, although the relationship with the host country is crucial to the way the diaspora constructs itself, as has been shown in previous chapters, the relationship with the homeland remains equally relevant, constantly renegotiated and remade. National belonging, Triandafyllidou explains, is often rediscovered through distance, nostalgia and feelings of difference (Triandafyllidou 2009: 236). The uprooting is one of the most important experiences of those that define diasporic life. Sever explained in one of his posts that 'you come away from your world [–] . . . you uproot [–] . . . and hope to return as soon as you can[,] . . . even though you "pretend . . . not to"' (*Români Online UK*). This pretence is indicative of an internal rupture and a displacement of huge importance. Like the amputee that can still feel the missing part, the migrant perceives the homeland as a phantom limb. It often prevents a permanent mental settlement, but it also incites a perpetual search for new routes: new meanings.

Migrants' second lives are defined by precariousness and suspension, as the following comment confirms:

> We have everything that Romania cannot offer us, and yet we are not completely happy. I'm surprised to discover how many of us are caught between these two worlds, without being sure of where we would like to live the rest of our lives. (Suciu, *Români Online UK*)

A long-lasting and self-generating Purgatory emerges, which is often populated by old traumas and disillusions, but also by waiting and hoping. As one online user observed: 'you start to believe that you can't find your place . . .

[. T]here is a period of adaptation which for some lasts a few years, for others a lifetime' (Lori, *Marea unire, Spania*). This in-between space of diasporic suspension leads to self-actualization and has been metaphorically described by most theorists of the diaspora. Sayad saw migrants as being 'torn' between times, countries and conditions, living 'in transit' (Sayad 2004: 58). Cora, for example, on *Români Online UK*, explained her transitory existence by observing that 'nobody knows me. I feel like a foreigner among foreigners'.

The split has also been interpreted as a 'bifocality' (Roger Rouse, quoted in Vertovec 2004: 974) or dual orientation and a plethora of useful concepts such as 'third space' (Bhabha 1994), 'double consciousness' (W.E.B. Du Bois, quoted in Gilroy 1993), 'in-between' culture (Bhabha 1996), 'perpendicular' worlds (Ignacio 2005) and 'place-polygamy' (Georgiou 2006), attempt to capture the negotiation, translation and mobile repositioning between 'here' and 'there'. Baronian and colleagues also talk of a 'triple belonging': to co-members of the diasporic community, to other diasporic groups around the world and to the imagined homeland or 'point of origin' (Baronian et al. 2007: 11).

These terms depict a symbolic geography that migrants need to negotiate. Like Dante before ascending the mountain of Purgatory, migrants have to self-purge and turn their gaze inwards, while at a crossroads of complex spatial and moral configurations. It is not the relationship between 'here' and 'there' that is problematic, but the continuous reevaluation of one's placeless and temporary existence. The mother country provides thus a point of reference from which different trajectories are calculated and reassessed. Also, what happens politically back 'home' has an impact on diasporic politics.

The painful result of this constant double negotiation is perfectly captured in the following comment:

> What do you do when you feel lost? Whenever you are alone in a foreign country you occasionally feel that you belong nowhere. . . . I cannot find my place in Romania anymore . . . but I will never feel 100% that this is my country, because it isn't . . . [. W]henever I have these feelings, they make me feel more immigrant. (Grecu, *Italia România*)

Grecu arrives at self-actualization and assumes his immigrant persona, because of the in-between position he finds himself in. Marta expressed similar feelings when she said: 'I can't yet call Italy my second *patria*, because *patria* has a special significance for me. At the same time, whenever I go back home [*în ţara*], I feel a bit alienated' (*Realitatea din Italia*). Marta used the word *patria*, which in Romanian has deeper patriotic connotations than the term 'mother country', and also used the expression *în ţara* (in the country), with the meaning 'home' or 'at home'. In Romanian, country and home are almost one. Their absence and distance lead to diasporic self-awareness. The double spatial distancing provides a necessary critical distance in the same way that Du Bois's and Gilroy's concept of 'double consciousness' (in Gilroy 1993) supplies an intellectual departure from cultural fixities into a realm defined by the mutability of meanings. The pitfalls of this spiritual journey are made even more acute by the suspension of cultural geography in cyberspace, which once more makes the online medium an ideal source of diasporic reflections.

The abundance of spatial metaphors encountered in diasporic literature indicate a core concern with critical repositioning vis-à-vis various geographical and cultural symbols. It is therefore important to acknowledge that critical distance and unremitting self-exploration are the basis for elaborating what Katherine Verdery calls in another context a 'language of claims' (Verdery 1996), a discourse that assesses a group's subaltern or unfavourable situation and attempts to find ways to remedy it. Increasingly, Romanian migrants start to appreciate the world transnationally, neither here nor there, neither home nor abroad (Sandu 2010: 132), prompting thus a new perspective. Placelessness, perpetual journeying and repositioning are therefore the premise for political awareness and activism. However, it is also apparent that the social Purgatory migrants inhabit is also a nowhere place, free for all, which is often the site of takeover attempts.

The Institutionalization of the Diaspora

While there are incipient indications that politicians in the West are finally becoming aware of the opportunity to exploit the political potential of diasporas, it is also overwhelmingly clear that home countries are increasingly interested in utilizing the political and economic support of diasporas, which is usually sought through institutionalization and renationalizing. Most emigrant nations have by now made some real efforts to reintegrate the parts that they have lost to the outside world in the process of emigration. As Sayad explains, referring to the case of Algeria, this is usually achieved through a patriotic discourse aimed at reminding the diaspora of its allegiance and a nationalist discourse professing the mother country's attachment to the diaspora (Sayad 2004: 111). Sayad rightly observes that it is precisely this double discourse that establishes the diaspora as an 'autonomous' reality, since diasporas become consequently present in their absence.

The Romanian government has also officially recognized the existence of Romanian diasporic communities. In 1995, the Departamentul pentru Românii de Pretutindeni (Department for Romanians from Everywhere, DRP) was set up, with most of its initial work focused on Romanian historic minorities living in territories now belonging to Romania's neighbouring countries (Trandafoiu 2006: 130; Culic 2008: 165). Overall, governmental actions directed at diasporic communities were defined by their invisibility (Sandu 2010: 13). However, several revamps later, most notably in December 2009 (when the department was renamed the Department for Relations with Romanians Living Abroad), have seen the link with Romanian émigrés become a key objective. While initially the government seemed unsure about how to accommodate the needs of the new labour diasporas (see Trandafoiu 2006), Romanian post-communist emigration has now become sufficiently established and substantial enough to raise concerns about the way diasporic communities preserve their ethnic, cultural, linguistic and religious identities. The concern that permanent migration leads to fewer links with the homeland and much reduced remittances is finally sinking in (Sandu 2010: 17). In view of the tensions Romanians encounter in some countries and the Western media's concern about migrants' criminal behaviour, image has also become as important to the Romanian government as it is for diasporans themselves. The DRP therefore now aims to establish partnerships with Romanian associations abroad to enhance the prestige and visibility of Romanian diasporic communities and promote Romanian culture among host societies and among the younger echelons of the diaspora, which have only feeble ties with their parents' homeland.

Interestingly, the DRP claims on its website that it now considers Romanian émigrés to be an integral part of Romanian 'spirituality'. This statement reintegrates Romanian migrant communities into the soul and body of the nation, the imagined community and the 'national spirit', and it also reminds Romanians abroad of their attachment and core identity. Through its activity and notably its long-term policies, the DRP is also keen to remind diasporans that they have not been forgotten. As we have seen in previous chapters, diasporans are somewhat cynical about governmental pledges and promises and quite critical of the lack of immediate reaction and support whenever the diaspora feels under attack. It may be that the complaints and lobbying of Romanian diasporic associations, as well as the numerous opportunities that governmental representatives have now had to meet the diaspora, have funnelled diasporic views towards governmental advisers. More likely is that renationalizing policies are caused by two important shifts in the attitude of the Romanian political class towards the Romanian diaspora. First, the Romanian diasporas are now formally addressed in political manifestos and governmental policy and this is due to the diaspora emerging as a key political player that can tip the political scales, as witnessed in the 2009 presidential elections. Second, Romanian foreign policy increasingly aims to use the diaspora as a tool in its activity, due to the diaspora's economic and political bargaining power.

As Romania has gradually evolved, from large political majorities winning landslides with some ease, to more fragmented and contested party politics often resulting in coalition governments, even a few diasporic votes (and the diaspora is constantly growing in numbers and political awareness) are becoming decisive. Romania's membership of the European Union that has come with free movement and work rights also requires a more active involvement of the government towards the wellbeing of a diaspora which now has legal status and thus visibility. Western countries, too, need to negotiate satisfactorily the tension between the demands for immigrant labour and the anxiety about ethnic diversity (Massey et al. 1998: 7) and are more willing to treat Eastern countries of emigration as partners in dialogue. Government policy in both home and host countries also heeds the economic power generated by the diaspora. In recent years, Romanian migrant workers have remitted on average more than four billion Euros each year (Trandafoiu 2006: 133; Culic 2008: 151). Remittances peaked in 2008 at over seven billion Euros, before the economic crisis took its toll. Romania's National Bank estimated at 5.5 billion Euros the total amount of remittances received in the first ten months of 2009, a drop of 26 per cent in comparison to the same period in 2008, but still a significant amount. A further 17 per cent slide in 2010 still put the total number of remittances at under six billion Euros. An analysis by the Statistics Directorate of the European Commission shows that Romania benefits from the highest amount of remittances in the European Union, which is twice the amount of direct foreign investments in Romania (source: http://www.balkaninsight.com, accessed March 2012).

In terms of impact, remittances have been blamed for an increase in the price of real estate and consumer goods, but they have also reduced unemployment pressures, which could have been a real issue during the economic transition (Delcea 2007: 115). Economic analysts like Delcea also agree that the impact of remittances could have been even more substantial if the government would have utilized them strategically, for example by encouraging private initiative. I myself complained elsewhere that the Romanian government was overlooking the business and technical skills of returning migrants and was not using a calculated approach to using remittances for economic growth (Trandafoiu 2006: 133). Remittances provide income, foreign trade opportunities and domestic demand for goods and services, but there also needs to exist an economic climate that encourages local investment and initiative (Massey et al. 1998: 253).

Some of the political, economic and technical potential of the diaspora remains untapped. However, in 2008, substantial governmental grants were made available to diasporic associations for projects that involved increasing the visibility of Romanian culture and improving Romania's image abroad. The news travelled fast. In August 2008, one of the users posted on *România*

Italia Net the news that the Romanian government was offering Romanian associations in Italy half a million lei (around ten thousand pounds sterling) for twenty-five projects aimed at improving Romania's image in Italy. This was a clear attempt to institutionalize the diaspora and rehome it, which has not gone unnoticed. In my interviews it quickly became apparent that there was concern that state financing could result in *divide et impera*. New, mostly family-run associations mushroomed, with the sole purpose of attracting financing. Many of my participants showed uneasiness at the hijacking of the diasporic agenda by the government and associations run by corrupt leaders. Although some associations coveted the grants for themselves, they also expressed concern for the rivalry and egocentrism of some diasporic leaders.

Online forum users criticized the inactivity of many organizations set up with the sole purpose of siphoning off governmental funds and overall, government sponsorship was seen as divisive. The president of PIR, Gianfranco Germani, also complained that 'the money that the Romanian government gave to diasporic associations was spent on mini-festivals with *mici* [Romanian-style kebabs] and *bere* [beer] when here, nobody really knows about Romanian culture' (Rome, 3 July 2008).

The financial crisis has, in 2009 and 2010, reduced the DRP to its old strategy of running smaller-scale projects like holiday camps by the Black Sea for young people of Romanian origin now living abroad, Romanian language classes for the same young Romanians and the sponsorship of numerous cultural events throughout the world. These initiatives remain important because they show a continued preoccupation with national image and renationalizing the diaspora, as well as attempting to maintain cultural ties. The DRP's intention is to return to a more consistent grant system in the future, the economic situation permitting. Their job is made more difficult by the fact that while in 2010 DRP was given a total budget of 7.5 million lei (approximately 1.8 million Euros), by May 2010 it had already received 464 requests for financing from diasporic associations, totalling over 438 million lei (104 million Euros).

A recent legislative proposal tabled by the parliamentary deputy William Brînză, who represents Romanian diasporas settled within the European Union, asked for 1 per cent of all remittances sent home by Romanians to be returned to diasporic communities in the guise of projects promoting national culture. This proposal, however, might pose redistribution problems. While Romanians in Italy and Spain remit almost 40 per cent of the total volume of remittances, Romanians in the UK and the US, the next most active remittent communities, only remit 5–6 per cent and Romanians in other countries even less (based on 2006–2008 data given in Sandu 2010: 37). The DRP policy, on the other hand, is to spread the income out, giving a little to everybody. Brînză's initiative was hotly disputed in Italy by PIR. At around the same time (July 2010), the online protest was extended to signature gathering and sit-ins in front of Romanian consulates in Italy, in relation to an increase in consular service fees. Overall many migrants remain sceptical of any 'help' from governmental departments. As one of my interviewees bleakly told me:

> Inside the Romanian Ministry for Foreign Affairs they have a department for relations with Romanians abroad and we contacted them to see whether they could support us financially. Romania doesn't really help Romanians abroad. Romania just 'helps' Romanians to emigrate. This policy works for Romania because we have become currency exporters to Romania. The government doesn't need to do anything, just create the right conditions for us to leave. In return, foreign currency just enters the country. (Mugur, Rome, 2 July 2008)

On the one hand, the attempt to symbolically bring the diaspora home, by recreating links and a certain notion of duty, is visible. On the other, the diaspora is being treated as a cash cow, able to prop up Romania's economy. These two tendencies are contrary in their effect and show tentative and shaky steps in forging a continuous relationship between the mother country and its diaspora.

Diaspora Home Politics

As explained at the beginning of the chapter, diasporic repositioning is a function of the point of reference provided by the homeland. It also can be argued that the political role that the diaspora plays at home, most recently in Romania as a political 'king maker', confirms its existence as a separate entity from the main body of the nation, a *deus ex machina* from afar.

The Romanian diaspora achieved political personality and recognition during the May 2007 referendum that decided against the suspension and impeachment of President Băsescu from parliament. The diaspora also played a key role in the 2008 parliamentary elections and especially the 2009 presidential elections. Vertovec correctly observes that lobbying and campaigning, establishing party branches, organizing collective action and militating for political change are common to many diasporic groups (Vertovec 2004: 982). However, the result of the Romanian presidential elections in 2009, in particular, calls for a reassessment of the diaspora's role as a political player in homeland macropolitics, its impact on future electoral policy and campaigning techniques aimed at worldwide diasporic communities, and the emergence of distinctively diasporic micropolitical phenomena.

The 2009 Presidential Elections

The Democratic Liberal Party (PD-L) candidate Traian Băsescu and the Social Democratic Party (PSD) candidate Mircea Geoană entered the deciding second leg of the presidential elections on 6 December 2009. Băsescu won and started his second presidential term after the closest political race in Romanian politics. Traian Băsescu and Mircea Geoană were separated by only 75,000 votes. Although in Romania Geoană obtained 14,738 more votes than Băsescu, in the diaspora 115,831 voted for Băsescu and only 31,045 for Geoană. It can be argued, and indeed the Romanian media did argue, that the diasporic vote decided who was to be Romania's president.

As polling stations were closing in Romania and the media were starting to report the results of the exit polls (out of four, three proclaimed Geoană the winner), most television news channels, most notably the popular *Antena 3* and *Realitatea TV*, gave Geoană as a sure would-be winner. At the same time, however, on the west side of North America, polling stations were just starting to open (the voting cycle in Romanian elections totals thirty-five hours, due to the time zones). The long voting cycle and the easy access to online news media offered the diaspora the opportunity to make a difference when diasporans became concerned about the claims made by the exit polls and Romanian media. In Canada, 81.64 per cent and 80.21 per cent in the United States chose Băsescu. The vote in Europe seemed similarly decisive for Băsescu: 77.76 per cent in Italy, 78.88 in the UK, 81.1 per cent in Spain. The irony of Mircea Geoană's promise to offer twenty-five thousand Euros to every Romanian migrant permanently returning to Romania did not escape political commentators.

In a note detailing the results, the administrator of the *Spania românească* forum described how Romanians abroad are sometimes better informed than Romanians in Romania. Not only do they have access to varied and unbiased information online (in his opinion most television stations in Romania, including the national broadcaster TVR, are partisan to Geoană), but their additional advantage is that they also understand how Romania is perceived by Western media. He declared: 'for the first time, Romanians abroad decided the future of Romania'.

He may be right if we look at the diasporic vote, although the total number of voters remained abysmal, well under two hundred thousand. Much of the blame was laid at the door of the Romanian government, which had designated only one hundred polling stations for Romanians abroad at the beginning of 2009. Multiplying the number of polling stations thus depended on local initiative. In the 2008 parliamentary elections I could vote in a polling station in Liverpool, near where I lived. I e-mailed its organizer in 2009 to see whether the Liverpool polling station would be again set up. Local polling stations can be set up with the help of local volunteers and under the supervision of Romanian consulate officials, but the initiative, time and costs have to be absorbed largely by the local organizers. However, she replied that she had been too busy to volunteer again. As a result, I faced a two-hour drive to Leeds, the nearest polling station for me.

Reports of similar, distance-related difficulties came from all over Europe and especially North America. The absence of facilities for electronic and postal voting (the threat of fraud is too high, according to many Romanian politicians) and distances of hundreds of miles between polling stations were not a new occurrence. In 2004 the Romanian Council in Atlanta had sent the Romanian government an official complaint about the lack of opportunities for exercising a constitutional right (Trandafoiu 2006: 136). Authorities were also seen to be uncooperative during the 2007 referendum. The president of PIR, Gianfranco Germani, explained that:

> The only time when Romanians in Italy voted in greater numbers (ten thousand) was the referendum for President Băsescu [2007]. At the time the government was against him, so they created a lot of difficulties for Romanians abroad: they never established enough polling stations for everyone. Our party has had to organise thirty polling stations. We obtained these stations from UDEUR [Unione Democratici per l'Europa, a former PIR ally]. I asked a representative at the embassy where Romanians from Palermo could vote; he told me they could go to Malta! We had to organise several polling stations in the south and in Sardinia. (Rome, 3 July 2008)

In 2009, Paris had two polling stations and 3,600 registered voters. By the calculations of the Romanian media, if all had voted, each vote could have lasted only nine seconds. In other words, Romania deliberately sabotaged one of the most important constitutional rights held by Romanian citizens abroad.

In addition to logistical difficulties, little effort was made by diasporic associations to galvanize the Romanians' involvement. Diasporic representatives were divided alongside political interests and some associations even chose to use the elections for self-promotion and media exposure. The Federation of Romanian Associations in Italy (FARI) claimed there was a massive amount of fraud in the fifty-five polling stations established throughout Italy, blaming 'electoral tourism' and bribery for the falsified results. On the other hand, PIR and other organizations accused FARI of being a 'phantom' association, which made unfounded accusations. On several blogs and online forums in Romania, many citizens vented their anger at the Romanian diaspora, asking, 'if you like Băsescu so much, why have you left Romania?' They claimed that polling stations abroad were insufficiently regulated, accused them of fraud and asked for the diasporic right to vote to be lifted. However, the overwhelming majority in favour of the incumbent president displayed by most diasporic communities put any accusations of fraud into doubt (my own experience in Leeds taught me that the voting procedure had been rigorously followed).

The result of the vote now compels any future candidates to campaign among the diaspora and design specific policies for Romanians abroad. At the beginning of 2009, the office of President Băsescu asked for and was granted an increase of 50 per cent in their travelling abroad budget in comparison to 2008. The budget thus totalled 2.3 million Euros, significantly more than the 1.9 million Euros the whole parliament had at its disposal for foreign trips. Despite obvious criticism, this seems to have been a well calculated, if morally dubious, strategy. President Băsescu became a popular face at diasporic congresses and appeared appreciative of each vote keeping him in power in 2007. Mircea Geoană, on the other hand, chose to treat diasporans rather dismissively when he promised them twenty-five thousand Euros to return, which was improbable in view of Romania's economic crisis. While farmers in Romania's rural areas looked favourably upon the plastic buckets they were promised if they chose the 'right' candidate (several PSD officials were briefly questioned by police about possible undue influence), diasporans were justly aware of an empty promise which presumed certain venal interests. The 2009 presidential elections thus wrote the book on political campaigning among the diaspora.

Political Representation in the Homeland

Theorists of the diaspora are right to detect an increase in specific home state policies aimed at diasporas who are becoming an integral part of the big imagined nation (Vertovec 2004: 983). Well known precedents include Vicente Fox's 2000 campaign among Mexicans in California (his opponent Cuauhtémoc Cárdenas also campaigned there) and Mary Robinson's embracing of the Irish community everywhere. Apart from the rhetoric, politicizing attempts have also become more decisive, long-term and strategic. Eriksen (2007) quotes the example of Chile, whose government promised diasporans the right to vote and reminded diasporans of a sense of national identity. Recently the two main Romanian political parties have opened branches in Athens, PSD in 2009 and PD-L in 2010, with similar branches already existing in other main European countries.

Many such initiatives are on the demand of diasporans themselves, disillusioned with the unprofessionalism of locally grown diasporic leaders. Italy, from whom Romanian policy took some inspiration, held the first conference of the Italian diaspora in 2000 and appointed the first minister for the Italian diaspora in 2001. In addition, legal modifications were made to allow Italians abroad to vote for the first time (Bonifazi 2007: 76). More recently, in 2010, Hungary proposed to offer citizenship to the ethnic Hungarian minority living in Transylvania, with the same aim of co-opting the diaspora back into the main national body.

The Internet, in particular, has helped politicians reach outwards and many have embraced this low-cost way of renationalizing and politicizing the diaspora. Eriksen envisages that the Internet will become a key tool for the homelands that aim to ensure the continued loyalty of their citizens, a sort of virtual nationhood (Eriksen 2007: 13). It is a definite sign of the way virtual nationalism changes more traditional forms of nationalizing. In Romania, in order to cut campaigning costs and access vast diasporic constituencies, the Internet has featured much more prominently in campaigns designed to attract the diasporic vote than it did in the 2008 parliamentary campaign conducted inside the country.

In 2008, for the first time, the Romanian diaspora was electing its own representatives. The thirty-eight candidates for the four deputies' and two senators' jobs were competing to represent four deputy 'colleges' or large constituencies (the European Union; Eastern Europe and Asia; America, Australia and New Zealand; and the Middle East and Africa) and two senatorial colleges (Europe and the rest of the world). Most candidates conducted busy online campaigns, setting up personal websites and Facebook profiles and using the e-mail lists of diasporic associations and diasporic websites to post their profiles and programmes. Most candidates promised stronger links between Romania and diasporans; proper representation of diasporic interests in the Romanian parliament; facilities for migrants who return; an improvement of the image of Romanians in Italy; efficiency in dealing with those who commit crimes in foreign countries – especially children; support for the establishment of churches for Romanians abroad; and preservation of the identity of diasporic communities. Many promises answered the concerns of the diaspora but were also blended with renationalizing interests and the wish to use the diaspora more effectively to represent Romanian interests abroad.

In Europe the campaign was carried out in traditional ways, adapted to suit a diasporic context. The National Liberal Party (PNL) set up liberal groups among diasporans willing to have an input. PD-L sent mobile campaign teams travelling around countries with large Romanian diasporas. New party branches were opened, especially in Italy and Spain. Campaigning on shoestring budgets of sometimes no more than ten thousand Euros per candidate and theoretically having to hop from one continent to another meant that the Internet became an indispensable tool. PSD used it primarily to reach communities outside Europe. William Brînză (PD-L), who was elected a deputy for the college representing the European Union, set up a website and a Facebook account, which he used to gather support and publicize his messages. In the UK he utilized the e-mail list of the Oxford Romanian Cultural Society and other similar associations to introduce his electoral manifesto. In an e-mail on 3 December 2008 he thanked diasporans for electing him and attributed his success – the highest number of votes received by any candidate – to his online campaign, which helped him achieve a popular profile quickly and made his name recognizable.

As discussed on the *Realitatea din Italia* website in April 2009, many Romanians in Italy expressed concern about diasporic political representatives who did not belong to the diaspora itself or lacked diasporic experience, and asked for a change in legislation. However, this initiative was opposed by some parliamentarians in Romania who pointed out that, with only one exception, all those elected had some experience of residency abroad. It is true that among the candidates, some banked on their previous fame, not on their current knowledge of diasporic contexts. The former Prime Minister Petre Roman (PNL) had, for example, only lived abroad during his doctoral studies in the 1970s (he was not elected). The more successful William Brînză had links with the Romanian diaspora in Spain, for whom he had helped establish a Romanian library in Castellon. He had also set up two legal consultancies in Madrid and Castellon, aimed at the Romanian community. Online he had also invited diasporic opinions and suggestions, such as the introduction of the postal vote for Romanians abroad, and during a trip to Italy promised new legislation helping those Romanians willing to return.

As we have seen, numerous countries now include diasporic groups into their national political community and one argument is that occasionally, diasporic support may influence 'disproportionately' the political outcomes (Brinkerhoff 2009: 9). The Romanian parliament has 137 senators and 322 deputies, elected by just over eighteen million voters. Between five and six million Romanians living abroad, who are still citizens and hence retain the right to vote, are represented by two senators and four deputies. The decision regarding the number of diasporic members of parliament took into consideration the measly 160,000 who voted in the 2007 referendum. Judging by this number, the diaspora would be overrepresented, since in Romania one senator represents 160,000 citizens. However, in Europe the diaspora is represented by two deputies and one senator. Somewhat unreliable calculations show that in Italy and Spain alone there could be at least 1.5 million Romanians (in Italy the estimates are around eight hundred thousand voters). If they lived in Romania, they would be represented by ten senators and twenty-four deputies. Hence many journalists and political commentators argue that in fact the diaspora is grossly underrepresented.

The problem remains, nonetheless, that in spite of the unique opportunity of electing its own representatives in the Romanian parliament, the diaspora's votes totalled a shockingly low twenty-four thousand in the 2008 elections. The explanations are numerous: the anger Romanians felt towards their 'bad' mother country; the disillusionment with homeland political corruption; pessimism regarding the future and uncertainty about an eventual return; the absence of a legal status that many migrants still retain; the lack of voting facilities; and the lack of professionalism displayed by candidates. Few candidates chose to engage the diaspora directly and mount large-scale campaigns online, which would have been the easiest and cheapest method. Most political manifestos aimed at the diaspora were written in general terms, promising better links with the country of origin, but lacking specific policies that would mean something to diasporans. Of course, campaigning among the diaspora is difficult because of the variety of migration circumstances and the complex geopolitical contexts. However, both the 2008 parliamentary elections and the 2009 presidential campaign indicate that a specific campaign aimed at diasporic communities is essential.

On an optimistic note, while in 2008 only 24,000 diasporans bothered to vote, 180,000 came out in 2009, when indeed every single vote counted in deciding the next president. Both the 2008 and 2009 results also show that the diasporic vote is distinctively different from the home vote. In 2008, PD-L came out ahead in 206 of a total of 221 polling stations abroad, taking 46.88 per cent of the Senate vote (a total of 9,781 votes) and 46.60 per cent of the Chamber of Deputies vote (a total of 9,759 votes). They were followed by PNL with over 20 per cent and, in third, the Social Democratic Party in alliance with the Conservative Party (PSD-PC) with over 13 per cent. The diasporic voting result was thus significantly different from the home vote, in which PSD-PC narrowly won the Chamber of Deputies (33.09 per cent in comparison to PD-L's 32.36 per cent) and the Senate (34.16 per cent over PD-L's 33.57 per cent) and PNL came third.

It is clear that in both recent national elections diasporic micropolitics acted to signal a significantly different political preference and expressed it most clearly in the percentages achieved by candidates. It is unlikely that politicians will be able to ignore the diasporic interest in future electoral encounters and dismiss the existence of a separate diasporic political culture.

Returning Acumen

Voting turnouts seem remarkably low for what is a rather large diaspora. Apart from the causes discussed above, it may be that the rehoming attempts made by the nationalizing state are not working. It may also be that many members of the diaspora are disengaging from homeland concerns, with a view to permanent settlement abroad. This raises questions about the way diasporans perceive an eventual return, how the returnees would reconcile their transnational capital with Romanian contexts and how the relationship with the mother country would be negotiated in the future, by those determined to settle abroad permanently. These issues, in turn, have an effect on the way Romanian diasporic culture continues to emerge as a distinct entity.

Among 830 Romanian immigrants living in the Madrid area polled in 2008, one-third expressed the wish to return in the next five years and one-third intended to settle permanently, with the rest envisaging a return at some point (Sandu 2010: 110, 113). However, the mass return envisaged by the Romanian media at the start of the economic crisis did not materialize. In spite of deterring policies, many work migrants plan to settle down permanently (even Sandu's small-scale research shows a large group willing to remain indefinitely and a majority perpetually postponing its return), giving the future of their children as the main reason and complaining about the unresolved economic and social situation back in Romania. Some talk about moving to another country in a migration model that has become itinerant.

The president of PIR, the largest Romanian party in Italy, told me:

> The data that we have shows that many of these Romanians will remain here. Many are now buying houses. Of course there are a few that come here to work and then go back home to build houses there, but a great majority of them are planning to stay here, most of these because of their children. Those who return to Romania often come back because they find that they are at odds with the Romanian mentality back home. (Gianfranco Germani, Rome, 3 July 2008)

History also teaches us that any period of mass labour migration results in large and permanently settled groups. In their extensive analysis of empirical data charting Mexican migration to the United States, Massey, Goldring and Durand found that the probability of settlement rose in tandem with the experience of migration (1994: 1502). At the end of 2008, less than one-third of Romanian migrants had thought about returning. Returning is also less appealing for those who already have families abroad. In Spain, those who expressed an interest in returning were labourers whose work had become insecure, those who earned less and those who had an irregular status (Sandu 2010: 42–3).

The likely prospect of future permanent settlement is somewhat recognized by Romanian authorities, who over the years have tried to entice migrants back with promises that were never fulfilled. Promises of various kinds are still brandished. During the 2008 parliamentary campaign, candidate William Brînză promised Romanians in Florence a new legislative proposal that would ensure that those returning and starting a business back home would not see their profit taxed for the first three years (if the turnover was not more than one hundred thousand Euros) and those buying a house (smaller than 150 square metres) would also not pay property tax for three years. Nonetheless, concrete working policies are still missing.

Migrants' accumulated capital of skills, networks and knowledge may be an important strategic advantage (Brinkerhoff 2009: 7) for those returning. Mr Germani reiterated this thought when he told me that 'the great richness of Italian or Greek societies has been their diasporas. They brought back to the homeland, not just money, but also new mentalities, new ideas, elasticity' (Gianfranco Germani, Rome, 3 July 2008). Some migrants do seem to relish the thought of returning. On *Români Online UK*, Romana boldly declared: 'WE, Romanians, will change the putrid political scene in this country [Romania]'. Another online participant, from Romania, also said hopefully: 'one of the few hopes that things will change here comes from you, those gone abroad. Only you can bring that "newness", that difference in mentality' (Lina, *Realitatea din Italia*).

However, regardless of what returning migrants could bring to the home-land, transcultural capital and complex migrant acumen preclude an easy reinsertion back into a society where 'some things are appropriate for 2008, but some are appropriate for the 1300s, particularly in the rural areas' (Gianfranco Germani, Rome, 3 July 2008). One would expect that those who had transited an accommodation process successfully would know how to approach a similarly painful adaptation 'in reverse'. However, most migrants point out that migration can rarely be reversed: 'I can't find my place there any more . . . [. I]t's not an easy feeling being a newcomer all your life among foreigners, but our own country pushed us to take this decision' (Anonymous poster on *Marea unire, Spania*). Monica added, referring to those returning:

> They will never find in Romania what they are hoping for. Many return on the basis of information received from friends and we all know how subjective personal views are . . . . They've just got over the trauma of integrating in a society which is somewhat culturally and linguistically different and they would need to readapt and start from scratch again. (Monica, *Italia România*)

These views confirm existing research showing that having left Romania with a clear strategy for life in the future, migrants constantly reexamine and compare their status with the aim to be achieved. If they do not accumulate enough money or the degree of institutional development in Romania is inconsistent with what they have found abroad, migrants will postpone their return (Sandu 2010: 119). This strategy is consistent with that observed by

Massey, Goldring and Durand, who notice that life abroad creates new expectations and desire for social mobility (1994: 1498).

Any hopes for a return are also tempered by worries related to the economic and political future of the homeland. Mugur, whom I interviewed in Rome in 2008, explained:

> I don't know what will happen to my children, but I hope to return with my wife at some point. I would like my children to be educated in Romania. We won't be able to repatriate if it gets to the point that our two boys finish secondary school here. I hope that the political and economic situation in Romania changes in the next five years so that we can return. I haven't got many hopes for the next five years, but I predict that after that things should get better.

Nick, a user on *Italia România*, confessed: 'I have lost hope that Romania would be able to entice us back in the next twenty years. There may be people who wish to return, depending on integration, professional satisfaction and the ambience in Italy'. However, he ruled himself out. Previous experiences in other countries with a similar mentality to the Romanian one signal caution. In the case of Greece, for example, another country of once significant emigration, returnees did not manage to use acquired skills successfully, due to the nature of Greece's informal economy, which favours connections and nepotism (Baldwin-Edwards 2007: 29).

The situation back home compels many to stay, even if the current economic context in the West is less auspicious and it is inevitable that many migrants 'cannot make it'. There is, however, reluctance to return, since Romania cannot offer a viable alternative; there, social mobility is slowing down and the disparities between rich and poor are getting bigger. Even if opportunities have diminished in the West, the economic crisis has hit Eastern Europe harder. It may also be that money has become an insufficient factor in enticing migrants back, as they now have expectations regarding institutions and lifestyles (Sandu 2010: 13).

One online forum contributor, Mircea, weighed up the importance of his heritage versus the opportunity for a better future. He came to the conclusion that: 'what we miss is our past . . . [. H]ere we only have a present and a future' (Mircea, *Italia România*). Many migrants tend to be realistic and focused on their future prospects. In addition, the choices they make do not have to be as decisive and definitive as they once were. Free EU movement means that Eastern Europeans have now the occasion for 'simultaneity', for exiting and conducting business in both home- and hostlands, through short-term 'shuttle' migration (Anghel 2008: 799). In his study of a small Romanian community's emigration to Italy, Anghel notes, for example, that freedom of movement has changed emigration from kin-based networks, which could efficiently organize labour migration (the Mexican model), to individual practices of irregular short-term migration (Anghel 2008: 792). Many migrants now conflate their lives at home and abroad to suit personal circumstances. They exist therefore in that placeless, Purgatory-like space that confuses statistical analyses, neither 'here' nor 'there' but en route to somewhere else.

This ambiguous relationship with the homeland poses dilemmas for both homeland and hostland governments. While hostlands must be prepared to cope with different lengths and types of settlement, homelands need to allow a diasporic culture to flourish and provide relevant support for it. Placelessness and existing intermediately are redefining identity politics in the new millennium and are prompting a reassessment of macropolitical strategies as well.

Conclusions: The Role of the Internet in Identity Politics

Cyberspace, the 'nowhere' land, is the most appropriate realm for expressing migrant cultural mobility and repositioning. With its multiple geographical anchors, easily attachable and detachable, cyberspace allows for the relationship with the homeland to be continuously refashioned and remade.

Cyberspace also provides the space for information and discussion, which allows diasporans to gain a more complete view of institutionalizing attempts. Patterns of institutionalization emerge in time, of which online participants seem to become progressively aware. Cynicism against home governments emerges, but it does not dent nostalgic feelings for the homeland. Nostalgia and selective remembering are obvious in the way websites are designed, but the practicalities of migrant life, the real concern with the here and now, prevent migrants from overindulging and losing track of the realities back home.

Digital diasporas have rewritten the book on political campaigning. As we have seen in the case of successive legislative events in Romania, campaigning online and publicizing political programmes via e-mail and diasporic websites ensures a higher degree of success. The Internet was also instrumental in gathering information about Romanian realities from a distance, obtaining a clear perspective on Romania's direction for the future and intervening in the outcome of the elections whenever there was an undecided electoral outcome, in order to tip the scales towards more liberal candidates, with a clearer international outlook. This was particularly evident among Romanian diasporas in North America, as the following chapter will show.

Chapter Seven

'America, Romanian Land'

Diasporic Identity Politics in the United States and Canada

The introductory discussion of the state of current theory applicable to East–West migration within Europe at the start of this book raised two important points. First, that there is little specific theory derived from the phenomenon of post-1989 Eastern European migration towards Western Europe and North America; and second, that the comprehensive study of American immigrants, so far focused on Latin Americans, has something to teach us, though this should only be the starting point for elaborating a separate theoretical strand. Many authors agree. Salomone (2008) writes on the appropriateness of looking at the American experience in order to avoid instances of isolation and poverty for the '1.5 generation' – the label for those who migrate as children and are brought up in the United States. Other authors confirm the need to derive a specific understanding of the Eastern European migratory experience in North America (Robila 2007, 2008 and 2010; Culic 2010), which at the moment is sparse. Although a comprehensive account of the use of the Internet for Romanian professionals migrating to Canada was provided by Nedelcu (2009), who focused on one website in particular, little has been written about life after immigration from a comparative point of view.

This chapter begins to sketch the differences between various migratory waves in terms of associative models, self-identity reflections, political engagements and comparisons that migrants themselves make with the experience that their compatriots have had in Europe. However, this chapter can only offer a rudimentary initiation of research that could also take into account various more migratory settlements over the past one hundred years, and a Europe/America comparison of migration policy and its effects on migrant demographics and transnational patterns.

Migrant Engineering

Similar to recent developments in the European Union, United States immigration policies have been circumscribed by increasingly restrictive strategies (Massey et al. 1998: 68) that attempt to limit the number of immigrants and reduce welfare entitlements (Hollifield 2004: 900). Pressure from countries such as Mexico and general public hostility towards immigration ensure that, like Europe, North America has long ceased to be an easily reached destination.

Unlike the European Union, both Canada and the US have a tradition of selecting the best brains (Favell 2008: 707) by cherry picking through their skilled workers scheme and green card system, respectively. This allows the economy to stay more competitive (Hollifield 2004: 900). From a comparative viewpoint, it also ensures that most immigrants arriving in North America from Eastern Europe are better qualified than their compatriots who immigrate to Western Europe (Baldwin-Edwards 2007: 18), and they migrate legally, with a career plan and life project for long-term settlement. However, while it is true that Eastern Europeans tend to be better professionally trained than Latin Americans, there are also big differences between various Eastern European immigrant groups. As Robila (2010) explains, some countries have a much higher level of graduate and professional degrees (Bulgaria, Russia), while others have a low level (Bosnia, Macedonia, Serbia). This is reflected in the income, which displays huge differences: 70 per cent of immigrants from ex-Yugoslavia, Belarus, Moldova and Albania earn less than US $25,000 a year, while Romanians seem to have the highest income, with almost 24 per cent of them earning more than US $50,000 (they are closely followed by the Czechs and the Slovaks).

Robila (2007) links educational level to income and health insurance, which she considers to be the premise for a smooth adaptation in the host society. However, while it appears that Romanians in North America might have an easier insertion into the host society and achieve more economically, Robila also hints at other types of difficulties. Even skilled workers can encounter problematic adaptations, despite a thorough premigration preparation and the accumulation of cultural capital. Culic refers to Canada's skilled workers and professional immigration scheme to describe the lengthy adaptation process that Romanians undertake premigration, when during the forty-eight-month application process, premigrants familiarize themselves with the languages and cultures of Canada, establish personal and professional links and start inhabiting a new mental space, as if the Romanian realities became an extraterritorial extension of the Canadian state (Culic 2010).

Culic does not specifically say how much of the cultural shock this preparation manages to absorb. However, Robila talks of a cultural fault line that is anyway likely to emerge. She notes, for example, that Eastern Europeans are more reserved and less assertive than their American counterparts, a cultural difference which leads to adjustment difficulties (2007: 114). Culic, too, mentions the 'unsettling' of male and female roles by the application process, which allows women to be main applicants, in contrast with the Romanian patriarchal approach in which the man is always seen as the head of the family and the main provider. Migration thus restores women's agency (Culic 2010: 354–5), but it is likely to have an effect on family and social dynamics post-emigration.

My own research highlighted the role of geographical distance, which makes the migration act permanent, gives little opportunity for return and severs the link between generations, especially grandparents (left behind) and grandchildren. This observation is confirmed by Robila's research (2007: 116). Having dismantled their former lives completely, migrants can feel trapped in US and Canadian realities, as the analysis of the online discussions will show. As a result, migrants continue to maintain an appetite for homeland politics, which is avidly consumed online and via satellite. Premigration preparation, education, income and even distance might create the premise for deeper integration, yet migrants in North America tend to be more nostalgic, more aware and reflective about the rupture they experience.

United States and Canadian immigration policies have always entailed a type of social engineering that to some extent has now been replicated in Western Europe, where the aim is to match the right workforce to the right economic needs. Skilled or seasonal workers' schemes are attempting to follow, to some degree, the North American model. The results have been divergent nevertheless. In Europe, the immigrant demographics have become split between highly skilled (and long-term settled) Romanians working for the financial services and the cultural economy on the one hand, and seasonal, manual workers (itinerant and returning) on the other. In North America, the focus on professional skills has ensured more homogeneous demographics, coupled with a different approach to rights and citizenship. Culic's excellent research shows, for example, how Canadian immigration policies legitimize the state and produce enactments of statehood and citizenship in premigrants (2010).

While many work migrants who emigrate to Western Europe are motivated economically by the desire to improve their living standards, Easterners who emigrate to North America are by and large professionals keen to exercise specialist skills and knowledge, with a view to achieving a more fulfilling career than the homeland economy would normally facilitate (Qiu 2003: 148). Canada, in particular, seems to be constructed as a land of professional opportunities and it is often imagined as a civilized, 'middle class habitus' (Culic 2010: 353). In comparison to European immigrants, those migrating to Canada (although not the United States) have the opportunity to become permanent residents upon arrival and have the right to apply for citizenship after three years. This, observes Tudoroiu, discourages circular migration and encourages settlement (Tudoroiu 2007: 26). It also encourages a thorough preparation and the progressive building of social and professional networks of premigration support (Culic 2010).

Migration to North America is the outcome of the development of migratory social capital. Once capitalism penetrated the local community, skilled workers saw the potential brought about by emigration to the global cities. They began to strategize their tactics, which then spread to the whole group (Massey et al. 1998: 133). The North American model of immigration necessitated, therefore, a community base, which was readily offered by the already existing migrant communities and various professional networks (Nedelcu 2009), as well as rediscovered friends and family members (Culic 2010). New networks were added through increased migration, which were shaped by origin, kinship and friendship (Anghel 2008), necessary in a system that required a permanent commitment and made return economically unfeasible.

Nedelcu (2009), who studied the emigration of IT specialists from Romania to Toronto, analysed the way professional channels and networks that could facilitate preparation and settlement appeared online. These networks became self-replenishing, as more and more migrants contributed to what became a generous pool of migratory resources. As a result, by the time of the 2006 Canadian census, Romanians had become the eighth largest group of educated immigrants (Plante 2010). As Robila points out (2010: 14), Romanian migrants are among those Eastern Europeans who are self-selected (like the Russians and Bulgarians) and hence many are better educated than those remaining at home or those belonging to ethnic groups that migrate as a result of persecution or displacement (e.g. Bosnian).

Certain migratory trends were initiated therefore by the specific labour needs of North American industry, which led to assiduous recruitment of certain skills, primarily by IT companies. Annually, 'talent scouts' travel to Eastern Europe to invite applications and job interviews follow in Eastern European capital cities. The 'American dream' is also cultivated by the United States' visa lottery, which within a few years after the 1989 post-communist revolution had achieved an almost mythical status at the level of Romanian popular culture.

A total of 98,000 Romanians arrived in the United States between 1995 and 2006 (Robila 2010: 2). There has been a small but steady flow of around two thousand Romanians arriving every year into both the US and Canada since 2000 (Baldwin-Edwards 2007: 18). By the 2006 census there were 192,170 Romanians living in Canada. The website of the Romanian Embassy in the United States puts the current number of Romanians in the US at one million, settled mostly in New York, California and the Midwest, and this number is confirmed by Popescu (2005: 462) and Robila (2010: 2).

Both online and offline Romanian communities differentiate between old and new (post-1989) Romanian migration. At the turn of the twentieth century, 'new immigration' from the East included many peasants from Transylvania, due to land shortages and ethnic discrimination in the Austro-Hungarian Empire (Popescu 2005: 461–2) and resulted in around one hundred thousand Romanians in North America by 1914. The oldest Romanian Orthodox church was established in Regina Canada in 1902. During the 1950s, more urbanized and better-educated immigrants arrived as the result of communist abuses (Popescu 2005: 462). In the 1980s and fleeing the communist regime, around thirty thousand Romanians arrived in the United States (Daniels 2004: 215). These older migratory cycles formed immigrant communities populated by second-generation Romanian-Americans who are fully integrated and participate in established diasporic organizations. The post-communist migration has enlarged this diaspora, but it has also altered the diasporic landscape with new needs and outlooks and new diasporic websites have been established as a result.

The 'new immigration' was at first attempted by those with family relations abroad and those fearing social instability (Sandu 2010). Baldwin-Edwards confirms that between 1996 and 2001 Romanian permanent migration to the US and Canada increased to the detriment of migration towards Western Europe (2007: 7). From 1996, the migration corridor towards Germany (established by the emigration of German Saxons from Romania immediately after 1989) was replaced in popularity by emigration to North America. In 2001 the North American corridor peaked, with 25 per cent of all Romanian emigrants leaving for Canada and 19 per cent for the United States. The Italian corridor started to dominate after 2004, but since 2007 both Canada and the United States have risen again in popularity, each taking about 20 per cent of all Romanian immigrants in 2007 and 2008 (Sandu 2010: 40–1).

In recent years, questions have been asked about the ability of the Canadian job market in particular to absorb these highly skilled migrants (Tudoroiu 2007; Nedelcu 2009) and websites (such as *Immigrant in Montreal – Canadian Reality*) have been set up to tell the story of those unable to find jobs proportionate to their education and experience. Those who emigrated without families also found the distance difficult. In her analysis of highly skilled Romanian migration, Anna Ferro noted that while migrants maintained diffidence with regards to a change for the better in Romania, many of those living in North America said they would welcome a move to Europe, citing geographic and cultural proximity among the reasons (Ferro 2004: 385). However, permanent migration also entails the burning of bridges, typically selling property and other resources to fund the emigration project, as well as quick family reunifications at the destination. The uncertain economic situation in Europe also dissuades any would-be returnees.

With a few exceptions that will be discussed further on, diasporic websites are popular with premigrants, already arrived migrants who still vacillate between Canada and the United States before settling permanently and migrants who have emigrated over the last two decades for professional reasons and family reunifications. While traditional community associations are firmly anchored in the new US and Canadian localities and are frequented by those from the 'old' migration, the websites are transnational, connected to both the homeland and to other diasporic cyber-networks, forming linkages across the North American territory. They are mainly populated by those from the 'new' migration. In terms of political activism, those from the 'old' migration have the associative tools and resources to lobby governments and international organizations on behalf of Romania. The more recent migrants engage online in political debate, but rarely action. However, these new migrants remain constantly engaged with issues of collective identity, as will be discussed later.

Associative Models

In Popescu's view (2005: 462), the nineteenth-century Romanian migration to North America was very dependent on setting up community institutions like churches; whereas subsequent waves (in the 1950s, for example) became less dependent on this factor, with only a fraction of Romanian immigrants participating in organizational activities and most Romanians preferring to assimilate. However, Popescu acknowledges that business interests, community institutions and press remain well organized and occasional events attract even those Romanians who choose not to engage with the community on a permanent basis.

The difference between the old and new migrants is marked. The established community has garnered, in time, an important lobbying voice, especially in the United States. Its identity claims are rooted in a sense of nationhood that entails references to Great Romania of 1918, as well as a prestigious high culture, mixed with folkloric and hence nostalgic overtones. Its sense of community was achieved through protest against the communist regime and political defection. By comparison, the more recently migrated community is more diverse and utilitarian in outlook. Its motivation lies in economic and professional hopes. Its reflexivity derives from ongoing identity interrogations and an ambiguous relationship with the homeland, but is less utopian in its outlook.

There is, of course, a dialogue between the two waves. While researching for this project I came across a festival entitled *Spirit of Romania*. Since 2007 it has become the largest concert series in Canada, bringing the best Romanian musicians to Toronto, Montreal, Ottawa and Kitchener. An initiative of the diasporic newspaper *Acasă* (Home), it claims to celebrate a thriving culture that emerges beyond its origins. Among the guests are diasporic artists living in Canada, alongside celebrities from Romania. There is a sense of nostalgia intertwined with the desire to create something less traditional and more in line with the tastes of the newer immigrants to Canada. In conditions of acculturation and integration, which define North American migratory settlement, ethnicity is often expressed merely symbolically through nostalgic allegiance and essentialized and visible symbols (Gans 1999: 392, 400). Many of the diasporic musical events I have encountered have been of this kind. 'Authentic' folkloric music and 'traditional' dancing make one wonder whether much heritage is really preserved in the process (Gans 1999: 394). *Spirit of Romania*, on the other hand, wants to synchronize itself with contemporary Romanian music and aspires to create something new.

In terms of associations, the landscape is dominated by organizations of some age and pedigree, of which the following are among the most typical. Consiliul Mondial Român (The Romanian World Council, CMR) is primarily active in the field of human rights protection, but it is also involved in charity initiatives. Its stakeholder base is not just Romania, but also former Romanian territories which still hold a strong Romanian presence, such as Bukovina and Bessarabia. CMR accepts both individual members and organizations, mostly from the US, but also from Romania, the Republic of Moldova and Canada. However, only ethnic Romanians can become full members. CMR's website set up a forum in January 2005, which has several hundred members and two hundred posts per month on average. Some of its aims are to create a diasporic network and maintain national identity in all territories where Romanians live. The association's mission, membership and ethnic policy indicate a pre-1940 vision of Great Romania, like that of the 'old' Romanian migration to the United States. Its activity consists of a variety of online petitions, from the denouncement of the Ribbentrop–Molotov pact (under which Romania lost several territories to the Soviet Union) to traffic issues and animal cruelty.

The Union and League of Romanian Societies has existed in a different form since 1906, but it was only in 1924 that two separate diasporic organizations came together under the current name. It therefore claims to be the oldest Romanian association in North America and is still working on the basis of fraternities established in several US states and Canada. It organizes cultural events aiming to preserve Romanian cultural heritage. Like CMR, its website is written in English and speaks proudly of fully integrated generations of Romanian-Americans.

The Romanian Canadian Cultural Association of Calgary (RCCAC) is the modern face of one hundred years of Romanian existence in Canada. It aspires to be the voice of the community and its focus, like in most other cases, is to preserve Romanian heritage while also supporting, more generally, life and culture in Alberta. It has a strong relationship with the Government of Alberta, which has financed several of its events, including folk dancing. It also has its own football team. Its online presence offers basic information about cultural activities and meeting opportunities, but fails to foster the emergence of an online community. This model is typical for associations that have existed for a long time, are anchored in the local community, have a physical base and have established services and activities. The websites only serve to pay lip service to the newer technologies and help inform newcomers and future members of events. The association websites differ radically, therefore, from the online discussion forums, which are mainly populated by newer migrants.

Both visually and discursively the websites belonging to Romanian associations in North America provide a double anchoring and aspire to become a bridge, a link and a channel translating between two cultures. However, due to the older establishment of the community as a diaspora and the nature of North American statehood (the 'melting pot' model), American realities often take precedence. This is why, in comparison to Europe, where all diasporic websites are in Romanian, in North America they are in English (e.g. The Congress of Romanian Americans, The Romanian Canadian Cultural Association of Calgary) or bilingual (*Români în Alberta*, whose website seems to have been abandoned after 2007). It is a more traditional model, preferred by homogeneous and established communities, who are still keen to preserve a link with the homeland and remain proud of their heritage, but perform citizenship at a distance, fully aware of their diasporic remoteness and individuality.

The aspiration of Romanian diasporic societies in North America to become two-way translators that can influence mental and geopolitical maps is evidenced in their desire to lobby the United States government in favour of Romania, which has occurred since 1997 when these societies accepted finally that Romania's closeness to the West was undeniable and its democratic path clearly chosen (Popescu 2005: 460). Popescu analyses the most important such attempt, which started with NATO's announcement in 1996 that Poland, Hungary and the Czech Republic would become members. At the time, Romania, another applicant, was not deemed ready and came to be admitted only in 2003. However, the 1997 public relations campaign and lobbying attempts strategized by the Romanian diaspora in the United States helped improve Romania's image and its chance of becoming a full NATO member later on. Popescu alludes to an ambiguity of feeling regarding certain neo-communist tendencies in Romania, which I have also noticed in the online discussions. This suspicion was certainly caused by US-influenced anti-communist fears and the disjunction between Romanian diasporic communities in North America and the homeland in the 1950s and subsequent decades. However, once mistrust was set aside, the support for NATO membership was pan-diasporan, with various Romanian organizations, media and individuals being equally involved and committed.

The most important organizations involved in the lobbying campaign of 1997 were the Congress of Romanian-Americans (CORA), the Union and League of Romanian Societies from America and the Romanian Orthodox Episcopate of America (Popescu 2005: 466). CORA, an umbrella for numerous associations and individuals, remains one of the most engaged organizations and has a clear political edge. It aims to represent Romanian interests and lobby on their behalf, involve itself in bilateral relations, fight for freedom and democracy and help preserve Romanian ancestry. It has provided so far sixty million US dollars of aid to Romania.

The North American diasporic associative model is traditional and steeped in culture and heritage, maintaining a historical approach that has been essentialized and pickled by time. The frequent emphasis on Romanian folklore and village traditions in most diasporic events is a clue to its traditionalism. These are associations that have been established for decades, combining the double pride of Romanian roots and North American opportunities and catering for a well established and fully integrated community. These organizations have a maturity that is lacking in the case of Romanian diasporic associations based in Europe, who still beg the financial help of the Romanian government and are unable to perform bilateral negotiations or lobby effectively.

The newer, post-1989 migrants have thus found an established physical network, which eases integration to some extent, but also causes tensions. The folklore and rural traditions of the old generation have been perverted by communist nationalist propaganda and have been cheapened by attempts to 'modernize' tradition during the post-communist transition. Furthermore, the love–hate relationship with the homeland inspires less nostalgic attachment in the new arrivals. Many newer migrants thus turn online, to forums populated by like-minded individuals, eager to conduct a critical discourse of a different kind. While those from the 'old' migration have a conservative online presence, the new community proposes a more dynamic cyber-engagement.

These associative models show that North American diasporic associations carry out nostalgic politics: for the people and the past; against politics and the present. This view is informed by classic conservative nationalism that still refers to 1918's Great Romania. This is not unique, however. Cid and Ogando (2010: 325) describe how the iconography of Galician immigration has become fossilized in time, due to being handed down through generations, without any major changes. However, liberal frames are present in the human rights and anti-communist campaigns that these North American associations undertake. A new breed of cultural organizations is making attempts to integrate new immigration waves through a cultural populist approach, marrying folklore with modern Romanian pop within events centred on national feasts and key religious dates. This newer model is more simplistic and less politically attuned but works within a physical environment enriched by diasporic diversity.

North America's Romanians Online

The online presence of North America's Romanians combines wikis (*Comunitatea română portalul diasporei române US*), magazine-style websites (*Romanian Times*) and Yahoo Groups (*Pro Vancouver*). Yahoo Groups are mainly used for posting messages and viewers can e-mail by way of reply. This system works well for information and two-way communication, but is awkward for group debates. Yahoo Groups therefore continue to wane in popularity. While in 2002, 2003 and 2005, the *Pro Vancouver* group registered up to seventy-four messages each month, in May 2010 it counted only six, most of them general announcements and classified advertisements. It has now faded away.

Another category is represented by the magazine forum *Romanian Times*, which has branches in Portland (Oregon), Phoenix (Arizona) and Atlanta (Georgia). It has a more elaborate printed version, which is made available online after a time delay. The magazine aspect is represented by general and human-interest articles and essays, some sent in by users and some written by permanent collaborators. The forum generates free debates and contributions by readers. This online diasporic presence is coordinated by the Phoenix Mission and has, therefore, a strong religious and charitable flavour, with news about Romanian religious communities and churches in the US and Canada featuring prominently. Numerous occasional collaborators from within the community join the permanent editorial team. The magazine has a separate online page for classified advertisements and a separate forum for the development of 'Romanian spirituality'.

A singular presence in the landscape of Romanian diasporic websites was *Royouth* (Ethnic Christian Romanian Youth), created in 2002. It had an active forum with no fewer than 12,446 threads and 409,071 posts created by 31,194 members (although the number of active members was, in June 2010, only 312; in 2011 the site closed to be redesigned, but has not reopened). Most of the discussions were in English. Users confessed that their mastery of Romanian was inadequate, as most users emigrated as children or were born in the US (although there were some users based in Austria, Canada and Australia). The site's founder and administrator did not find the Romanian language very useful outside the Romanian community and considered that maintaining it was just a matter of national and ethnic pride, which accounts for the site's bilingualism. Most forum debates were on religious topics mixed with the concerns of the young, such as: 'is make-up a sin?'

Apart from these special types, numerous Romanian diasporic websites in both the United States and Canada aim to inform, advise and help the socialization of the new community that has been trying to establish itself since the 1990s. The role of such forums is therefore not that distinct from similar sites in Europe. However, North America-based websites tend to be built on a larger scale, with many more active users and several administrators for each site. Due to the geography of North American communities, they tend to be localized to a specific state or province or alternatively they may contain a chain link of several communities in various states. Another peculiarity is the large amount of advertising and promotion, which indicates that North America-based diasporic websites tend to be much more business and revenue oriented.

A whole category of North America-based diasporic websites seems to be dedicated almost entirely to advertising, product promotion and classified advertisements. These websites usually lack the identity given by diasporic symbolism or imagery and are not interested in fostering a sense of community, although much of the content still features diasporic products and services. Some hover between a strong business concern and a weaker diasporic identification. *Rovancouver – Comunitatea Română Virtuală din Vancouver* (The Virtual Romanian Community of Vancouver) provides a simple list of messages grouped according to various categories falling mainly under the umbrella of news and classified advertisements. This site's specialty is a virtual advertising board, containing classified advertisements and several pages that provide an extensive guide to emigration and life in Canada. The founders have aimed to create a site dedicated to information exchange and product promotion and they have attracted so far over three hundred thousand visitors, but only thirty-four of them are active members, while the rest are just dropping by for the odd job offer or to look for a flat to rent. Sites of this type are heavily criticized in the European context by established migrants for lacking community spirit, but they are abundant in the North American environment.

The advertisements and other content hosted by *40 Romania* falls into several categories: Romanian 'Yellow Pages' and information about mortgages, real estate, credit cards and online shops selling Romanian products are combined with chat facilities and announcements about Romanian events and gatherings. *40 Romania* is primarily concerned with the North American day-to-day life of the Romanian diaspora, while advertisements for cheap phone calls and flights and a gallery of photographs from Romania show only a brief attempt to reconnect with the homeland. It would therefore be difficult to classify this website as transnational. The website lacks any ethnic markers, so its diasporic status is hard to recognize; diasporic life is not highlighted as a clear feature and hyperlinking is basic, with users simply selecting links to goods and services, news, diasporic newspapers and radio, without being able to interact, play clips or have an input.

On the British Columbia website *BC Romanian Community Center*, even the forum is hijacked by promotional announcements. With on average one hundred viewers, these posts have no replies, with the result that the forum ceases to act as a debating *agora*. These websites help migrants keep in touch with events happening in their locality, but they are less interested in building an online community and are geared instead towards helping Romanians meet at various functions and fairs. Economically, the website is viable due to heavy sponsorship placed on parallel continuous strips on the left and right hand side of the screen, which leave no room for diasporic imagery. Nonetheless, the colonization of forums by business interests can lead to conflicts. In a post from March 2010, one user accused the site administrators of censorship. Negative views had been exchanged about companies providing services to Romanians. These posts were hastily deleted but censorship was strongly denied by the volunteers who maintain the site. The incident raised the question of a conflict of interest if administrators (some of them volunteers) also have business interests, which are promoted online.

Other discussions in the *BC Romanian Community Center* relate to customary diasporic concerns – particularly the image that Romanians project in contact with others and the tricky relation with the official structures of the Romanian government – but they are also specific to the Canadian context. Concerns about the recognition of diplomas and driving licenses are no longer an issue in the context of EU membership in Europe, but remain an important matter of practicality in Canada. Promoting Romanian culture and preserving elements of national identity also take centre stage. The Romanian diaspora in Canada is more mature, permanently established and one would presume from previous studies (Nedelcu 2009; Culic 2010), better educated than the Romanian diaspora in Italy or Spain. This group thus takes inspiration from the Italian, French, Spanish and British model of diasporas, who prefer to promote prestigious elements of their national culture, language and civilization.

A network of three sister websites dedicated to Romanians in Chicago, New York and Los Angeles combines classified advertisements with useful online guides for new or future migrants. Visually, the websites are anchored in US imagology, featuring graphic outlines of skyscrapers, while the content is clearly diasporic. However, content pertaining to contemporary Romania is almost absent, suggesting a clear orientation towards life after immigration. *Români la Chicago/Los Angeles/New York* could be one website, but the founders explained that websites focusing on local realities and with locally relevant classified advertisements provide a better business model. This web chain has evolved from a former Yahoo Group, which has been gradually replaced by increasingly expanding forum facilities. This reinvention is part of an evolutionary process that aims to modernize the website in order to attract more traffic. It seems to be working. The *Români la New York* Yahoo Group registered only a handful of messages in 2009 (from one to eighteen per month) and these were mainly announcements not leading to discussions. By comparison, the new website registers on average three hundred visitors each week. According to the statistics publicized on the website itself, first time visitors outnumber returning visitors by at least three to one. This suggests that these web chains are useful sources of information, but their ability to encourage the long-term formation of an online community is still unproven. Their anchoring in locality suggests a desire to replicate the cyber-community in the physical world.

In comparison to Europe-based websites, some North American sites lack a strong diasporic personality or double anchoring, since visually they speak more about North American imagology. Both the visual appearance and content of *Din State* (From the States) show the site's focus on the local, US context. The Statue of Liberty and the United States flag at the top of the site are a clear indication of its geocultural orientation, as is its opening statement. The site wishes to describe Romanian lives in the US, including issues such as immigration, discrimination, intergenerational differences and the maintenance of culture and tradition, but also aspires to analyse the US lifestyle and culture. The information is parcelled into twelve video episodes containing interviews telling the story of settlement and life in the United States.

Another online model is represented by *Români în America* (Romanians in America). It is more promotion oriented than the Europe-based websites. However, it is comparable in terms of diasporic visual identity, forum facilities and double diasporic repositioning. At the top right-hand corner of the site, the outline of the United States is filled in with the colours of the Romanian flag, which itself is shown beside every menu. Information for new migrants and announcements about Romanian events in the US are available alongside links to news from the homeland, live webcam feeds from main Romanian cities and photograph albums. The news is clearly Romanian oriented, focusing on bilateral official visits, Romanian personalities with achievements in the US and Romania's current economic situation.

RomPortal is devoted to information and discussion. Advertising is unusually absent. The site's logo includes a globe, the letters *rom* in the colours of the Romanian flag, and a star in the shape of the US flag. In October 2012, the website had 7,355 users and 47,227 threads, with a total of 74,223 posts. A large number of posts were exchanges about immigration procedures and achieving legal status, targeting both premigrants and newcomers or individuals whose legal status has changed while in the US. This is a useful resource, due to the complexity of the US immigration system and the diversity of visa types available. The relevance of the forum is obvious in the number of people who read this advice. One thread on the topic of legal status had, in May 2010, no fewer than 93,378 readers and 349 posts. Sending private messages to users is not accepted by the forum administrators, so all messaging has to be conducted publicly for the benefit of all users, who are rewarded with points in accordance to the number of contributions.

The *RomPortal* forum is also a useful source of information about the Canadian, Australian and New Zealand immigration systems. As the United States is becoming less welcoming, itinerant migrants plan to move to more appealing countries. The discussions help premigrants decide on the best target. The forum has many users located in Romania but also many in Italy, a proof that itinerant migrants are emerging as a distinct category of immigrants who will relocate to more favourable economic and cultural climates.

Another unusual feature of the website is 'soft' topics proposed as 'round table' exchanges coordinated by returning users. Soft topics are well attended and have longevity. A thread about babies elicited 850 posts between May 2006 and August 2009; another round table about perfumes and cosmetics elicited 110 replies from November 2005 to July 2009; and exchanges of jokes and humour account for 253 posts from November 2005 to July 2009. These topics help the community form groups around gossip and practical information exchanges in a friendly atmosphere, but the forum has also mobilized users politically, mostly during the Romanian national elections when relevant posts accumulated hundreds of readers.

All the above websites share certain commonalities: they provide an excellent base for building labour networks and receiving complex legal advice; they straddle large geographical territories and the forums tend to be larger than those based in Europe, but still dominated by a handful of 'debaters'; because some have multiple authors, administrators and moderators, they tend to be less visually distinct and more fragmented; and they are colonized by advertising and promotional messages. All these features seem to suggest fewer opportunities for sustained political engagement than those evident in Italy, for example. However, as we shall see in the remainder of this chapter, there is a constant effort to expand identity discourses through a double referent (Romanian and North American) and there is political engagement and reflection, but these aspects are circumscribed by homeland events. For various reasons already mentioned, the Romanian diaspora based in North America tends to be less dynamic and less politicized by the local immigration context than Romanian diasporas in Europe.

In-betweeners

In North America-based discussion forums diasporans speak about the normal concerns of migrants. Conflicts and the negotiation of online hierarchies take place in the same way they pepper the online life of Europe-based diasporic communities. In the *BC Romanian Community Center* forum a user took a stand against the pro-religious posts of the user Decebal. Roza asked the administrator to set up a separate topic so that 'we don't have to read his posts anymore, he's becoming annoying'. In addition, but also alluding to the fact that the forum was set up by Romanians from Transylvania, known for their taciturn nature, Daciana added the comment:

> This has started to look like a Transylvanian forum. Few people read the posts, not many contribute opinions, the subjects are amorphous, lacking in taste and colour. Only Decebal used to wake us up with his sermons. Where is the art of conversation? Do we lack topics? I don't think so. I asked a question in the forum six months ago; it was read by 275 pairs of eyes, but nobody answered.

Another user defended the running of the forum with: 'The fact that Transylvanians are unconcerned by "hot news" (gossip) is laudable. I first think and then write' (Horea, *BC Romanian Community Center*). This exchange shows that administrators need to resuscitate the conversation whenever it is languishing and also manage conflicts derived from controversial views. However, often administrators wait and take the pulse of the thread and contributors first. This has the double advantage of allowing them time to decide the nature of the intervention and also garnering some interest in the forum.

In this particular case, a heated debate followed, after one of the administrators declared he was unwilling to move certain discussions elsewhere. This sounded like a provocation and so it garnered lot of interest. Daciana was right to observe that such exchanges were rare, the majority of topics being announcements and questions requiring practical information about Canadian life. Like in many other forums, users have to openly negotiate the terms and rules and it is important to have personalities causing dissent in order to reinvigorate the public sphere aspect of the website. Interestingly, as this exchange shows, users are split among regional provenance. This is typical for diasporic sites based in North America. While in Europe regional provenance does not seem to matter as much, in some North America-based forums popular humour, friendly banter and even competitive challenges often mention the area users come from, which becomes a weapon of sorts, with Transylvanians enjoying a special reputation.

The ambivalence expressed by migrants in Europe towards the mother country is replicated by diasporans settled in North America. There is a vivid criticism of the way Romania is progressing en route to democracy and prosperity and the same disparaging attitude towards Romania as a nation is obvious. On *RomPortal* in December 2006, Maricica quoted a migrant from Spain who had said:

> Being a migrant has become a burden. I lived in Italy and France and I am now in Spain. After learning of other cultures and mentalities I can say I am sick of Romanians . . . . It may be nice abroad, but we will always be immigrants and so will our children. I would take up arms and return to clean Romania up . . . . Are you not fed up? . . . We need a real revolution.

Maricica's quote received 160 replies, which were read by 14,600 people. Magdalena contributed by saying: 'It's not easy to be an immigrant, I can feel that every day, but I prefer to be an immigrant here and live a decent life, than be in my own country right now.' Ciprian summarized the discussion in a slightly bigoted fashion, by repeating the usual clichés about Romanian inadequacies:

> Don't generalise, there is people and people. If you despise Romanians, you despise yourselves. We have Latin blood and many nations of Latin origins display the same shortcomings. Secondly, we are closer to the Orient and we borrowed bad traits from them. And then we lived under communism, which brought us the worst traits, depersonalisation included. Don't admire other people; can't you see how many weirdoes Americans have? They were lucky to be colonised by the English who brought them everything, language included . . . [. J]ust think what would have happened if they were colonised by the Mexicans[:] . . . we would have never come[,] . . . although slowly the little people from the South are starting to make progress.

These migrants replicate the discourse about Romanian inadequacies that has been described in previous chapters, but the addition of stereotypes learnt within the North American context is also evident, particularly feelings of superiority to the Latin population. Ciprian paradoxically compares himself with the Spanish in Europe, but views Mexicans differently. The same interplay between complexes of inferiority and superiority is a feature of Europe-based diasporic forums.

In January 2008, another user on *RomPortal* posted weblinks to negative headlines about Romanians published in a number of countries. Aurelia expressed her ambivalence in the usual gloomy fashion:

> Sometimes I'm glad Americans are so full of themselves that they don't see further from their borders, otherwise . . . where can I emigrate, somewhere nobody['s] heard of Romanians[?] . . . I don't want to change the topic, which is about Romanianness and patriotism, but whenever one person manages to achieve something (you've read the post about Mungiu's film), another ten contribute to theft, crime and violence [that appears] on the front pages of newspapers.

Aurelia's post marks the divide once more between supposedly opposite types of migrants, showing the difficulty of integrating various diasporic groups under one identity and alluding to the never ending quest for meaning among a complex mosaic of identities. Romanians in North America seem to perform their identity quest by looking at otherness within, rather than a foreign other. The nature of the Romanian demographics in North America, the absence by and large of illegality in status and the peculiar characteristics of American integration models, have shielded Romanians from the ethnic tensions and the legal backlash that has affected Romanians in Europe. The emphasis on (North) Americanness seems to offer them the opportunity for integration without overt discrimination. While the geographical distance and the North American nationalizing processes help them perform a strategy of identity distanciation from the homeland, they continue to harbour rancour against a homeland that has symbolically expelled them.

In a thread that started in January 2007 one participant in the *RomPortal* forum posted an interview with President Băsescu in which the Romanian president considered the return of migrants to be a priority. Maricica wrote the following comment:

> Yes, higher wages would be the best solution; however[,] this works for those who only left to make money and who then return to buy a home. But for those who go outside and realise that life can be different, the system is different, life in general is better[;] there is nothing Băsescu can do, they won't return.

Maior added: 'You get used to normality and start to see the REAL face of Romania' (emphasis in original). Romulus, on the other hand, became critical of Romanians back home, who continued to put up with the situation:

I have to start by saying that in my soul I will always be Romanian, I will maintain Romanian traditions and my children will speak Romanian. But I am angry with the attitude of Romanians. . . . Instead of wanting to live better, speak up when we don't agree, stop giving bribes, learn to respect others . . . we prefer to say 'this is Romania', as if nothing can ever change.

Most users agreed that immediate changes were not to be expected and that for them there was no return. Maior retorted: 'All these issues depend on civic attitudes, WHICH DO NOT EXIST IN ROMANIA. This is the biggest crime of the communist regime' (emphasis in the original); and Rita observed that 'IT migrants would be unemployed if they returned to Romania'. Only Silvestru disagreed somewhat: 'Băsescu said that wage increases would convince migrants to return. I'd say not everybody, but many would feel better working in Romania on half the salary they have abroad, but in positions which are higher up.' The thread amassed a total of eighty-seven replies and was read by 8,560 people. From these comments we have to understand migration to North America as a process of burning bridges and adopting a critical distance in which a certain sense of nostalgia remains but anger and discouragement about everything Romanian dominate.

The Electoral Politicization of the Diaspora

Romanians in the United States and Canada seem to enjoy easier social integration than those in Europe in the absence of legal issues, curtailment of the right to work or criminalization by media and politicians. This means that political activity online is significantly reduced and whatever exists is orientated towards the political relationship with the homeland.

Comunitatea română portalul diasporei române US (Romanian Community, Portal of the US Romanian Diaspora) is a wiki set up in January 2004. Discussions are often suffocated by the high number of promotional posts, which register very few replies. However, discussions gathered pace in the context of the referendum calling for the impeachment of President Băsescu in May 2007 and the parliamentary elections taking place in November 2008. Most of these discussions were steered by the administrator, through relevant messages. In April 2007, the administrator posted the news that the president had been suspended. His pro-Băsescu interventions attracted the opposing views of another user. In a long and personal exchange analysing the president's political decisions, Marcu and the administrator reflected the opposing views of many Romanians and the thread attracted 5,750 readers. This exchange provided a necessary dialogue that helped users prepare for voting decisions. In a separate thread, the administrator linked to all the pro-Băsescu electoral posters, providing thus a visual collage of the president's campaign and this thread, in turn, was viewed by 3,033 users. After the vote, observing that 96.85 per cent of Romanians in Seattle voted against the impeachment (from a total of 444 votes), one user considered it a good, if unnecessary, democratic lesson.

In November 2008, Sorin Udroiu, the PNG (New Generation Party) candidate to represent the US diaspora in the Romanian parliament, posted his electoral programme in the *Comunitatea română portalul diasporei române US* forum. He received only one reply, but the post was read by 786 users. He also used the *RomPortal* forum to publicize his programme, but here he was met with irony. Sorana made new policy 'recommendations' that poked fun at the party's president, a Romanian magnate and football club owner. The candidate thanked her for the humour, to which she replied, 'please convince me that your party is a model for the Romanian society and your programme makes sense when your leader bad mouths other candidates publicly and tells foreigners to "remain where you are"!' As Udroiu's cyber-mishap shows, making political promises is insufficient in a context in which users have developed a critical distance from the homeland and relish the opportunity to exchange views. They can also enter into a personal relationship with the candidate, taking thus the real measure of that person.

The exchange between Sorin Udroiu and Sorana opened a full polemic, which provided a critical analysis of parties, candidates and electoral programmes. Radomir entered the debate by openly addressing the PNG candidate:

> Don't you understand we have our rules, our preferences? For me RP [*RomPortal*] represents Ro [Romania], with our laws, manners and information . . . [. W]hy are you talking about your elections, when we have a verified system, experience and our way of spelling things out[?] From recipes to health, immigration, houses, divorces, love and whatever, we talk about everything . . . all without pressure.

Radomir's post shows displeasure with the transgression of rules. In his view, the honesty of the forum seemed to have been tainted by a promotional post. The candidate is accused of not understanding the system that makes the forum work. Sorana also questioned the integrity of any PNG candidate and users agreed. The candidate replied asking potential voters to check out his YouTube videos, where his policies were explained in more detail. He continued to reiterate that those who were serious about politics should contact him privately. Users seemed interested in the candidate's diasporic experience and reacted negatively when they found out that he had travelled abroad for work, but had no actual immigration experience. Firu asked: 'How will you represent me, a Romanian citizen resident abroad, when you never ate immigrant bread? Three months here and there, amounts to a holiday!'

Two issues were brought to light by this exchange. First, the inability of the candidate to recognize the internal unwritten rules of the forum and campaign accordingly, by asking for permission, for example, or spending some time with the online community to get to know them. Second, the issue of representation became a key one. Like their colleagues in Italy, diasporans based in North America seemed reluctant to offer their vote to somebody who did not share their experience of immigration and life in the diaspora.

Radomir observed that most candidates had similar electoral programmes and that some of their proposals, such as lifting visas for Romanians travelling to the US, were not decisions that could be readily influenced by Romanian politicians. Users were also not best pleased to find the candidate campaigning on *Italia România* on behalf of a colleague who was unable to use the Internet (Italy was not part of Udroiu's electoral 'college'). This clearly indicates an extensive research being carried out by the online community on the candidate's pedigree and the work of his party and colleagues. After the elections, Sorin Udroiu posted another message to thank diasporans (although he was not elected) and tell them of a business proposal. Having not learnt his 'lesson', the former candidate was asking those interested in setting up a tourism agency to contact him. The message created consternation among users, who suspected that his candidacy was a pretext for starting a business in the US. He was thus accused of insinuating himself on a false pretence into the soul of the online community in order to derive some profit. The thread closed after 115 posts, read by 20,849 people.

On *Comunitatea română portalul diasporei române US* Bebe asked for advice about the various diasporic candidates and programmes: 'I feel tempted to vote, because for the first time, we are electing our own representative in Parliament and I want a change because this government has forgotten about us', he explained. One user recommended Anna Birchall, the PSD candidate and a Yale graduate, who had been his teacher. In a separate thread, another user sang the praises of the independent candidate Constantin Timoc, a Californian resident. In the aftermath of the online discussion, a makeshift public debate between Constantin Timoc and the PSD candidate Anna Birchall was organized by the diasporic paper *New York Magazin* on 23 November 2008 and the video footage of the event was posted on YouTube. However, the footage had been heavily edited and claimed Birchall was only a 'visitor' to the US, while Timoc, having lived for forty years in the country, was introduced as the more 'authentic' choice. While the organization of the debate seemed a good idea, in the process of transposing the online discussion into real life, the event was hijacked by partisan anti-PSD interests. This shows that online communities remain vulnerable to some extent to exploitation by certain community leaders, but they also remain a great source of inspiration and reflection.

On general election day, *RomPortal* members used the web to avidly look for early results and exit poll data. The news that PSD-PC might have come first by a slight margin was quickly distributed. Romulus expressed his amazement that Romanians still believed in 'this party', which some diasporans suspected of having crypto-communist tendencies. Firu replied: 'it's our fault; we are detached from Romanian realities. As for "our" elections, it's still too early, still many more hours till polling stations close here. All I know is that turnout is currently low'. In this case, the online diasporic community expressed again its critical distance from Romanian realities, positioning itself as politically different and hence more liberal than people back home. Amarena commented:

> We still have five hours, the last polling station to close is Portland OR. I am watching what is happening and I feel sick. . . . I used to watch the Antena TV stations before, but now they are all biased for the PSD-PC alliance. When I read the papers, I also have to interpret the news according to who owns them. I haven't seen bigger shit than this. Plus, look at the war fought in *Români la Chicago Yahoo Group*, where the campaign is still taking place.

These kinds of exchanges, which characterized many online forums in North America that day, were ongoing while voting was still taking place in the diaspora. This prompted Romanian political analysts to suspect an impact of the time zone-related delays not only on voting participation, but also on the overall result of the elections, since the diasporic vote was more favourable to the Democrats.

This suspicion was confirmed in the 2009 presidential elections, when the diasporic votes made an even bigger difference (see Chapter Six). In the aftermath of these elections, participants on *Québec Ro* discussed cleaning politics up, the need for a new generation of politicians and Romania's unfortunate history. In their analysis of the results of the presidential election, users congratulated each other for 'winning against communism' and claimed that while the diaspora voted correctly, the Romanians back home 'voted badly'. Communism was thus not completely defeated and more action was needed. Users called for postal or electronic voting to be instated. Electronic voting, due to the distance between polling stations in North America, was also the main desiderate of *Romanian Portal US* users.

Romanian Portal US (which had almost twelve thousand forum members in October 2012 and is not to be confused with *RomPortal*) aims to embrace the Romanian diaspora everywhere and become a transnational website. In fact it centres on the US and Canada. The forum is split regionally between different areas in the US (Midwest, Southeast and so on), with the purpose of creating sub-forums discussing locally relevant issues. Similarly, Canada is split between Québec and Ontario and other much smaller (fewer than one hundred threads each) sub-forums are available for different communities in Europe, Australia and New Zealand. Usually, political threads are relegated to the mixed open or general discussion area, but this is one of the few forums with a separate politics category. In a thread debating the right of the diaspora to get involved in Romanian politics in December 2009, Irimie's opinion was:

> Romanians in the diaspora have a better vision, they live in democratic civilized countries, so they know how things should be and understand the anomalies in Romania. Although we may not be physically there, ninety-nine per cent of us still have families there. So the argument that we know nothing and we don't care is not valid. We are directly involved through our families. In addition, the diaspora has a huge impact on the Romanian economy, remittances are higher than foreign investment.

The same superiority and critical distance encountered on most diasporic sites is manifested here. Diasporans claim a pivotal role in Romania's affairs due to the economic impact of remittances and assumed know-how in democratic matters.

Before the elections, between November and December 2009, a dedicated thread on *Romanian Portal US* discussed the candidates and users posted articles and video clips, featuring and about the candidates, sourced from the Romanian media. 12,945 viewers read the 382 posts. The online discussion was totally divorced from the activity of Romanian associations in the physical world, who did not intervene in the political debate prior to elections. Wild ideas, put forward by the occasional guest with an unlikely project or people in search of self-promotion, were usually ignored. The election occasioned a larger discussion about Romanian geopolitics, the country's relationship with neighbours and the impact of the Hungarian minority on Romanian politics. Like in all other diasporic forums, US politics was little discussed, although some users proffered pro-Obama views, attempting to link the two distant political realms. There was more interest in issues related to the US health system and the US economy, but not necessarily the way the political system works.

During the electoral presidential campaign in Romania, a pro-Geoană (the main opponent of the incumbent president) message was posted by one of his public relations advisers, but the promotional campaign was soon criticized by users for being 'amateurish'. After censuring the spin doctor for claiming that Geoană had a decisive role in Romania becoming a NATO member, Irma remarked:

> I had a precise economic question to ask, but in view of your latest cam-
> paign messages, I give up. You insulted the intelligence of *Romanian-Portal*
> users. Please desist or adapt to the medium. If you have the professional
> ability, that is.

As in previous instances, diasporans rejected general and unsubstantiated claims and responded with analyses that showed a detailed knowledge of political news. This forum is, after all, the only diasporic forum that polls its members regularly, including on voting intentions. There was, once more, criticism of the inability of candidates and their advisors to understand the online community and the diasporic experience, and tailor policies accordingly.

Conclusions: Syncopated Micropolitics

North America-based websites share the same concerns with national image, the relationship with the homeland, life and identity as an immigrant and the impossible return as their counterparts in Europe. However, the websites and their online communities are shaped by the specificities of the North American context. Romanians in the United States and Canada have not been radicalized by the legal and political context and therefore they politically mobilize only during electoral events that allow them to fulfil their roles as voters and Romanians. They show mistrust in direct political approaches and especially unsubstantiated political promotion, although users' personal views are largely tolerated. This new diaspora has also inherited from the old diaspora and from North American popular discourse a preoccupation with the survival of communist tendencies. The mistrust in political leaders encountered in Europe is coupled here with a fear of communism creeping back in. There is limited evidence suggesting that the Romanian diaspora based in North America leans towards the right of the political spectrum. Anti-communist views are probably to do partly with the ability of the old diaspora (clearly anti-communist) to influence general discourses, but also with the migrant demographics (more middle-class professionals than in European diasporas) and with the general experience of North American capitalism. Certain electoral choices may also be dictated by the way Romanian candidates fail the online test, unaware of the need to modify their messages in line with diasporic expectations and the rules of the online community. This demonstrates again the lack of professionalism that still defines Romanian politics, but offers the diaspora the occasion to come together as a group at key political moments and express itself with a deep understanding of issues, strategies and programmes.

Online electoral politicization shows that diasporic websites (some, at least) have reached a maturity that enables them and their members to conduct a sophisticated political analysis and translate it into voting behaviour. Geographical and cultural distanciation becomes political distanciation through reflexivity. Micropolitical reflection enables the diasporic forum to come of age, reassert its rules and strengthen its identity around core views and behaviours. It is probably the strongest proof, so far, that online interaction works as a political tool in diasporic contexts and this is a lesson no politician can ignore.

PART IV – SECOND LIFE

'Voir, c'est avoir à distance'

CHAPTER EIGHT

Diaspora Online

Hierarchies and Rules

Previous chapters have followed Romanian migrants on their diasporic journeys, from symbolic distanciation to actual departure, from arrival to settlement, and finally, from reflection to activism. These journeys were made possible by diasporic websites that performed a multitude of roles. This final chapter represents an assessment of some of the most important functions of Romanian diasporic websites, as well as their future potential. Diasporic websites are characterized by developments taking place as a result of diasporic needs and the meanings invested in them over time. However, diasporic websites also evolve and will continue to evolve as a result of external circumstances, responding to new challenges.

This chapter explores the structural formation of Romanian diasporic websites, including individualization and customization, and explains the evolution of discussion forums in relation to online hierarchies, roles and rules. The chapter also explains how the formal appearance of a website, as well as its structural content, can incubate certain cultural and political expressions.

Ethnic Branding

All diasporic websites construct 'Brand Romania' by providing recognizable icons. This starts with the name of the website, which always includes words such as 'Romania' or 'Romanian' and 'identity' or 'community'. Pictorial and graphic representations of the national flag and elements of heraldry are common to most sites (*Români în UK, Spania românească, FEDROM, Italia România, Identitatea românească, Ora Turin*). Occasionally, the red, yellow and blue of Romania's flag are woven throughout the entire site (*Romanian*

Portal US, Italia România, Străinatate). The tricolour represents a crumb trail that prevents users from getting lost within the symbolic geography of the online space whilst scrolling down or accessing various parts of the website. The yellows, blues and reds subconsciously remind them of due national allegiance and help provide a pathway for the visual identity narrative. They are a form of 'banal nationalism', to appropriate Michael Billig's term (1995).

The iconography of architectural landmarks and maps adds another layer of visual recognition, recalls a sense of nostalgia (Hiller and Franz 2004) and reenacts home culture (Siapera 2005: 512). The home is reimagined through remembering and reinterpreting and a new, symbolic home is reconstructed. The relationship between the two homes, one remembered, the other imagined, is defined, in terms borrowed from Sayad, as a simultaneous 'presence' and 'absence' (2004: 82). Diasporic culture cannot be easily homed, but it is not homeless. Online, it is expressed through vivid exchanges of music, art, amateur photography, food and humour, which become defining elements of any diasporic website. Diasporic culture thus uses national culture as a point of reference but achieves an individual personality. Through multiple anchorings and its existence among compounded simultaneous geopolitical spaces, online diasporic culture forms a separate event horizon.

In addition, the choice of images can emphasize the feeling of pride in national cultural achievements. Brâncuşi's famous sculpture 'Table of Silence', for example, appears as the logo of the site *Comunitatea română portalul diasporei române US*. While in *aggiornamento* (reconstruction) in the summer of 2008, the opening page of *România Italia Net*, whose forum was still functioning unimpeded, featured only the outline of Romania, filled with photographs of places: city centres, iconic buildings and famous landscapes. *Italia România* used a similar map, coloured in red, yellow and blue. These devices indicate that symbols of roots and rootedness are recuperated in order to verify provenance and heredity, ensuring that websites are legitimate, as far as their diasporic identity is concerned.

The various visual, textual and discursive elements also claim cultural and historical pedigree. Often they reproduce stereotypical images and expected associations. Orthodox monasteries and Bran Castle (what tourists presume to be Dracula's castle) hardly speak of the Romania most Romanians know, but play up to the internalized stereotypes that make Romania visible or recognizable to non-Romanians. This is the Romania that can support a dialogue between Romanians and others. This is an ideal Romania, so the emphasis is on landscapes and historical buildings that cannot be easily altered by political and economic crises or views and hence remain untainted and immortal. Most websites contain a photomontage or slide show, depicting the timeless beauty of the Romanian landscape: an invitation to tourism perhaps for foreigners; a nostalgic view of idyllic Romania for diasporans. Nationalist topoi steeped in the naivety of the village and the purity of the landscape are appropriated within the framework of environmental animism and geographical determinism (already discussed in Chapter One). A paradox emerges here: on the one hand, diasporans are critical, as exemplified in this book time and again, of nationalist propaganda and Romanian realities; on the other hand, they appropriate and internalize clichés, as if this was compensating for 'betraying' the mother country.

Cultural specificity provides a sense of recognition, and eases accessibility for diasporic users. Language, icons and other ethnically specific imagery produce collective cultural meanings. Users return to a symbolic home that is instantly recognisable visually: a shorthand to Romanian identity. The door is left open for 'outsiders', as well. The symbolism is not fully exclusionary, because it also contains various levels of diasporic double anchoring: Romanian icons stand side by side with flags and pictures of landmarks belonging to the host country (*Români în UK, Italia România*).

Although less colourful, with the exception of websites dedicated to music and parties (websites like *RomNights – Romanian Nights in New York* and *RoNights, chefurile româneşti din Chicago* – Romanian parties in Chicago), the Romanian websites based in North America always bear the United States or Canadian flags and some might even exclude Romanian iconology. In the case of wikis (*Comunitatea română portalul diasporei române US*), there is little structural input and, because the design has several authors, the visual identity is less pronounced. The absence of the Romanian flag on some sites also indicates a clearer separation from the homeland and a stronger anchoring in American realities.

The relationship between location, ethnicity and symbolic attachment recalls Appadurai's well known concept of 'ethnoscape' (1990). Diasporic websites become ethnoscapes of multiple belongings, as they look both towards 'there' and 'here', past and present. This multiplicity typical of identity in flux, this diasporic imaginary, has had many definitions: 'Third Space' (Bhabha 1994), 'cultural assemblage' (Gilroy 1993), 'cultural *bricolage*' (Androutsopolous 2006) or 'place-polygamy' (Georgiou 2006), which try to explain the reelaboration of identity narratives though new cultural referents. The *bricolage* of user avatars, global brands and internationally relevant imagery speaks of the inherent transnationalism encapsulated in diasporic online presences. Transnational imagery and multiple anchorings add to the dynamism observed already in forum discussions and speak of the awareness that results from migratory trajectories and experiencing the diasporic condition. These qualities qualify diasporic websites as sites of identity reimagining, cultural diasporism and diasporic micropolitics.

To sum up, the ethnic branding: (1) refashions the national home through presences and absences that require multiple anchorings, simultaneous remembering and forgetting and, above all, the ability to negotiate symbolic geography, often imbued with political connotations, flexibly and reflexively; and (2) gives the online community a pedigree that serves as a basis for the recognition of the community itself, its history and its cultural achievements, which form the basis for a new language of political claims. At the same time, the cultural *bricolage* contributes to the formation of a separate diasporic culture, transnational and in flux, which creates a new identity with the potential to express itself politically.

Partial Institutionalization

A separate, diasporic identity, able to express itself, is also acquired while negotiating institutionalization attempts. As Nedelcu observes, the diaspora represents 'a new cultural market' (2009: 291), which is attractive to many institutions and entrepreneurs. Diasporic websites have multiple publics. Apart from the diasporic one, Siapera counts the host public and the business public (Siapera 2006: 11), in addition to which we need to add the home public, represented by media and governmental institutions.

The host public has been, so far, largely ignored by Romanian diasporic websites. Apart from websites belonging to diasporic parties or official diasporic associations (*Identitatea românească, FEDROM*), bilingualism is rarely present. Furthermore, in the absence of colonial ties, the links with the host culture are weak. This has a double effect. On the one hand, when there is a need for public political action, the diaspora often finds itself isolated, its voice unheard. For all the shouting and complaining that may take place online, very little is being done in practical terms, because the diaspora lacks allies. On the other hand, it leaves the diaspora open to being influenced by organizations and institutions belonging to the home country, whose aim is often to use the diaspora in local political games. We have seen the evidence in Chapter Six.

The business public also remains rather small and dominated by products and services relevant to the diaspora. All the websites feature rolling advertising banners (usually at the top or side of the site) for flights, currency, remittance services and cheap telephone rates. Links to Romanian shops and restaurants are also a feature. Some US sites feature advertising from US manufacturers looking for business opportunities among the diaspora or in Romania.

A few searches among web resources that offer value calculations and income data for websites reveal just how untapped the business potential remains. Most Romanian diasporic websites are credited with earning US $1–2 per day by *SiteLog* (accessed 9 February 2010) and considered to be worth not much more than between US $600 (*Spania românească* or *Québec Ro*) and US $1,200 (*Italia România* or *Români Online UK*). Another website value calculator, *Cubestat* (accessed 9 February 2010), reveals that *Români în UK*, one of the more established sites, has daily advertising revenues of just over US $5 and that it is worth only US $3,800. Advertising is not completely absent, but the advertising income indicates that this is not the main 'business' of the websites.

While diasporic websites may not yet be money-making machines, there is evidence of attempts to institutionalize them in other ways. The renationalizing drives of the mother state, the craving to absorb diasporic culture into 'national' culture, have led to much more involvement on the part of the official arms of the state abroad – embassies and cultural institutes. *Români Online UK* has a close association with the Romanian Embassy in London, and also with the RCC, a private charity-based enterprise. The website often acts as a promotional platform for their activities. Embassies and cultural institutes have also used the websites to build e-mail lists and contacts within the diasporic community. Although these databases have not yet been misused or misappropriated (for political propaganda, for example), there is a clear drive to acquire a more detailed picture of the diaspora. One of the aims is to tap into the diaspora's skills and financial resources and, in the long run, use the diaspora as a voice, a spokesperson for Romania's interests abroad. Funding earmarked for diasporic associations by the Romanian government was one of the first attempts to partially institutionalize the diaspora. The effect was twofold: the positive multiplication of Romanian associations, with clearer cultural and political projects, occurred; but alongside this came negative competition and squabbling for finances. Particularly on Italian websites, the enrolment of the diaspora into the service of specific political and financial interests has led to some tensions (see Chapter Six). The ambivalence that Romanians feel towards the homeland and their negative experience with highly factionalized home politics are bound to spark further tensions in the process of forging links between the diaspora and its political home. However, homelands continue to want to maintain links with the diaspora (Laguerre 2006), in a case of forced love that has clear underlying interests.

These features reveal that:

- Romanian websites remain defined by a gaze firmly turned towards the diasporic community, with only isolated attempts to reach out. This is typical for relatively new online communities, which are prepolitical in their attempts to rationalize their mission;
- Financial, cultural and political potentials remain untapped. On the positive side, the Romanian diaspora online displays a certain innocence; on the negative side, any institutionalizing attempts are likely to lead to conflict and tension and a definitive loss of innocence (see also Sheffer 2003: 201);

- The diaspora remains isolated and is hence inefficient in political terms. However, it is necessary to spend time on the process of building community identity before any action is conducted within the larger social field.

Individualization and Hierarchy

Diasporic websites have already made progress in understanding their own relevance and identity and this is beginning to be expressed in the look and content of sites. Initially, most Romanian diasporic sites were produced cheaply without much sophistication, with limited and limiting features, the offspring of diasporans with plenty of enthusiasm but restricted financial means and basic design skills. Some websites evolved from Yahoo Groups, which represented, at first, the most common way of keeping in touch with community events. Even when full sites were developed, they did not require specialized technical knowledge on the part of the users and were free of corporate or political interests. The advantage was threefold: the websites were not clogged by advertising; they were of little interest to embassies and other state-sponsored institutions; and the basic and most sought after information was obviously placed and easily accessible. Through recurrent updates and redesigns, the websites have now become more sophisticated. Increased competition for a ready-made but limited audience has naturally boosted complexity, in order to maintain appeal and a unique selling point.

In the UK, for example, *Români în UK,* the longest-serving site, has a tabloid look, publicizes celebrity news and music events and seems to be aimed at fun-loving Romanians, while *Români Online UK* is the more professional-looking site for 'heavier' subjects. *Spania românească* embellishes the site with photographs of Miss Diaspora contestants and the 'most beautiful Romanian girls in Spain'. *Italia România* and *Romanian Times* are known for the amount of international news they provide. *Québec Ro* specializes in classified advertisements. Originality is not essential in countries where the diasporic demographics are large enough to accommodate two or more very similar websites. There is little glaring difference between *România Italia Net* and *Italia România*, both of some longevity, both geared towards providing survival information and both with active forums. Nevertheless, even when the diaspora is significant, it is important for websites to establish their uniqueness and identity. This is illustrated in the North American case. From *Comunitatea română portalul diasporei române US*, which is a very general, all encompassing initiative, to the Arizona-based *Romanian Times*, with its distinct religious flavour and heartfelt life stories; from *Québec Ro*, which caters heavily to premigrants and newcomers, to *Romanian Portal US*, set up by

Romanian web designers in the US, which aims to become, in time, a global diasporic network, there is something for everybody.

A website may choose to stand out from the crowd by responding to specific events and taking advantage of the temporary political climate. *Ora* (The Hour) in Turin is both a website and a newspaper belonging to *Romanian Hour*, an association for social and cultural promotion. On 10 October 2007, the website initiated the 'Campaign to remove all Romanian criminals – United Against Crime!' which lasted for almost a year. While not a roaring success, judging by the rather paltry 273 signatures I counted in June 2008, at the height of the 'Gypsy problem' in Italy, the website came to prominence with its virulent campaign against the Roma. The online petition, which featured a raised fist, asked for the immediate expulsion of all Romanian Gypsies who tarnished Romania's image and reputation in Italy. It was a reverberation of the aggressive discourse of the Italian right-wing government, eager to impose more stringent immigration laws. It also played a tune favoured by many online users in Italy-based forums. Although ethically dubious and morally questionable, the campaign fitted in well with the views of the radicals in the diaspora and gave the site distinctiveness in the process.

In their look and functions, all diasporic websites are relatively similar. They all cater for three main audiences: premigrants, migrants who have been in the host country for less than five years and settled migrants who have achieved some continuity and permanency (Hiller and Franz 2004: 737). This typology may not take into account repeat migrants or returnees, but it provides a useful compass for the way websites are shaped to accommodate these main categories. The need for basic information required by the first category collides with the survival and socializing needs of the newcomers, as well as with the achieved status, financial wellbeing, reflective self-awareness and political needs of the third, 'settled', category. Most sites try to cater concomitantly to all, which accounts for commonalities between sites. Websites display extensive menus for premigrants, which include host country guides, immigration and work rights information, embassy locations and document requirements. Newcomers can find menus or links that take them to Romanian organizations and associations, churches, communities, news, diasporic radio and newspapers, permits, health-related resources, shops and restaurants. The menus for these two categories of users are usually very prominent and easily accessible, while the content answering the needs of settled migrants is buried within the site's inner layers.

There are concomitant demands placed on diasporic services, resulting from the co-existence of different types of audiences. As Andrei explained, referring to the needs of premigrants and newcomers on the one hand and settled migrants on the other: 'as long as the forum remains a "public information office", the old members will refuse to enter, fed up with cyclical questions, while the new ones will find out what they want and "beat it"' (Andrei, *Români în UK*). Increasingly, diasporic websites have had to reinvent themselves, in order to resolve the tension between offering recycled information, necessary for the survival of newcomers who keep asking the same questions, and catering for the more sophisticated and demanding habitual users, who not only search for interesting and topical discussions, but also want to have a say in the way both structure and content are being shaped.

The true soul of the website is therefore embedded in the inner belly of the beast, defined by the historical and social contexts that have shaped a particular website, the activity in the forum and the relationship between the website administrator or webmaster and members. Once peeled like an onion, the inner layers of a site reveal forum and chat facilities, which open up a new and interactive diasporic world, a second life. It is the forum that gives the site individuality. One online forum participant, Cerasela, explained: 'I found a united community, which I never expected, due to what one hears about Romanians abroad'. Marieta also added: 'I found all my answers and the help I needed on this site' (*Români Online UK*).

Settled migrants are probably the more elusive and also intriguing category. These are people who have minimal survival needs, but a huge cultural, social and political appetite. As a result, they are active and tend to stick around longer. They treat the forum as a second home, understand hierarchies and play the role of advisers to premigrants and newcomers. They form an accidental and, at times, dysfunctional family. Clashes of interests and personalities – between newcomers and settled migrants; those who intermarry and those who do not; and those who dream of returning and those who turn their backs on the homeland – are essential for attracting viewers and participating members. This diversity also shapes political attitudes. Websites want to attract and retain settled migrants in the forum, in order to ensure the survival of the website. Depending on its history and the personalities, achievements and clashes that have shaped it, each site will acquire its own uniqueness. However, there is a constant process of change at work. 'The forum needs to keep up with new fashions, ideas' (Rareş, *Români în UK*), commented a Romanian user, aware of the necessity for renewed relevance.

Most forums are defined by the interplay between presences and absences. A high number of visitors and lurkers and a small number of posters represent the usual norm. Tynes, for example, reports that while the Sierra Leone listserv *Leonenet* had around four hundred members at the time of his research, only about forty regularly posted e-mails and even in this case, their contributions ranged widely from two words to ten pages (Tynes 2007: 503). The temptation to use the free information and resources without reciprocating is often very strong (Nedelcu 2009: 207). Online diasporic forums assume that a high number of members will be simply lurking out of curiosity, some will remain dormant and only a few dozen contributors will keep the forum debates alive. In October 2007, when *Români Online UK* celebrated the 4,000-member milestone, the administrator concluded his congratulations with, 'many find necessary help here and many also stop by to help others, perpetuating thus our attitude and spirit'. One user quickly reminded him that out of the 4,000, 2,500 had never written any messages. However, other users intervened to point out that widespread activism was idealistic and it was more important for the forum to keep growing. *Români Online* now has almost 17,000 members (October 2012).

Rewarding strategies are deployed to keep users engaged. By applying web semiology to cyber-research, Smart and colleagues (2000) arrive at the conclusion that websites need to find ways to be appealing, arouse and sustain curiosity and interest, but also reward users for their achievement. On the homepage, content such as success stories, photographs and news from diasporic events act as a way of building confidence about the efficacy of the site (Brinkerhoff 2009: 199). In addition, users are able to derive certain degrees of interactivity and satisfaction from search features, chat, e-mail, links, animations and emoticons, as well as a sense of control, achievement and satisfaction during and at the end of each browsing session. This is usually indicated not just by users' commitment to the site, but also by the length of time spent on each session, when, rather than occasional posts, whole dialogues ensue, lasting weeks. Habitual returns, cyber-time and number of posts, as well as the passionate language used, indicate the amount of value placed on online interactions.

Members can build distinct personalities online, through customization features: creative avatars, emoticons, sign-off animations and quotes, which are 'emblematic' representations (Androutsopoulos 2006: 524). The space has to be personalized and owned, and emotions need to be expressed somehow in the absence of face-to-face interactions. Emotion is also an indication of the value of some of the debates to the personal experiences of the migrant and can reveal the user's political attitudes.

Some users may choose to reinvent themselves by deleting their avatars and reappearing under a new guise. However, the accumulation of points or stars for prolonged and frequent participation discourages this practice, as does the community's reactions when such users are found out. When the *Romanian Community of Ireland* forum discussed the community's governing rules in January 2005, one of the most disputed issues was that of users with multiple avatars and online presences. Some argued that it was necessary to be able to maintain privacy and anonymity from spouses or friends, who also frequented the forum. Switching from one online persona to another thus helped them preserve their freedom of opinion. However, Horațiu was one of several users who raised the following point: 'it is incorrect for some to mislead people' and multiple avatars were discouraged thereon.

Users are rewarded with stars, points or designations similar to the eBay system, which prove not only the degree of participation, but also the user's place in the online hierarchy. *Români în UK* is a typical example. It has an administrator (webmaster) and also moderators. Participation is graded, with the avatars carrying up to five points (up to five coloured squares, to be more precise) and a label describing the position the user is assigned within the hierarchy. One point carries the label 'I read in the shadow'; two, 'I have a question'; three, 'Interested in the forum'; four, 'I like it a lot'; and five points go hand in hand with 'I have a lot to say' or 'veteran'. The administrator and moderators all have five points. This system is emblematic because it presupposes a number of lurkers who 'read in the shadow'. The forum considers that those who only venture to ask for information can be rewarded with the 'I have a question' label. Those who clearly show an interest in the forum are those with roughly seventy posts or more. Five points are assigned to users who have contibuted over one thousand posts. This categorization provides instant visual recognition for the user's place in the online hierarchy; it gives full or partial symbolic rights and it invites a specific treatment of the user.

Irony and humour are often exercised on new members, usually without malice, as seasoned users assert their position and precedence in the hierarchy and test the boundaries of the new relationship. For example, when I posted details about my research, inviting users to e-mail me their views and meet me in Valencia in the summer of 2008, Enache (*Marea unire, Spania*) replied, 'if you are under thirty-five, young, beautiful, with money, a house in England, a house back home and unmarried, I will be waiting for you, eager to share my experience of life abroad'. He retuned to a serious tone giving me his e-mail and prompting me to: 'write only good things about us'. His ironic message was a strategy of verification; Enache was trying to get the measure of the person I was or pretended to be.

Monica on *Italia România* took a similarly humorous approach to 'rules of integration into the forum'. She ironically recommended newcomers to at first approve everything and use plenty of smileys/emoticons; check how much support people enjoy before attacking them; attack in a pack because it was more efficient; always ask people's opinion because people love to be consulted; start only fashionable topics (government, Italians, football, Gypsies); and remember that those who use an elevated and grammatically correct language become unpopular. With this tongue-in-cheek post, Monica in fact pointed out some of the perceived ills of life in the diasporic forum, so her post represented both a critical commentary and a helpful warning.

Online hierarchies test normal social boundaries, but provide important functions:

- Sometimes online hierarchies mimic existing social and institutional practices. Other times, through conflict and disruption, they create new value systems, new hierarchies of power, individual to each forum and website. Power games prepare the online community for political expression;
- Diasporic websites function in consultation with users. *Romanian Community of Ireland* was redesigned in 2010 and users were consulted about its sections, content and facilities and a competition was launched for designing a new logo. Webmasters now choose to redevelop through participation and consultation, and this becomes a new form of micropolitics, a symbolic contract between the website and its audience;
- Forum users perpetually joust for a position from which they can impart advice, vet new members, earn respect and gather a following. Hierarchies are thus made and remade constantly, on a daily basis. This allows for a certain dynamism to evolve, which serves the online community well at times when important issues need to be debated and decisions taken and enacted.

Webmastering the Rules

Webmasters, administrators and moderators have the power to shape online hierarchies. Diasporic webmasters share information, help new migrants and often provide friendship and support (Chan 2006: 13). Day-to-day webmastering activities entail greeting new members, organizing subject categories, monitoring discussions and intervening when rules are infringed (a substantial percentage of the job, according to Wise, Hamman and Thorson 2006: 26).

When webmasters do not react promptly, users become frustrated. Quick reaction times and calming interventions to flaming situations can increase the trust that members and visitors place in the site, in the same way the frequency of messages shows the level of engagement and sociability (Wise et al. 2006: 27). On *Spania românească* in October 2006, one user suggested to the moderators to use *România Italia Net* as a model, in order to create a more animated virtual relationship among Romanians. When neither webmaster nor moderator acted, users starting feeling despondent about the future of the forum and in time the online activity declined, putting the site's viability into question.

A crucial role for webmasters is posting messages and starting threads that stimulate discussions (Chan 2006: 12). They also make attempts to reactivate 'sleepers' or lapsed members by circulating e-mails, containing news about new posts and online activities. The webmaster's role is slowly becoming differentiated from the moderator's role. While the webmaster looks after design, technical specifications, general rules and member numbers, the moderator becomes crucial for the day-to-day health of the forum, especially when it comes to forum organization and policing behaviour. A discussion about what the role of the moderator should be took place on *Români în UK* in February 2009. It started with one user observing that the webmaster was too busy to constantly police the forum. He asked for a moderator who would display neutrality and balance, not like Rada, 'who overreacts at each message', or Vasile, 'who doesn't want to upset anybody'. Proposals came quickly, users preferring people who were respected, showed good judgement, had ideas for new discussions, knew the difference between opinion and insult, had patience and time, and did not exacerbate conflicts. The requirement for neutrality dominated overall, yet some also appreciated polemics that did not display threatening behaviour.

When someone asked for a cloaked or hidden moderator, the webmaster rejected the idea for being unethical and lacking transparency. Gender came into discussion, but was dismissed as unimportant. Romanian diasporic web-sites are heavily populated by women, reflecting the great proportion of women migrants, and women hold their own online, but are not necessarily viewed as the better communicators. A few users declined the offer of a mod-erator altogether, arguing that self-censorship should dominate. These users encouraged others to take responsibility for their own online behaviour. Andrei considered that there were two sides to the job, one 'artistic' (stimulat-ing debates) and one 'technical' (enforcing rules). He added: 'the moderator is the glue of the community, impartial and creative, a good organizer; he or she mobilizes users to participate in the forum, creates topics, discusses new ideas. The moderator needs to maintain the life of the forum.' As a result, two moderators were named, one male and one female, their personalities being considered a good balance for the forum; the webmaster had the casting vote.

Apart from electing moderators, members also shape many of the online rules in accordance to their own preferences and pet hates. A good example is the *Romanian Community of Ireland* diasporic site. In January 2005 a poll was posted in the forum, inviting users to vote on new forum rules. The discus-sions showed users to be split down the middle about some of the rules, prompting one user to ironically predict the dissolution of the forum. Some members proposed moving any deviations from the topic thread to the general category 'place to bang heads together' (reserved for 'off topics'); others proposed that conflicts were moved to a separate discussion area because, as Ieremia noted ironically, 'contradictory discussions help us to know each other better'.

The debate highlighted not only that the majority of users had not read the existing forum rules, which they implicitly signed up for when registering, but also two other major concerns. One related to flaming, which was considered a serious issue, but not serious enough to justify banning or out-right exclusion. Some users even thought that conflict drew out the real personality or 'face' of the contributor. A second major concern was deviations from the subject, which many users found annoying and in breach of netiquette. Users discussed, although could not come up with a definitive solution for, the need to remove threads that had become inactive or had deviated from the initial topic.

Flaming, particularly trolling – posting with the sole intent of provoking dissension – is commonplace in diasporic forums. Graham and Khosravi explained how the Iranian forums they studied contained confrontational language, which was otherwise avoided in face-to-face interactions. One Iranian chat room based in Toronto even specialized in cursing (2002: 238). Their presupposition was that anonymity and lack of consequences led to a certain degree of irresponsibility. However, Graham and Khosravi also agreed that the airing of conflicts and contradictions perpetuates collective identity through ongoing, if acrimonious, dialogue (Graham and Khosravi 2002: 243).

In the *Români în UK* forum, the webmaster had to ask users to keep the threads 'clean' (January 2009). In his support, Andrei was of the opinion that those who thought that living the 'Romanian way' was enough to claim participation in the life of the community were misguided. He gave the example of 20 May 2008, when Romanians gathered at the feet of Churchill's statue near Westminster, to manifest their support for President Băsescu. Such actions of unity, he claimed, helped create a more real 'portrait' of the community. Participation, he added, was about action, common projects and volunteering skills and time.

The same thread, discussing the involvement of Romanians in community projects, contained a post which is illustrative of the source of much online diasporic flaming. A (newer) user took issue with the term 'Romanian community', asking polemically, 'Romanian community?????! What on earth does that mean, are we some kind of sect?' To this Adina, one of the oldest contributors, replied, 'is it difficult to restrain yourself when you have nothing constructive to say? Where did you come from, have you got nothing else to do?' Traditional research often assumes the homogeneity of diasporic groups, whereas my own research points towards a more mobile identity, shaped by discordant tussles and a rejection of inherited traditional identities. However, this exchange also shows the way the group readjusts by attempting (through Adina) to eliminate dissension (sometimes unsuccessfully). Flaming and deflaming or deflating are the opposite sides of the same coin in online identity-making strategies.

When, in September 2008, *Români în UK* discussed its own rules, users focused on finding a balance between freedom of expression and inappropriate

language or personal attacks; the relationship between webmaster or administrator and moderators; and instances of deleting messages, a practice that was
overwhelmingly condemned (one of the moderators admitted deleting messages that did not fit into any of the preexisting categories). The main rules
resulting from the debate were: no personal contact details, intentional off-
topic posts, bad language, ill-tempered reactions or returning to the same
subject repeatedly. The thread was locked after hundreds of posts, which
occasionally resulted in verbal blows. The heat of the discussion showed that
the forum mattered to users and conflict was a means of thrashing out key
issues. Continuous discussion can develop the community in a certain way
(Brinkerhoff 2009: 93), which can prove crucial in the future development of
political activity.

Such debates display an online hierarchy loosely engineered by webmasters, but also fought on the ground through heated debates. It is here that
rules can be created and modified, exclusions can be symbolically enacted and
webmasters can meet with open challenges to their authority. Undermining
the webmaster is a rare occurrence, but can happen. In June 2009 on *Români
în UK* Dorel attacked the webmaster for the quantity of banners and advertising on the website, which he considered to be a violation of trust and an
abuse. The webmaster pointed out that the absence of any revenue from users,
who can sign up freely, had to be compensated by online advertising. He also
claimed that only the server costs are met in this manner, while attending
events, news gathering, site administration and updates were paid for from
personal funds.

The language used in these forums is emotional, categorical and only
occasionally rude, all part of the arsenal of symbolic power. In July 2008 on
România Italia Net, Mela protested that the language was too 'robust' for a
forum that was public. The user explained she did not want to redraft the
rules, because that was the task of the administrator and the moderators who
decided what image the forum should carry, but she thought that a clear differentiation between public and private discussions needed to be made. Rude
language raises the prospect of deleting offensive messages. However, as
Brinkerhoff noticed in her study of several diasporic forums, removal of
content and member ejection is very rare (Brinkerhoff 2009: 93). The inde-
pendence and openness of the online diasporic forum is jealously guarded and
the online communities are usually 'self-regulating' through registration,
moderation and participation (Brinkerhoff 2009: 46).

The administrator of *Italia România* informed users in May 2008 that he
had deleted two posts by Ceanu, one of the most active members, in a thread
discussing what Romanians admired about Italy. The administrator explained:
'I don't like eliminating messages, there is in fact a certain freedom in this
forum, but only up to a point. Don't be upset, these are *"incidenti di percorso"*

[small accidents along the road]'. Ceanu apologized by mentioning that his irreverent posts had been a 'joke'. In the *Români Online UK* forum, there were several cases of locked threads, where the thread was still available to view, but posting technically impossible. When in October 2007 one user complained about locked threads, a moderator, Ariana, responded: 'we do not police, but it is normal to intervene to keep the peace[:] . . . locking threads is always the last solution'.

Freedom and self-expression have always defined online media and so attempts to delete messages and threads under the pretence of tidying up, cleaning or maintenance are usually met with protests. When such an attempt took place on *Români în UK*, between August and December 2008, the user Rareş made the point: 'this is a forum[:] . . . we need minimal rules'. As a result of the users' enthusiasm for openness and freedom, only very few forums have developed a strict system of sanctions. One such forum belongs to *Romanian Portal US*, which covers primarily the United States and Canada. One of its forum sections is dedicated entirely and unusually to admonishments and suspensions. The first temporary suspension is enacted after at least three admonishments; two temporary suspensions lead to a permanent suspension. Suspensions can vary in length from two weeks to three months. The forum polls members about the best sanctions for rule infringements, so there is a certain 'tyranny of the majority' at work here, which can be justified by the sheer size of the forum, that requires that interactions be channelled and categories of topics clearly structured.

The major lessons learnt by observing the making and remaking of online rules are:

- Both flaming and trolling can provoke conflicts and lead to symbolic exclusions. However, some degree of conflict is necessary to keep discussions alive and users engaged, as well as purge tensions. Tynes is of the opinion that conflict and cajoling serve to strengthen the social bond (2007: 508): the group comes together as an ethnic entity, united by a common purpose. In a well established forum, occasional flaming acts as a necessary carnivalesque act, a common purge of pent-up anxieties. It tests the community and its ability to measure up to the challenge. Its outcome is therefore significant for the group's ability to debate, take decisions and implement actions;
- In her analysis of the way four ethnic communities in the United Kingdom interacted online, Siapera noted that websites recreated enclosed communities and repeated the process of community formation, which is exclusionary to a certain extent (Siapera 2006: 6). All the above examples show an attempt to establish structure and law in a medium that should be chaotic and anarchic. Yet, online the law is not laid down in an absolute

manner; rules are negotiated and tweaked constantly, evolving in relation to specific users, needs and the wider online context. The role of the webmaster is often symbolic; laws and punishments are often renegotiated. These may be mini-societies, but they are societies of a special kind, defined by not just constant compromises but also conflicts, leading to the development of new forms of banal politics.

Conclusions: Projecting the Diasporic Self

In an article published in 2007, which prepared the way for the publication of his book *Communication Power*, Manuel Castells proposed the term 'mass self-communication' to describe a new form of socialization through communication. Digital media offer the opportunity for autonomy and confronting established institutions through activities that challenge their power. This slightly Durkheimian advent of an individualistic culture that puts 'I' and 'me' at its centre might recall Ellul's technological anxieties and the rise of the 'mass man' (Ellul 1973) until we understand that mass self-communication offers equal opportunities to small or marginal groups, as well as individuals, to challenge established political actors.

As Castells explains in another article, an important shift takes place from institutionalized political systems to fluid and informal associations founded on particular interests and needs, able to act within the public sphere (2008: 84). This new civil society, which from my perspective includes diasporic groups congregating online, is able, with the help of technology, to exist independently from institutions (Castells 2008: 86). Coupled with the weakening of the nation-state, this empowerment allows diasporans to engage in critique of both the homeland (Sheffer 2003: 254) and the hostland. However free of institutional characteristics online diasporic communities are, there is still a need for minimal structures and rules. As a result, in their prepolitical and identity-building phase, diasporas online engage in the establishment of hierarchies and power relations, the negotiation of new rules and values, and the selective appropriation of ethnic iconography that is reelaborated to reflect transnational experiences and multiple geographical anchorings. The online diaspora has thus the potential to become the locus of new and still incipient forms of political activism (Laguerre 2006: 2).

The Story Is Still Being Written

As Antonia, one of the diasporans in the UK, said, referring to Romanian migrants, 'their story is not over yet, their story is still being written' (Antonia, *Români în UK*). What I have observed online amounts to a continuous process that is making and remaking a community with its own ideals, rules, conflicts and negotiations, as well as claims and actions. Migration is a political act and the existing ruptures at the level of the collective consciousness, as well as the perpetual reexamination of the performance of the migrant body, constantly reformat identity and rearticulate what being Romanian in the world means today. The diasporic self-awareness, reflection and action I observed throughout this project are part of a longer process of maturation that warrants further investigation. The story does not finish here.

As someone writing from inside, having gone through the migratory experience, with both a sense of achievement and unavoidable regrets, I often observed, the extent to which migrants and migration are still being ethicalized. Alongside appreciation for the enrichment that migration brings, migrants themselves dwell upon the implied betrayal of their migratory act, a sign that national attachments hold fast and strong still. Judgements about someone's motivations for migration, which are by definition rather complex, are better withheld. I have tried instead to discuss the historical, social and cultural contexts that lead to migration, which are often overlooked in the case of Eastern Europeans who are simply classified as temporary 'work migrants'. Yet at the same time, I tried to avoid diasporic idealization, often observed in our field, and spoke openly about discrimination and racism when I encountered it, placing it again in the context of the migration experience.

My aim was to describe a unique diasporic culture in continuous making and remaking, that occasionally is at odds with rehoming and renationalizing attempts by the homeland, but which cannot exist in a vacuum, so naturally presents itself as a contradiction: an extension of national culture that wishes to act autonomously. This unique culture comes alive through the migrant voices that we hear in the numerous quotes used. My strategy was to let them speak; I only intervened and commented occasionally, thus placing them on an equal footing with traditional academic discourse. The book represents a reexamination of the politics derived from both emigration and immigration and the role that the Internet plays in supporting and facilitating different types of micropolitics. However, it represents but a transitory phase in a long and complex development that merits further investigation and reference to a range of migrant groups from Eastern Europe. I remain committed to the idea that the mental aspects of migration (lived experience, psychological phenomena) need to be examined as much as those physical aspects (migrant numbers, jobs, remittances), which have so far dominated the academic discourse on migration.

I plan to continue to develop this area of research in the not so distant future, by focusing on the role of memory in the elaboration of diasporic identity projects (which encapsulates place, trauma, amnesia, shame, denial, sublimation, rewriting, erasing, rupture, displacement, repression and fossilization). My inspiration for this aspect of the diasporic experience is my correspondence with the Romanian American artist Marius Lehene, who explained what role memory plays in his own work:

> I simply pick an entity that has a history to itself: a T-shirt that I wore in Romania before knowing I'd ever travel abroad; the Department of Homeland (strange word for an immigrant) Security letter granting me the permanent resident status, etc. In the "Absence" series, I either physically worked with or depicted empty clothing items that posit an absence, [a] metaphor for the emptiness of memory, for the fact that its contents are continually changed – I believe we only think we remember the same event/feeling/etc. because we have somehow accessed the same tag/label, but what's underneath is subtly changing every day. In short, I think my artworks should reveal in some way this precariousness proper to memory, because memory (*n'est-ce pas?*) is at the foundation of any sense of identity. (E-mail correspondence with the artist, 24 July 2010)

While particular care needs to be paid to the dangers of emphasizing diasporic nostalgia at the expense of the more complex phenomena revealed by Lehene in this extract of our online conversations, undoubtedly memory deserves a more in depth assessment. Diasporic experiences, as revealed by many online contributors, are more about interruption than continuity, syncopated experience rather than logical sequencing. The role of imagination, but also trauma therefore, cannot be underestimated.

The research has proved that the Internet allows diasporans to: reinvent identity, domesticate distance, alleviate social exclusion, produce a collective migratory expertise, mobilize transnationally and in dialogue with the nation-state, help shape a transnational civil society and develop a cosmopolitan imagination (Nedelcu 2009: 285–6); it allows migrants to produce and explore 'imagined worlds' (Appadurai 1990) that both expand and subvert Anderson's original concept from a transnational perspective. The Internet also relieves 'identity stress' and provides opportunities for organization and mobilization (Brinkerhoff 2009: 235), while also allowing once fixed ideas of national culture, race and ethnicity to be altered by online discussions (Ignacio 2005: 8).

From a methodological point of view, this research proves once more that the Internet can help researchers examine identity in the making and remaking, which, as Brinkerhoff points out (2009: 223), they have few opportunities to do elsewhere. This research has also confirmed that the kind of governance expressed by the nation-state is being affected by a crisis of efficiency, legitimacy, identity and equity (Castells 2008: 82), allowing for the rise of challenges to power. However, the nation-state is unwilling to whither and die and it is reinventing itself as the 'network state' (Castells 2008: 88), which includes diasporas in a transnational game of identity cat and mouse.

Although this research has highlighted, once more, the potential of online spaces, future research would also need to engage much more with how identity is performed on- and offline, at the border between 'scapes' (to use Appadurai's language, 1990), between cyber- and physical spaces, spaces of immigration and spaces of reflection, as well as immigration borders that migrants both dread and eagerly anticipate, which have significant symbolic meanings. Possible future research engaging with the issue of the immigrant body's performance in such liminal spaces was suggested by an online conversation with Rozalinda Borcilă, an artist based in Florida, and her work *Geography Lessons*, an ongoing archive of video images shot in airport security zones (Borcilă 2002). She reflected:

What kind of space is this, and how is it produced??? How is it produced right now, as it is always under construction, so my own engagement with it is part of the process of producing it? There are material dimensions to the border device which I could attend to as a sculptor (materials, dimensions, architectural layouts, equipment and so forth), and also representational dimensions (codes, tropes, laws, corporeal practices and choreographies) – but perhaps my concern was primarily with how to grasp these from a micropolitical perspective – from the territory of the body, of affect, of the ways in which we internalise ourselves as subjects at the border. (E-mail correspondence with the artist, 10 July 2010)

Borcilă's words recall many online diasporic reflections, which described in minute detail the 'out of body' experience of migration. They often referred to the shame associated with migration and the loss of control over how the migrant body behaved in between spaces of experience. These aspects of identity (the political relevance of spatial hierarchies, the way belonging and rejection are internalized, the performance of otherness or of difference) deserve a closer look (see also Culic 2010).

While conducting the research and writing the book I was surprised and occasionally shocked by the Romanian sense of loss, anger, social implosion and complete disintegration of moral values, for which both history and its politicians have a lot to answer for. However, I also saw glimpses of pride. Romanians have a deep sense of their own intimacy with great European culture and living abroad has given them a sense of their own value, professionalism and talents. Over the few years I have studied both online and offline communities, I have witnessed the slow maturation of their sense of kinship. There are numerous examples in this book showing the strategies that Romanians deploy to develop a language of political claims and constitute themselves as political subjects. I believe in their (our) ability to act out their (our) universal responsibility as Romanians, European citizens and diasporans.

What I have not encountered so far is a sense of responsibility in Western politicians and institutions, for the values that should define our journey into the twenty-first century. In Europe, the anti-immigration discourse continues to elect governments. As we have seen in the case of Italy and France, European politicians are willing to stand aside and accept illiberal and illegal laws that make a mockery of European Union freedoms. Non-citizens are barely tolerated in order to fill jobs that Westerners are no longer willing to do or bring skills that the economy needs. There is no willingness to treat these 'workers' as rational political subjects, able to develop complex transnational discourses from their multiple positions.

Recommendations

One role of academic discourse can be to highlight social injustices and propose remedies. Diasporic research has become one of the most important forces in addressing some contemporary issues. It is important to bring a humble contribution to what is already a respectable theoretical corpus, so that mistakes are not repeated and injustices perpetuated for the next generation. At the end of this book and with the future in mind, there are a few recommendations or rather wishes I feel compelled to make:

- European Union members need to solve the liberal paradox and reassess their handling of basic political rights. The European Union has to look more closely at the ability or rather inability that many diasporic groups have to exercise such rights in Europe today;
- There is an obvious problem with the way diasporic groups are represented and politicized at various levels in both homeland and hostland. Social mobility is also problematic and largely mythical. A reassessment of the multicultural discourse is desperately needed;
- Increased criminalization of ethnic groups through state policy and public discourse is dangerous and should be penalized;
- The normalization of East–West relations in relation to migration can be achieved through education and a set of policies devised bilaterally, as well as reexamining both media and political representation in relation to migration;
- Homeland policies must adjust to the needs of the emerging diasporas. Their value as a resource has begun to be recognized, but there is no comprehensive support for their settlement and return, nor any comprehensive state action on their behalf;
- Diasporic online communities have a few things to teach campaigning politicians. There are specific rules of engagement that define diasporic groups and online interactions have their own language and code that should be respected;
- The Internet has become a level playing field for politically engaged migrants, politicians, government bureaucrats and academics. It is the appropriate space for argument, rationalization and decision making;
- The diasporic language is too emotionally loaded. In order to become a language of political claims and match that of politicians and policy makers, it needs rationality. In other words, we need a professionalization of the diasporic discourse that migrants themselves use. This language can evolve in time, only if migrants are allowed to speak with their own voice.

Bibliography

Agudelo-Suárez, A. et al. 2009. 'Discrimination, Work and Health in Immigrant Populations in Spain', *Social Science and Medicine* 68(10): 1866–1874.

Alighieri, D. 1993. *Tutte le opere*. Grandi Tascabili Economici Newton: Rome.

Amersfoort, H.V. and J. Doomernik, 2002, 'Emergent Diaspora or Immigrant Communities? Turkish Immigrants in the Netherlands', in P. Kennedy and V. Roudometof (eds), *Communities across Borders: New Immigrants and Transnational Cultures*. Routledge: London, pp. 55–67.

Andreescu, G. 1996. *Naţionalişti şi antinaţionalişti. . . O polemică în publicistica românească*. Polirom: Iaşi.

Androutsopoulos, J. 2006. 'Multilingualism, Diaspora, and the Internet: Codes and Identities on German-based Diaspora Websites', *Journal of Sociolinguistics* 10(4): 520–547.

Anghel, R.G. 2008. 'Changing Statuses: Freedom of Movement, Locality and Transnationality of Irregular Romanian Migrants in Milan', *Journal of Ethnic and Migration Studies* 34(5): 787–802.

Appadurai, A. 1990. 'Disjuncture and Difference in the Global Cultural Economy', *Public Culture* 2(2): 1–24.

Baldwin-Edwards, M. 2007. 'Navigating between Scylla and Charybdis: Migration Policies for a Romania within the European Union', *Southeast European and Black Sea Studies* 7(1): 5–35.

Balibar, É. and I. Wallerstein. 1991. *Race, Nation, Class: Ambiguous Identities*. Verso: London.

Baronian, M., S. Besser and Y. Jansen (eds). 2007. *Diaspora and Memory: Figures of Displacement in Contemporary Literature*. Rodopi: Amsterdam.

Bernal, V. 2006. 'Diaspora, Cyberspace and Political Imagination: The Eritrean Diaspora Online', *Global Networks* 6(2): 161–179.

Bhabha, H.K. 1994. *The Location of Culture*. Routledge: London.

Bhabha, H.K. 1996. 'Culture's In-between', in S. Hall and P. du Gay (eds), *Questions of Cultural Identity*. Sage: London, pp. 53–60.

Billig, M. 1995. *Banal Nationalism*. Sage: London.

Blaga, L. 1994 [1936]. *Spaţiul mioritic*. Humanitas: Bucharest.

Blanchflower, D.G. and C. Shadforth. 2009. 'Fear, Unemployment and Migration', *The Economic Journal* 119(535): F136–F182.

Boia, L. 1997. *Istorie şi mit în conştiinţa românească*. Humanitas: Bucharest.

Boia, L. 2001. *Romania*. Reaktion Books: London.

Bonifazi, C. 2007. *L'immigrazione straniera in Italia*. Il Mulino: Bologna.

Borcilă, R. 2002. 'What to Do with a Disturbing Body?', in T. Dörfler and C. Globisch (eds), *Postmodern Practices, Beiträge zu einer vergehenden Epoche*. LIT: Münster, pp. 147–154.

Boswell, C. and O. Ciobanu. 2009. 'Culture, Utility or Social Systems? Explaining the Cross-national Ties of Emigrants from Borşa, Romania', *Ethnic and Racial Studies* 32(8): 1346–1364.

Bourdieu, P. 1998. *Acts of Resistance: Against the New Myths of Our Time*. Polity: Cambridge.

Brah, A. 1996. *Cartographies of Diaspora: Contesting Identities*. Routledge: London.

Braziel, J.E. and A. Mannur (eds). 2003. *Theorizing Diaspora: A Reader*. Blackwell: Oxford.

Brinkerhoff, J.M. 2009. *Digital Diasporas: Identity and Transnational Engagement*. Cambridge University Press: Cambridge.

Bromley, R. 2000. *Narratives for a New Belonging: Diasporic Cultural Fictions*. Edinburgh University Press: Edinburgh.

Brubaker, R. 1996. *Nationalism Reframed: Nationhood and the National Question in the New Europe*. Cambridge University Press: Cambridge.

Brubaker, R.W. 1999. 'Membership without Citizenship: The Economic and Social Rights of Noncitizens', in S. Vertovec (ed.), *Migration and Social Cohesion*. Edward Elgar: Cheltenham, pp. 259–279.

Brubaker, R. 2005. 'The "Diaspora" Diaspora', *Ethnic and Racial Studies* 28(1): 1–19.

Brubaker, R., with M. Feischmid, J. Fox and L. Grancea. 2006. *Nationalist Politics and Everyday Ethnicity in a Transylvanian Town*. Princeton University Press: Princeton.

Castells, M. 2007. 'Communication, Power and Counter-power in the Network Society', *International Journal of Communication* 1(1): 238–266.

Castells, M. 2008. 'The New Public Sphere: Global Civil Society, Communication Networks, and Global Governance', *Annals of the American Academy of Political and Social Sciences* 616(March): 78–93.

Castles, S. 2004. 'The Factors that Make and Unmake Migration Policies', *International Migration Review* 38(3): 852–883.

Cesereanu, R. 2003. *Imaginarul violent al românilor.* Humanitas: Bucharest.

Chan, B. 2006. 'Virtual Communities and Chinese National Identity', *Journal of Chinese Overseas* 2(1): 1–36.

Cid, X. and I. Ogando. 2010. 'Migrate Like a Galician: The Graphic Identity of the Galician Diaspora on the Internet', in A. Alonso and P.J. Oiarzabal (eds), *Diasporas in the New Media Age: Identity, Politics and Community.* University of Nevada Press: Las Vegas, pp. 317–337.

Cohen, R. 2008. *Global Diasporas: An Introduction.* Routledge: London.

Colombo, A. and G. Sciortino. 2004. *Gli immigranti in Italia. Assimilati o esclusi: gli immigranti, gli italiani, le politiche.* Il Mulino: Bologna.

Csedő, K. 2008. 'Negotiating Skills in the Global City: Hungarian and Romanian Professionals and Graduates in London', *Journal of Ethnic and Migration Studies* 34(5): 803–823.

Culic, I. 2008. 'Eluding Exit and Entry Controls: Romanian and Moldovan Immigrants in the European Union', *East European Politics and Societies* 22(1): 145–170.

Culic, I. 2010. 'State of Imagination: Embodiments of Immigration Canada', *The Sociological Review* 58(3): 343–360.

Daniels, R. 2004. *Guarding the Golden Door: American Immigration Policy and Immigrants since 1882.* Hill & Wang: New York.

Delcea, A. 2007. *Remittances and International Migration: Romania in the Context of the European Union.* Paralela 45: Piteşti.

Deleuze, G. and F. Guattari. 1987. *A Thousand Plateaus: Capitalism and Schizophrenia.* University of Minnesota Press: Minneapolis.

Drăgan, I. et al. 1998. *Construcţia simbolică a cîmpului electoral.* Institutul European: Iaşi.

Düvell, 2007, 'United Kingdon' in A. Triandafyllidou and R. Gropas (eds), *European Immigration: A Sourcebook.* Ashgate: Aldershot, pp. 347–360.

Edemariam, A. 2009. 'Unhappy Return: Fear and Loathing Await Fugitives from Belfast Racism', *Guardian*, 26 June, Retrieved 15 June 2010 from http://www.guardian.co.uk/world/2009/jun/26/race-attacks-on-belfast-roma.

Einaudi, L. 2007. *Le politiche dell'immigrazione in Italia dall'Unità a oggi.* Editori Laterza: Bari.

Ellul, J. 1973. *The Technological Society.* Random House: Toronto.

Elrick, T. and O. Ciobanu. 2009. 'Migration Networks and Policy Impacts: Insights from Romanian–Spanish Migrations', *Global Networks* 9(1): 99–116.

Eriksen, T.H. 2007. 'Nationalism and the Internet', *Nations and Nationalism* 13(1): 1–17.

Faist, T. and A. Ette (eds). 2007. *The Europeanization of National Policies and Politics of Integration: Between Autonomy and the European Union*. Palgrave Macmillan: Basingstoke.

Fauser, M. 2007. 'Selective Europeanization: Europe's Impact on Spanish Migration Control', in T. Faist and A. Ette (eds), *The Europeanization of National Policies and Politics of Integration: Between Autonomy and the European Union*. Palgrave Macmillan: Basingstoke, pp. 136–156.

Favell, A. 2001. *Philosophies of Integration: Immigration and the Idea of Citizenship in France and Britain*, 2nd edn. Palgrave Macmillan: Basingstoke.

Favell, A. 2008. 'The New Face of East–west Migration in Europe', *Journal of Ethnic and Migration Studies* 34(5): 701–716.

Fekete, L. 2009. *A Suitable Enemy: Racism, Migration and Islamophobia in Europe*. Pluto Press: London.

Ferro, A. 2004. 'Romanians Abroad: A Snapshot of Highly Skilled Migration', *Higher Education in Europe* 29(3): 381–391.

Financiarul 2008. 'SOS pentru romanii care pun economia Italiei pe picioare', *Financiarul*, 21 June.

Fonseca, I. 1996. *Bury Me Standing: The Gypsies and Their Journey*. Vintage: London.

Gaiser, T.J. and A.E. Schreiner. 2009. *A Guide to Conducting Online Research*. Sage: London.

Gallagher, T. 2004. *Furtul unei naţiuni. România de la comunism încoace*. Humanitas: Bucharest.

Gans, H.J. 1999. 'Symbolic Ethnicity: The Future of Ethnic Groups and Cultures in America', in S. Vertovec (ed.), *Migration and Social Cohesion*. Edward Elgar: Cheltenham, pp. 392–410.

Garapich, M.P. 2008. 'The Migration Industry and Civil Society: Polish Immigrants in the United Kingdom before and after EU Enlargement', *Journal of Ethnic and Migration Studies* 34(5): 735–752.

Geddes, A. 2003. *The Politics of Migration and Immigration in Europe*. Sage: London.

Geddes, A. 2007. 'The Europeanization of What? Migration, Asylum and the Politics of European Integration', in T. Faist and A. Ette (eds), *The Europeanization of National Policies and Politics of Integration: Between Autonomy and the European Union*. Palgrave Macmillan: Basingstoke, pp. 49–70.

Georgiou, M. 2006, *Diaspora, Identity and the Media: Diasporic Transnationalism and Mediated Spatialities*. Hampton Press: Cresskill, NJ.

Gilroy, P. 1987. *'There Ain't No Black in the Union Jack': The Cultural Politics of Race and Nation*. Routledge: London.

Gilroy, P. 1993. *The Black Atlantic: Modernity and Double Consciousness*. Verso: London.

Goffman, E. 1990. *Stigma: Notes on the Management of Spoiled Identity.* Penguin: London.

González Enríquez, C. 2007. 'Spain', in A. Triandafyllidou and R. Gropas (eds), *European Immigration: A Sourcebook.* Ashgate: Aldershot, pp. 321–333.

Graham, M. and S. Khosravi. 2002. 'Reordering Public and Private in Iranian Cyberspace: Identity, Politics and Mobilization', *Identities: Global Studies in Culture and Power* 9(2): 219–246.

Grancea, M. 2002. 'Consideraţii pe marginea teoriei străinului şi aplicaţiile acesteia în cercetarea istorico-socială. Cazul ţiganului', in N. Bocşan, S. Mitu and T. Nicoară (eds), *Identitate şi alteritate. Sudii de istorie politică şi culturală.* Presa Universitară Clujeană: Cluj-Napoca, pp. 64–67.

Grancea, M. and A. Ciobanu. 2002. 'Criza identitară românească. Discurs istoriografic şi stereotipuri etnoculturale', in N. Bocşan, S. Mitu and T. Nicoară (eds), *Identitate şi alteritate. Sudii de istorie politică şi culturală.* Presa Universitară Clujeană: Cluj-Napoca, pp. 363–378.

Greenfeld, L. 1992. *Nationalism: Five Roads to Modernity,* Harvard University Press: Harvard, MA.

Hall, S. 2003, 'Cultural Identity and Diaspora', in J.E. Braziel and A. Mannur (eds), *Theorizing Diaspora: A Reader.* Blackwell: Oxford, pp. 233–246.

Hamelink, C.J. 2006, 'The Ethics of the Internet: Can we Cope with Lies and Deceit on the Net?', in K. Sarikakis and D.K. Thussu, *Ideologies of the Internet.* Hampton Press: Cresskill, NJ, pp. 115–130.

Hansen, P. 2004. 'In the Name of Europe', *Race & Class* 45(3): 49–62.

Hartman, K. and E. Ackermann. 2004. *Searching and Researching on the Internet and the World Wide Web,* 4th edn. Franklin, Beedle and Associates: Wilsonville, OR.

Hartman, T. 2008. 'States, Markets, and Other Unexceptional Communities: Informal Romanian Labour in a Spanish Agricultural Zone', *Journal of the Royal Anthropological Institute* 14(3): 496–514.

Hewson, C., P. Yule, D. Laurent and C. Vogel. 2003. *Internet Research Methods.* Sage: London.

Hiller, H.H. and T.M. Franz. 2004. 'New Ties, Old Ties and Lost Ties: The Use of the Internet in Diaspora', *New Media and Society* 6(6): 731–752.

Hitchins, K. 1997. *Mit şi realitate în istoriografia românească.* Editura Enciclopedică: Bucharest.

Hollifield, J.F. 2004. 'The Emerging Migration State', *International Migration Review* 38(3): 885–911.

Horváth, I. 2008. 'The Culture of Migration of Rural Romanian Youth', *Journal of Ethnic and Migration Studies* 34(5): 771–786.

Huysmans, J. 2006. *The Politics of Insecurity: Fear, Migration and Asylum in the EU.* Routledge: London.

Ignacio, E.N. 2005. *Building Diaspora: Filipino Cultural Community Formation on the Internet.* Rutgers University Press: New Brunswick.

Institute for Public Policy Research (IPPR), C. Drew and D. Sriskandarajah. 2006. *EU Enlargement: Bulgaria and Romania – Migration Implications for the UK.* Institute of Public Policy Research: London.

Kelly, T. and S. Reid. 2008. 'Revealed: How Romanian Pickpocket Gangs Are Building Palaces Back Home with Child Slave Labour', *The Mail*, 25 January, Retrieved 15 June 2010 from: http://www.dailymail.co.uk/news/article-510100/Revealed-How-Romanian-pickpocket-gangs-building-palaces-home-child-slave-labour.html.

Kennedy, P. and V. Roudometof (eds). 2002. *Communities across Borders: New Immigrants and Transnational Cultures.* Routledge: London.

King, T. 2003, 'Rhodesians in Hyperspace. The Maintenance of a National and Cultural Identity', in K.H. Karim (ed.), *The Media of Diaspora*, Routledge: London, pp. 177–188.

Kosic, A. and A. Triandafyllidou. 2007. 'Italy', in A. Triandafyllidou and R. Gropas (eds), *European Immigration: A Sourcebook.* Ashgate: Aldershot, pp. 185–199.

Kozinets, R.V. 2009. *Netnography: Doing Ethnographic Research Online.* Sage: London.

Laguerre, M.S. 2006, *Diaspora, Politics, and Globalization.* Palgrave Macmillan: Basingstoke.

Lazăr, M. 2002. *Paradoxuri ale modernizării. Elemente pentru o sociologie a elitelor culturale româneşti.* Limes: Cluj-Napoca.

Light, D. and C. Young. 2009. 'European Union Enlargement, Post-accession Migration and Imaginative Geographies of the "New Europe": Media Discourses in Romania and the United Kingdom', *Journal of Cultural Geography* 26(3): 281–303.

Lowe, L. 2003. 'Heterogeneity, Hybridity, Multiplicity: Marking Asian-American Differences', in J.E. Braziel and A. Mannur (eds), *Theorizing Diaspora: A Reader.* Blackwell: Oxford, pp. 132–155.

Macri, G. 2010. 'Who Do They Think They Are? Online Narratives among Romanian Diaspora in Ireland', in L. De Pretto, G. Macri and C. Wong (eds), *Diasporas: Revisiting and Discovering.* Inter-Disciplinary Press: Dublin, pp. 205–214.

Mandaville, P. 2003. 'Communication and Diasporic Islam: A Virtual Ummah?', in K.H. Karim (ed.), *The Media of Diaspora.* Routledge: London, pp. 135–147.

Mann, C. and F. Stewart. 2000. *Internet Communication and Qualitative Research: A Handbook for Researching Online.* Sage: London.

Marino, A. 1995. *Pentru Europa. Integrarea României. Aspecte ideologice şi culturale.* Polirom: Iaşi.

Marino, A. 1996. *Politică și cultură. Pentru o nouă cultură română.* Polirom: Iași.

Massey, D.S., L. Goldring and J. Durand. 1994. 'Continuities in Transnational Migration: An Analysis of Nineteen Mexican Communities', *American Journal of Sociology* 99(6): 1492–1533.

Massey, D.S. et al. 1998. *Worlds in Motion: Understanding International Migration at the End of the Millennium.* Clarendon Press: Oxford.

Meinhof, U.H. and A. Triandafyllidou (eds). 2006. *Transcultural Europe: Cultural Policy in a Changing Europe.* Palgrave Macmillan: Basingstoke.

Miglietta, A. and S. Tartaglia. 2009. 'The Influence of Length of Stay, Linguistic Competence, and Media Exposure in Immigrants' Adaptation', *Cross-Cultural Research* 43(1): 46–61.

Mihăilescu, V. 1999. 'Imaging the Other. An Anthropological Perspective', in I. Culic, I. Horváth and C. Stan (eds), *Reflections on Difference: Focus on Romania*, Limes: Cluj-Napoca, pp. 111–123.

Mitra, A. 2005. 'Creating Immigrant Identities in Cybernetic Space: Examples from a Non-resident Indian Website', *Media, Culture and Society* 27(3): 371–390.

Mitu, S. 1997. *Geneza identității naționale la românii ardeleni.* Humanitas: Bucharest.

Mungiu-Pippidi, A. 2002. *Politica după comunism.* Humanitas: Bucharest.

Nedelcu, M. 2009. *Le migrant online: Nouveaux modèles migratoires à l'ère du numérique.* L'Harmattan: Paris.

Noica, C. 1996. *Sentimentul românesc al ființei.* Humanitas: Bucharest.

Oiarzabal, P.J. 2010. 'Basque Diaspora Digital Nationalism: Designing "Banal" Identity', in A. Alonso and P.J. Oiarzabal (eds), *Diasporas in the New Media Age: Identity, Politics and Community.* University of Nevada Press: Las Vegas, pp. 338–349.

Outhwaite, W. and L. Ray. 2005. *Social Theory and Postcommunism.* Blackwell: Oxford.

Parker, D. and M. Song. 2006. 'New Ethnicities Online: Reflexive Racialization and the Internet', *The Sociological Review* 56(3): 575–594.

Pauwels, L. 2005. 'Websites as Visual and Multimodal Cultural Expressions: Opportunities and Issues of Online Hybrid Media Research', *Media, Culture and Society* 27(4): 604–613.

Pavlik, J.V. 2001. *Journalism and New Media.* Columbia University Press: New York.

Pecican, O. 2003. *România și Uniunea Europeană.* Eikon: Cluj-Napoca.

Piracha, M. and R. Vickerman. 2003. 'Immigration, Labour Mobility and EU Enlargement', in J. Smith and C. Jenkins (eds), *Through the Paper Curtain: Insiders and Outsiders in the New Europe.* Blackwell: Oxford, pp. 35–60.

Plante, J. 2010. 'Characteristics and Labour Market Outcomes of Internationally-educated Immigrants', *Statistics Canada*. Retrieved 30 January 2012 from http://www.statcan.gc.ca/pub/81-595-m/81-595-m2010084- eng.htm.

Pleşu, A. 2010. 'Ce este un forum?', *Adevărul*, 16 March.

Popescu, A. 1999. 'Interethnic Stereotypes and Identity Patterns', in I. Culic, I. Horváth and C. Stan (eds), *Reflections on Difference: Focus on Romania*. Limes: Cluj-Napoca, pp. 45–54.

Popescu, G. 2005. 'Diaspora Geopolitics: Romanian-Americans and NATO Expansion', *Geopolitics* 10(3): 455–481.

Preda, C. 1999. *Occidentul nostru*. Nemira: Bucharest.

Qiu, H. 2003, 'Communication among Knowledge Diasporas: Online Magazines of Expatriate Chinese Students', in K.H. Karim (ed.), *The Media of Diaspora*. Routledge: London, pp. 148–161.

Rantanen, T. 2005. *The Media and Globalization*. Sage: London.

Reynolds, M. 2010. 'Romanians Steal Man's Home', *Daily Express*, 23 March. Retrieved 25 March 2010 from: http://www.express.co.uk/posts/view/164583/Romanians-steal-man-s-home.

Robila, M. 2007. 'Eastern European Immigrants in the United States: A Socio-demographic Profile', *The Social Science Journal* 44: 113–125.

Robila, M. 2008.'Characteristics of Eastern European Immigration in the United States' (Report), *Journal of Comparative Family Studies*, 22 September. Retrieved 30 January 2012 from http://www.highbeam.com/doc/1G1-190260347.html.

Robila, M. 2010. *Eastern European Immigrant Families*. London: Routledge.

Rostás, Z. and S. Stoica (eds). 2006. *Tur-retur. Convorbiri despre munca în străinătate (vol. II)*. Curtea Veche: Bucharest.

Rushdie, S. 2009. 'A Fine Pickle', *Guardian Review*, 28 February.

Sabry, T. 2005. 'The Day Moroccans Gave up Couscous for Satellites: Global TV, Structures of Feeling, and Mental Migration', *Transnational Broadcasting Studies* Spring/Summer(14). Retrieved 2 February 2006 from http://www.tbsjournal.com/Archives/Spring05/sabry.html.

Salomone, R. 2008. 'Transnational Schooling and the New Immigrants: Developing Dual Identities in the United States', *Intercultural Education* 19(5): 383–393.

Sandu, D. 2005. 'Emerging Transnational Migration from Romanian Villages', *Current Sociology* 53(4): 555–582.

Sandu, D. 2010. *Lumile sociale ale migraţiei româneşti în străinătate*. Polirom: Iaşi.

Sayad, A. 2004. *The Suffering of the Immigrant*. Polity: Cambridge.

Schierup, C.U., P. Hansen and S. Castles. 2006. *Migration, Citizenship, and the European Welfare State: A European Dilemma.* Oxford University Press: Oxford.

Schöpflin, G. 2000. *Nations Identity Power: The New Politics of Europe.* Hurts & Company: London.

Schuster, L. and J. Solomos. 2004. 'Race, Immigration and Asylum: New Labour's Agenda and Its Consequences', *Ethnicities* 4(2): 267–300.

Sheffer, G. 2003. *Diaspora Politics: At Home and Abroad.* Cambridge University Press: Cambridge.

Siapera, E. 2005. 'Minority Activism on the Web: Between Deliberative Democracy and Multiculturalism', *Journal of Ethnic and Migration Studies* 31(3): 499–519.

Siapera, E. 2006. 'Multiculturalism Online: The Internet and the Dilemmas of Multicultural Politics', *Cultural Studies* 9(1): 5–24.

Sigona, N. 2005. 'Locating "The Gypsy Problem". The Roma in Italy: Stereotyping, Labelling and "Nomad Camps"', *Journal of Ethnic and Migration Studies* 31(4): 741–756.

Smart, K.L., J. Cossell Rice and L.E. Wood. 2000. 'Meeting the Needs of Users: Toward a Semiotics of the Web', *Proceedings of IEEE Professional Communication Society, International Professional Communication Conference and Proceedings of the 18th Annual ACM International Conference on 'Computer Documentation: Technology and Teamwork'.* Retrieved 5 January 2010 from http://portal.acm.org/citation.cfm?id=504884.

Tismăneanu, V. 1992. *Reinventing Politics: Eastern Europe from Stalin to Havel.* The Free Press: New York.

Tismăneanu, V. 1997. *Mizeria utopiei. Criza ideologiei marxiste în Europa Răsăriteană.* Polirom: Iași.

Tismăneanu, V. 1999. *Fantasmele salvării. Democrație, naționalism și mit în Europa post-comunistă.* Polirom: Iași.

Todorova, M. 2000. *Balcanii și balcanismul.* Humanitas: Bucharest.

Trandafoiu, R. 2006. 'The Geopolitics of Work Migrants: The Romanian Diaspora, Legal Rights and Symbolic Geographies', *Regio: A Review of Studies on Minorities, Politics and Society* 9(Autumn): 130–149.

Triandafyllidou, A. 2009. 'Migrants and Ethnic Minorities in Post-communist Europe: Negotiating Diasporic Identity', *Ethnicities* 9(2): 226–245.

Triandafyllidou, A. and R. Gropas (eds). 2007. *European Immigration: A Sourcebook.* Ashgate: Aldershot.

Tudoroiu, T. 2007. 'The Changing Patterns of Romanian Immigration to Canada, *Journal of Identity and Migration Studies* 1(2): 21–43.

Tynes, R. 2007. 'Nation-building and the Diaspora on Leonenet: A Case of Sierra Leone in Cyberspace', *New Media and Society* 9(3): 497–518.

Ulram, P.A. and F. Plasser. 2003. 'Political Culture in East-Central and Eastern Europe: Empirical Findings 1990-2001', in D. Pollack, J. Jacobs, O. Müller and G. Pickel (eds), *Political Culture in Post-communist Europe: Attitudes in New Democracies*. Ashgate: Aldershot, pp. 31–46.

Ungoed-Thomas, J. 2009. 'The Faraway Town Fat on UK Benefits', *The Sunday Times*, 23 August. Retrieved 15 March 2010 from: http://timesonline.co.uk/tol/news/uk/crime/article6806484.ece.

Van Hear, N. 1998. *New Diasporas: The Mass Exodus, Dispersal and Regrouping of Migrant Communities*. UCL Press: London.

Verdery, C. 1991. *National Ideology under Socialism: Identity and Cultural Politics in Ceauşescu's Romania*. University of California Press: Berkeley.

Verdery, C. 1996 *What Was Socialism, and What Comes Next*. Princeton University Press: Princeton.

Vertovec, S. 2004. 'Migrant Transnationalism and Modes of Transformation', *International Migration Review* 38(3): 970–1000.

Vidroiu-Stanca, A. 2008. *Liniştea începe niciodată. La tranquilidad empieza nunca*. Depósito legal V-1116-2008: Valencia.

Wakeford, N. 2004, 'Developing Methodological Frameworks for Studying the World Wide Web', in D. Gauntlett and R. Horsley (eds), *Web.Studies*, 2nd edn. Hodder Education: London, pp. 34–48.

White, G.W. 2000. *Nationalism and Territory: Constructing Group Identity in Southeastern Europe*. Rowman & Littlefield: Oxford.

Wise, K., B. Hamman and K. Thorson. 2006. 'Moderation, Response Rate, and Message Interactivity: Features of Online Communities and Their Effects on Intent to Participate', *Journal of Computer-Mediated Communication* 12(1): 24–41.

Wolff, L. 2000. *Inventarea Europei de Est. Harta civilizaţiei în epoca luminilor*. Humanitas: Bucharest.

Wright, S. and J. Street. 2007. 'Democracy, Deliberation and Design: The Case of Online Discussion Forums', *New Media and Society* 9(5): 849–869.

22 Revista Grupului Pentru Dialog Social. 2007. 'Românii din afara graniţelor. Cine le apără interesele?' 15(928). Retrieved 1 August 2010 from http://www.revista22.ro.

Websites

Acasă: http://www.acasamedia.com/

Acum, diaspora Moldovei: http://www.diasporamoldovei.org/start.html/ (no longer active)

AROVA, Valencia: http://www.arova.es/

Associazione Italia–Romania Futuro Insieme: http://www.irfionlus.org/ (no longer active)

BalkanInsight: http://www.balkaninsight.com/en/page/all-balkans-home/

BC Romanian Community Center: http://romanians.bc.ca/

Click Romania: http://www.clickromania.co.uk/

Comunitatea română portalul diasporei române US: http://www.romanian-portal.com/

Consiliul Mondial Român: http://www.consiliulmondialroman.org/

CORA Congress of Romanian Americans: http://www.romanianamericans.org/

Cubestat: http://www.cubestat.com/

Diaspora românească: http://www.diasporaro.com/

Din State: http://www.dinstate.ro/

DRP, Departamentul pentru Românii de Pretutindeni: http://www.dprp.gov.ro/

E-Migrant: http://www.e-migrant.ro/

FEDROM, Federația Asociațiilor de Imigranți Români din Spania: http://www.fedrom.org/

Gazeta românească: http://www.gazetaromaneasca.com/

Greg Hands M.P.: http://www.greghands.com/

Identitatea românească (PIR): http://www.identitatearomaneasca.it/ro/

Italia România: http://www.italiaromania.com/

Koolro: http://www.koolro.com/ (no longer active, but there is a Twitter presence: https://twitter.com/Koolro)

Marea unire, Spania: http://www.mareaunire.com/spania/

Marea unire, UK: http://www.mareaunire.com/uk/

Nou Horizont: http://nouhorizont.org/ (no longer active)

Ora Turin: http://www.oraromaniei.com/

Petition Online: http://www.petitiononline.com/

PIRUM: http://www.partidulromanilordinspania.blogspot.co.uk/

Pro Vancouver Yahoo Group: http://groups.yahoo.com/group/Pro_Vancouver/

Québec Ro: http://www.quebec.ro/

reAct!: http://www.reactgroup.org.uk/

Realitatea din Italia: http://www.realitateadinitalia.com/ (no longer active)

Romanian Canadian Cultural Association of Calgary: http://www.romanianscalgary.ca/

Romanian Community of Ireland: http://www.romaniancommunity.net/

Romanian Cultural Centre, London (RCC): http://www.romanianculturalcentre.org.uk/

Romanian Portal US: http://www.romanian-portal.com/sua-comunitatea-romaneasca/

Romanian Times: http://www.romaniantimes.com/
Românca Society: http://romancasociety.blogspot.co.uk/
România Italia Net: http://www.romaniaitalia.net/
Români în Alberta: http://www.romaniinalberta.ca/
Români în America: http://www.romani-in-america.com/
Români în UK: http://www.romani.co.uk/
Români Online UK: http://www.romani-online.co.uk/
Români la Chicago/Los Angeles/New York: http://www.romanilachicago.org/
    (Chicago version)
RomNights – Romanian nights in New York: http://www.romnights.com/
RomPortal: http://romportal.com/default.aspx/
RoNights, chefurile românești din Chicago: http://www.ronights.com/
RoVancouver (Comunitatea Romana Virtuala din Vancouver):
http://www.rovancouver.com/community/intrare.htm/
Royouth: http://www.royouth.com/
SiteLog: http://www.sitelogrs.com/
Spania românească: http://www.spaniaromaneasca.com/
Străinatate.org: http://www.strainatate.org/
The Union and League of Romanian Societies: http://www.romanian
    societies.com/
William Brînză: http://www.williampdleuropa.eu/
Ziarul românesc: http://www.ziarulromanesc.net/
40 Romania: http://info.40romania.com/

Index